HISTORY OF ANCIENT
Greece

HISTORY OF ANCIENT
Greece

NATHANIEL HARRIS

hamlyn

Executive Editor: Julian Brown
Senior Editor: Trevor Davies
Art Director: Keith Martin
Senior Designer: Claire Harvey
Design: Marc Burville Riley
Picture Research: Zoe Holtërman
Production Controller: Lee Sargent

First published in Great Britain in 2000
by Hamlyn, an imprint of
Octopus Publishing Group Limited
2–4 Heron Quays, Docklands, London
E14 4JP

ISBN 0 600 59808 X

Distributed in the United States and
Canada by Sterling Publishing Co., Inc.
387 Park Avenue South
New York, NY 10016-8810

A catalogue record for this book is available
from the British Library

Produced by Toppan
Printed in China

CONTENTS

INTRODUCTION

THE ANCIENT GREEKS ARE THE FIRST PEOPLE IN HISTORY WHO SEEM TO SPEAK TO US FULLY AND FREELY. THEY GIVE VOICE TO FAMILIAR THOUGHTS AND FEELINGS, AND ADOPT A HUMAN-CENTRED VIEW OF ART AND LIFE; BY COMPARISON, THE GREAT CIVILIZATIONS OF WESTERN ASIA AND EGYPT INSPIRE AWE AND ADMIRATION BUT REMAIN SOMEWHAT REMOTE AND STRANGE. MODERN SCHOLARS EMPHASIZE HOW MUCH THE GREEKS OWED TO THESE OLDER CIVILZATIONS, AND POINT OUT THAT, WHEN EXAMINED CLOSELY, GREEK CULTURE PROVES TO BE LESS RATIONAL AND 'MODERN' THAN IT APPEARS. YET IT REMAINS TRUE THAT THE GREEKS THOROUGHLY ABSORBED WHAT THEY LEARNED FROM OTHERS AND TRANS-FORMED IT INTO SOMETHING NEW OF THEIR OWN; AND THAT ANCIENT GREECE WAS A DIRECT ANCESTOR OF PRESENT-DAY WESTERN CIVILZATION. IF THE GREEKS SEEM SO FAMILIAR, IT IS BECAUSE WE HAVE INHERITED SO MANY OF OUR WORDS, IDEAS AND IMAGES FROM THEM.

The earliest Greeks we know about were Bronze-Age warriors, the Mycenaeans, who learned their arts and skills from the neighbouring civilization of Crete. The Mycenaeans built imposing fortress palaces and were a force to be reckoned with in the Mediterranean during the 2nd millennium BC. Their deeds, worked on by time and imagination, became the basis of Homer's epic poems and of adventure-myths such as the Trojan War and the voyage of Jason and the Argonauts, which have never ceased to haunt the human imagination.

After the collapse of the Mycenaean world and the passage of obscure centuries, the Greeks re-entered history as inhabitants of small rival city-states, of which Athens became the most famous. Greeks settled as colonists and traders in many parts of the then-known world, influencing the development of other peoples from France and Spain to the Crimea. But the most momentous events took place in Greece itself, especially during its great Classical age, the 5th and 4th centuries BC. Unprecedented experiments in political organization led to the emergence of Athenian democracy and the military totalitarianism of Sparta, vying for pre-eminence in Greece. Meanwhile Greeks defeated the might of the Persian Empire on land at Marathon and at sea off Salamis. Having earlier invented philosophy, Greece now produced thinkers - Socrates, Plato, Aristotle - whose contributions to fundamental questions about ethics, politics and the nature of

the good life have never been surpassed. The first dramas were written and performed at Athens, sculptors and painters glorified the human form, and the Parthenon and other masterpieces of architecture were created.

Constant wars between the city-states drained them of some of their vitality. But after they fell under the domination of Macedon, a monarchy on the fringes of the Greek world, Alexander the Great led an all-conquering Greco-Macedonian expedition into Asia. Alexander's brief, spectacular career ended in 323 BC, but its consequences were far-reaching for the Near and Middle East, which were to be culturally and politically Greek for hundreds of years.

In antiquity the Greeks made their presence felt from Spain to India; and later ages have also fallen under their spell. This book aims to describe, in words and pictures, not only the deeds but also the world-changing works, thoughts and way of life of this extraordinary people.

1 ORIGINS

THE GREEKS LOOM SO LARGE IN WESTERN CONSCIOUSNESS THAT IT IS EASY TO FORGET HOW MUCH THEY OWED TO THEIR PREDECESSORS IN THE PREHISTORIC AND HISTORIC PAST. THE FIRST CIVILIZATIONS AROSE NOT FAR AWAY, IN THE NEAR EAST, AND THESE INTERMITTENTLY INFLUENCED GREEK LIFE, THOUGHT AND ART OVER TWO MILLENNIA. AND ALTHOUGH FLOURISHING BRONZE-AGE SETTLEMENTS DEVELOPED ON THE MAINLAND AND THE AEGEAN ISLANDS, THE FIRST CIVILIZATION IN THE REGION GREW UP ON THE ISLAND OF CRETE. NOW KNOWN AS MINOAN, THIS CIVILIZATION ESTABLISHED CONTACTS ALL OVER THE EASTERN MEDITERRANEAN BEFORE DECAYING AND BEING TAKEN OVER BY A PEOPLE FROM MAINLAND GREECE: THE MYCENAEANS. THEY WERE THE FIRST GREEK-SPEAKING PEOPLE THAT WE KNOW

Ancient and modern. Over four thousand years old, this marble figure of a woman looks strikingly modern. Its simplified, geometric style is typical of the art of the Cyclades, the main group of Greek islands in the southern Aegean.

OF, AND THEIR DOINGS GAVE RISE TO LATER LEGENDS, INCLUDING THE EPIC EVENTS OF THE TROJAN WAR. DESPITE THEIR REPORTED SUCCESS IN THIS CONFLICT, THE MYCENAEAN KINGDOMS COLLAPSED IN THE 12TH CENTURY BC AND GREECE ENTERED ITS DARK AGE. WHEN IT EMERGED INTO THE LIGHT OF HISTORY A FEW HUNDRED YEARS LATER, GREEK CIVILIZATION HAD ALREADY BEGUN TO TAKE ON THE FORMS FAMILIAR TO US.

THE NEAR EAST AND CRETE

Glorious though their achievements were, the Greeks built on solid foundations. In the course of many millennia, human beings had begun to transform their habitat and, inadvertently, to change themselves. Over wide areas of Europe and Asia they had discovered how to grow crops and domesticate animals, and had given up hunting and settled down as farmers. Spinning, weaving and the art of pottery had been invented. Tools and weapons of stone had been supplemented by more effective objects of copper and bronze. Trade was carried on by land and sea. And, even before the emergence of the earliest civilizations, human beings had begun to develop complex societies and form settled communities large enough to be described as cities.

The first civilizations developed in the great river valleys of the Tigris-Euphrates and the Nile, which were capable of yielding rich harvests if they were properly irrigated. This became possible once a large organized labour force could be deployed, and that in turn depended on the existence of a strong state apparatus, specialized administrators and reliable records; hence the earliest of all civilizations, Sumer in Mesopotamia, gave birth to the earliest known form of writing. The surpluses produced by successful farming of the rich alluvial soils of Sumer and Egypt went to strengthen the state, priesthood and army still further, and also to finance monumental art and great building projects such as the pyramids. (However, less advanced societies along the shores of the Mediterranean and Atlantic also proved capable of monumental building; surviving examples include the megaliths of Stonehenge in England and Carnac in Brittany.)

In the 3rd millennium BC civilization began to spread from the older centres. The Indus Valley in India became the site of a vast and enigmatic society that may have evolved independently or through some degree of contact with Sumer. Asia Minor (roughly the area of modern Turkey-in-Asia) developed a distinctive culture through such contacts, and other parts of the eastern Mediterranean were affected as trade brought them in touch with both Mesopotamia and Egypt.

The bull-leaper fresco shows what must have been a spectacular display. The women are distinguished by making their bodies paler, a convention often found in Greek pottery painting a millennium later. 15th century BC.

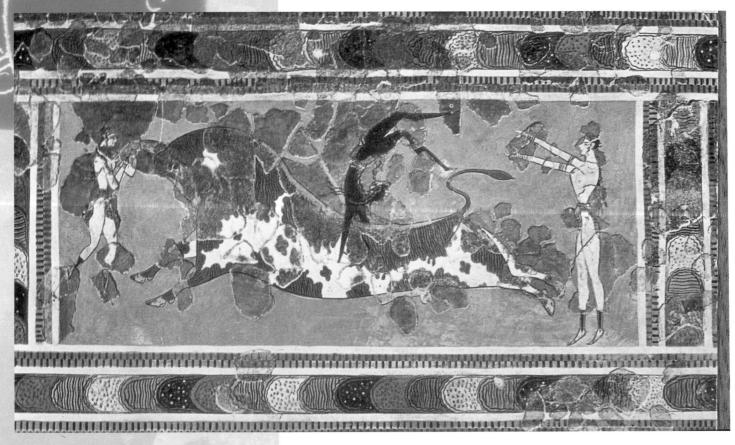

The 'snake goddess' is a small faience (glazed pottery) figure from Knossos in Crete. Dating from about 1600 BC, this fierce, snake-wielding, bare-breasted female has a fine feline headdress and an elaborately flounced costume.

As yet, there were probably no Greeks on what is now the Greek mainland, or on the islands of the Aegean. One or more Greek-speaking peoples are believed to have invaded the mainland from the north somewhere around 2000 BC, almost certainly conquering and absorbing the non-Greek inhabitants, whose existence can be inferred from the presence of a number of unknown alien words in the Greek language.

At about the same time as these obscure events were taking place, Europe's first civilization was emerging on the large island of Crete, only

100km (60 miles) to the south-east of the main-land. Initially, when Cretans met Greeks it was the Greeks who copied and learned from their island neighbours, although eventually the Greeks also had a hand in destroying the culture they had learned from.

This relationship appears to be reflected in one of the best-known of the Greek myths. It pictures Crete as the domain of King Minos, who is said to have exacted an annual tribute from Athens of seven youths and seven girls; these were sacrificed to the Minotaur, a monstrous man-bull who was housed in the centre of a labyrinth. The sacrifices went on until the Athenian hero Theseus managed to slay the Minotaur with the help of the king's daughter, Ariadne, who provided him with a magic sword and the length of thread he needed to find his way out of the labyrinth.

Like many ancient legends, this one probably has some kind of basis in fact, however distorted it may have become in the folk memory. The *labrys*, a double-headed axe, was a widely used symbol in Crete, evidently with a cultic significance; and labyrinth is now taken to mean the palace or hall of the double axe. The bull too was the object of a Cretan cult, though it seems to have been the animal itself, not human beings, that suffered at sacrificial ceremonies. The surviving pictorial evidence shows only one kind of young man or woman who had to face an enraged bull: the bull-leaper, a trained acrobat whose role was apparently to seize the bull by its horns and somersault right over it. It seems likely that the story of Minos incorporates confused recollections of palace complexes that seemed like labyrinths to their rustic Greek visitors, and perhaps also of Greek casualties among the less skilful or less fortunate of the acrobats.

After its fall, Cretan civilization was forgotten until about 1895, when the island's great palaces began to be uncovered by the British archaeologist Sir Arthur Evans. He called the entire culture 'Minoan', after the legendary Minos; and in spite of obvious objections to this fantasy title, it has been generally accepted. But if the name of Minos suggests cruelty and gloom, almost everything else we know about Minoan culture suggests the the opposite. The palaces at Knossos, Phaestos,

Mallia and Zakro seem to exude an atmosphere of tranquil gaiety and civilized leisure. They are complexes of rooms (guest-, store-, administrative, cult, work-, and public rooms) built round an open courtyard with an eye to comfort rather than grandeur. Since Minoan writing has not been deciphered, 'palaces' is no more than an educated guess, but the character of the layout and the arrangements for storing substantial amounts of grain, wine and olive oil (perhaps taxes in kind) make it difficult to interpret them as anything else. The buildings were sophisticated constructions of stone and wood, yet there are no traces of fortifications; and the impression of peace and security is reinforced by the fact that Minoan soldiers do not appear to have worn body armour until late in the history of the culture, when it was unmistakably in decline and possibly controlled by outsiders. The rest of our picture of Minoan society comes from surviving fragments of the bright, cheerful frescos that covered the walls, executed in a vividly expressive cartoon-like style; and from statuettes, plaster reliefs, painted pottery, sarcophagi and stones carved for use as seals. Minoan writing has been preserved on clay tablets but is less informative; it initially took the form of hieroglyphs, which were later replaced by a linear script (called by scholars 'Linear A'); but all attempts to relate the signs to any known language have so far failed.

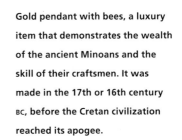

Gold pendant with bees, a luxury item that demonstrates the wealth of the ancient Minoans and the skill of their craftsmen. It was made in the 17th or 16th century BC, before the Cretan civilization reached its apogee.

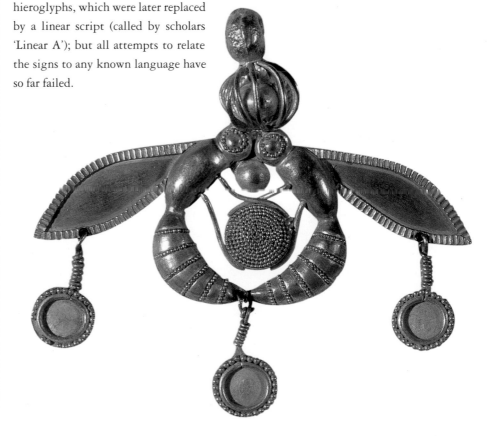

The ruined grandeur of the palace at Knossos, unearthed around 1900 and restored by the British archaeologist Sir Arthur Evans. It was the greatest of the Minoan palaces, remembered centuries after its fall in Homer's epic poem the *Iliad*.

The palaces are the most striking feature of Minoan society, apparently forming self-contained communities of impressive complexity. But town life also flourished, and there is evidence of considerable luxury in the larger houses. In paintings the people of Minoan Crete seem relaxed, attractively dandified creatures – the men striding about in neat loincloths and boots, the groups of gossiping women well-made-up, with puff-sleeved tunics, open at the front to show their breasts, and flounced skirts. Much of the island's wealth must have been generated by trade, and it seems certain that Crete possessed a large merchant navy; the Minoans had a marked taste for marine subjects on their frescos and pottery, accommodating dolphins, octopi and other sea creatures to the spiral and tendril-like patterns they favoured. But this was only one aspect of a wider love of nature that expressed itself in paintings of flowers and birds,

executed with a freedom most unusual in the decorative arts of the ancient world.

These attractive features enhance the favourable effect made by most other remains of Minoan culture; but it is always possible that Cretan brightness and cheerfulness are illusions created by partial evidence and wishful thinking. Evidence of human sacrifice, uncovered in relatively recent times, demonstrates that there was certainly a dark side to the culture, but at the moment it is impossible to be sure whether it was a permanent element in Minoan life or an aberration (perhaps a panic response) caused by one of the disasters that intermittently overtook the island.

One such disaster – probably an earthquake – struck around 1700 BC, but Cretan prosperity was at its height and recovery was swift. The destroyed palaces were rebuilt on an even larger scale than before, and Minoan colonists began to settle in some of the Greek islands and (perhaps more tentatively) at Miletus on the coast of Asia Minor. In fact Minoan civilization reached its apogee in the 17th and 16th centuries, when it exercised an unmistakable and strong influence on the more backward culture of the mainland Greeks. Then, from about 1500 BC, a decline set in, hastened by one or more unidentified catastrophies that wrecked most of the palaces and left the culture too weakened to rebuild.

The part played in these events by internal conflicts and external aggression is largely a matter of speculation. Even more controversial is the role of the volcano-island of Thera (modern Santorini) to the north of Crete. Originally circular, Thera is now moon-shaped as a result of the colossal eruption that blew its centre apart in ancient times; and it has been plausibly suggested that the destruction of Thera was the origin of the legend of Atlantis, the vast continental civilization said to have disappeared beneath the waves. The layer of volcanic ash that settled on Thera had the effect of preserving the town of Acrotiri, which has been uncovered by archaeologists in recent decades. The excavations prove that Thera shared the Minoan way of life (which does not necessarily mean that it was politically linked to Crete), with busy streets of two-storey buildings containing Minoan-style frescos, pottery and other goods.

More devastating than Krakatoa or Mount St Helens, the eruption on Thera was long believed to have occurred around 1450, poisoning the atmosphere and possibly creating an enormous tidal wave that hit Crete with terrible destructive force. The theory provided an attractively neat explanation for the decline of Cretan civilization; but the question of dates is crucial – and accumulating evidence from scientifically verifiable sources such as tree rings and polar ice cores suggests that the eruption took place much earlier, in about 1628 BC. This is currently the majority view, although the evidence is not entirely one-sided and the debate has certainly not yet ended.

Whether an eruption or some other event weakened Crete, the island declined further as a result of Greek attacks and a Greek occupation that began around 1450; all the palaces were burned with the exception of Knossos, which appears to have served as the headquarters of the island's new masters. For reasons unknown they abandoned it surprisingly quickly, around 1400, and at this time, or perhaps somewhat later, Knossos too went up in flames. Crete subsequently recovered some of its prosperity and importance, but its distinctively Minoan culture had collapsed and the island was no longer a dominant presence in the eastern Mediterranean. The immediate future belonged to the warrior society on the mainland, which has come to be described as 'Mycenaean'.

Left: the fisherman and his catch, the best-preserved wall-painting from Acrotiri on the island of Thera. Culturally related to Minoan Crete, Acrotiri was destroyed in the 2nd millennium BC by a volcanic eruption that blew away the centre of the island.

Far left: sophisticated lady. The impression made by this fragment of a Minoan fresco from Knossos is so strong that it is universally known by the nickname 'La Parisienne'. The painting is believed to represent a priestess. 15th century BC.

Cyclopean masonry: the east gallery at Tiryns, one of the principal Mycenaean strongholds. The rugged grandeur of such drystone constructions (that is, set firmly in place without mortar) makes it easy to overlook the skill with which they were made. 15th–13th century BC.

MYCENAE, RICH IN GOLD

The people who entered mainland Greece around 2000 BC soon spread out and settled in its lowland and coastal areas. The most abundant evidence of their culture has been found in the Peloponnese, the large peninsula comprising the whole of southern Greece. Here, at Mycenae, Tiryns and Pylos, chiefs or kings lived in forbidding, strongly fortified palaces sited on strategically located hills. Mycenae occupied a particularly powerful position, controlling the land route to central Greece through the Isthmus of Corinth, and the Greek myths and the epic verses of the first great Greek poet, Homer, confirm its importance. Homer's Mycenae is the stronghold of the High King of all the Greeks, and the site has in fact yielded the richest finds to the archaeologist; as a result, the entire early Greek culture from about 1600 BC has been labelled 'Mycenaean', and all Greeks of the period are often indiscriminately described as Mycenaeans. In central Greece, Athens and Orchomenos were already of some importance, but the most powerful centre outside the Peloponnese was probably Thebes, whose legendary history also played a part in later Greek myth; it was said to have been ruled by King Oedipus, who solved the riddle of the Sphinx but was doomed unwittingly to murder his father and marry his mother – hence 'Oedipus complex', the psychoanalytical term for the jealous hostility said to be displayed by the boy child towards his father.

Somewhere around 1600 BC Mycenae became really wealthy, as the contents of its graves have shown. Homer called Mycenae 'rich in gold'; and so it proved when, 3,500 years later, the settlement was excavated. Mycenae's rulers were buried with gold face masks and quantities of swords, daggers and ornaments, made of gold, bronze or rock crystal, hammered, engraved, inlaid or carved with impressive skill. The influence of Minoan art was very strong during this period, and intensified contacts between the two cultures, whether political or economic, may well account for the sudden appearance of so much wealth at Mycenae. But there is no evidence, or likelihood, of a Cretan occupation or colonization of the mainland. Despite the Mycenaeans' cultural debts to Crete, their way of life and values were very different from those of the islanders. Among the most splendid archaeological discoveries at Mycenae were the masks of beaten gold placed over the faces of dead kings; and these portray the kings with beards and moustaches, unlike the clean-shaven Cretans. The kings' skeletons indicate that they were also taller than the islanders. Unlike the Minoans they valued amber goods, which had to be imported from the Baltic, and their carvings on stone grave markers show that they were familiar with the horse-drawn chariot, which was still unknown on Crete. (The horse had been domesticated on the Eurasian

Mask of beaten gold, placed over the face of a dead Mycenaean king. A number of these masks were found by Heinrich Schliemann, who believed that he was looking upon 'the face of Agamemnon'. It actually dates from the 16th century BC, even earlier than the time of the semi-legendary hero.

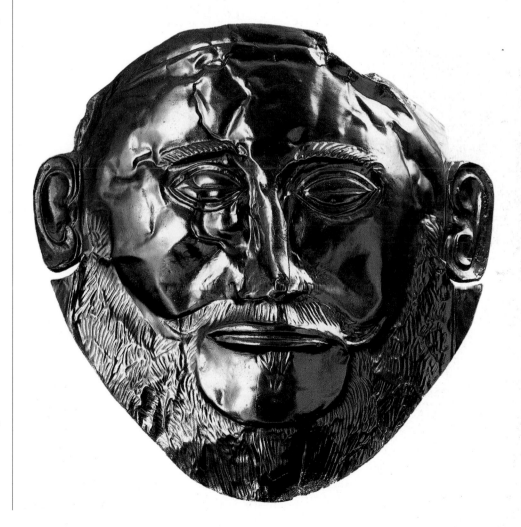

The imposing Lion Gate at Mycenae has the oldest known monumental sculpture from ancient Greece (c.1250 BC), set in a recessed triangular area which serves to lighten the weight on the lintel.

lization in the 16th and 15th centuries gives the impression of a rugged and vigorous warrior society that has not yet been tamed or sapped by the wealth it has acquired.

Although the greatest treasures have been found at Mycenae itself, the entire Mycenaean world flourished during this period. Supplies of gold, silver and bronze (which is an alloy of copper and tin) can only have been acquired from abroad, and if this was done by trade the Mycenaean kingdoms must have had a surplus of produce such as wine, wool and olive oil to exchange for them; whether the surplus was created by improved land use, or by taxation of a helpless peasantry, is a moot question. Not surprisingly, it has been suggested that this warrior people owed their wealth to piracy and war, as well as to trade or home production; in either case they must have been experienced seafarers.

Pottery and other evidence indicates a Mycenaean presence in the Cyclades, on Cyprus (a prime source of copper), and of course on Crete from about 1450 BC. Though we cannot be certain that it was the Mycenaeans who destroyed the Minoan palaces (their successful invasion may have been a result rather than a cause of the destruction), their presence at Knossos is beyond question because it is confirmed by written evidence. The clay tablets found at Knossos are written in the script that scholars call Linear A, and also in a later script employing many of the same signs, Linear B. Both remained undeciphered until as recently as 1952, when a brilliant scholar named Michael Ventris was able to show that the language of Linear B was an early form of Greek. This was not true of Linear A, which evidently recorded the now-lost language of Minoan Crete and is consequently still undeciphered. Clearly the Mycenaeans learned to write from the Minoans, adapting their Linear A script to put down Greek words; they may well have done so during their brief occupation of Crete. Linear B tablets have been found not only at Knossos, but also on the mainland at Pylos, Mycenae and Thebes. They owe their survival to the terrible fires that occur in the wake of earthquakes and invasions: the records

steppe a century or so earlier.) The emphasis on weaponry, the massiveness of the citadels and the organization of the palace, centred on a great hall of the type that inevitably suggests the roistering feasts of Homeric heroes – all of these are distinctly un-Minoan. Altogether Mycenaean civi-

scratched on to tablets of damp clay were baked hard by the fires and survived the great palaces in which they were kept. Apart from a few inscriptions painted on pottery, there are no other relics of Mycenaean writing, although it is at least possible that the Minoans and Mycenaeans confided some significant communications to skins or other perishable materials. However, in most societies writing has started as a humdrum form of record-making, and this is certainly the case in the surviving Mycenaean tablets. Their contents are essentially civil-service memoranda – lists of stores, allocations, jobs scheduled to be done for the authorities, and so on. They reveal that Mycenaean society was complex and highly specialized (from a separately functioning king and commander-in-chief down to distinctions between crafts whose meaning we can now only guess at); and also that it was strictly controlled from the top. It was, in fact, a small-scale version of the great empires of Mesopotamia and Egypt.

Although they left or were driven out of Crete around 1400, the Mycenaeans were more prosperous than ever in the 14th century. They had contacts with the Lipari Islands and the Italian mainland, and established trading posts in Syria. In Egypt, Mycenaean pottery has been found in the ruins of the Pharaoh Akhenaton's capital, Tel-el-Amarna, some 300km (190 miles) up the Nile. And around 1300 the ruler of the Hittite empire in Asia Minor wrote a diplimatic note to a fellow-sovereign who is generally believed to have been the king of Mycenae, explaining his violation of some territory on the west coast of Asia Minor belonging to his correspondent. The injured party was addressed as the 'king of the Ayyiwah'; and 'Ayyiwah' has been interpreted as a Hittite's attempt to get his tongue round 'Achaeans', Homer's name for the Greeks of Mycenaean times. Rulers of empires sometimes have good reason to cultivate their lesser brethren, but if the 'king of the Ayyiwah' *was* the king of Mycenae, with an outpost in Asia Minor, he must have carried a fair amount of political and economic clout. The assumption that the Greek king in question was the ruler of Mycenae is not, of course, unchallengeable; but both later tradition and the wealth of Mycenae – far exceeding that of any other 14th-century site – argue strongly in its favour.

Dagger blade from a royal shaft grave at Mycenae. Made of bronze and inlaid with gold, niello and silver, it shows hunters attacking a lion, which has slain one of them; c.1500 BC.

THE TROJAN WAR

The Trojan Horse. This relief on an amphora is the earliest known image of the Horse, made c.675 BC and found on Mykonos. It includes a set of panels revealing the Greek warriors hidden inside.

During the 13th century the Mycenaean kingdoms were under pressure and beginning to show the strain. At Mycenae itself there is evidence of declining trade and less competent home production. As precautions against real or imagined dangers, the massive cyclopean walls of the citadel were extended and an underground passage was constructed that linked it to a spring outside the walls.

Similar measures were taken at Tiryns, and a defensive wall was built across the Isthmus of Corinth, implying that the Peloponnese faced a threat from the north. An underground stairway has also been discovered at Athens, which has otherwise left few traces in the Mycenaean record.

If the legendary Trojan War ever took place, it must have been in this troubled century. The war is supposed to have been caused by the elopement of Helen, Queen of Sparta, and Paris, one of the sons of King Priam of Troy. The deserted husband was Menelaus, King of Sparta and brother of Agamemnon, who was King of Mycenae and, as such, High King or overlord of all the Greeks. Under Agamemnon's leadership a Greek armada sailed for Troy to avenge Menelaus and bring back Helen; and in the course of a ten-year siege heroes on both sides, such as Achilles and Hector, found glory and death. Finally the city was taken by a ruse: the Greeks sailed away as if despairing of victory, leaving a gigantic wooden horse on the shore; the rejoicing Trojans hauled the horse into the city; and in the dead of night Greek warriors emerged from their hiding-place in the horse's belly, opened the gates to their comrades, sacked and burned Troy, and led the survivors away into slavery.

Nobody can be certain that any of these events took place. But the story would need to be outlined here even if it were known to be wholly fictitious, since it occupied a vital place in Greek culture. For the Greeks, the war was at once heroic history and a kind of archetype of human experience – particularly those parts of the action described in Homer's great epic poem *The Iliad*, dating from several centuries later. The works of Homer acquired a unique authority: they were not only great literature but also ancestral history, repositories of wisdom, and an inexhaustible quarry for later writers, who might bring radically diverse attitudes to bear on the same materials. The only rough equivalent in our culture is the Bible, whose sayings are also quoted in all sorts of contexts and whose stories have also been retold and reinterpreted many times. The Trojan War and its aftermath, like the story of Oedipus and his children, permeated the Greek imagination for well over a thousand years after the events on which they were based.

The site of Troy remained unknown until 1870, when it was discovered by the German businessman-turned-archaeologist Heinrich Schliemann. He succeeded where others had failed because of his passionate belief in the accuracy of *The Iliad*. The clues provided by the epic encouraged Schliemann to excavate a mound

on the north-west coast of Asia Minor; and it is generally agreed that the city beneath it must indeed be ancient Troy. This was by no means Schliemann's last contribution to archaeology. He went on to make the first serious excavations at Mycenae and Tiryns, and his fabulous finds included the gold death masks in the Mycenaean graves – masks that he wrongly but understandably took to be those of the Trojan War heroes. After examining the most noble-looking, he wrote with touching enthusiasm: 'I have looked upon the face of Agamemnon!'.

Later excavations revealed not one but nine Troys: the site was a good one, controlling the entrance to the Black Sea, and it had been settled, razed and re-peopled again and again from the Early Bronze Age to Roman times. Homer's Troy is now thought to be 'Troy VIIa', which was destroyed by fire in about 1220 BC. Large storage jars have been found buried in the floors of the houses, suggesting careful preparations to withstand a siege; and there are various indications that the end was accompanied by human violence. So it looks as though here, too, Greek legend has a basis in fact.

The fall of Troy also dooms its ruling family. In this vase painting the Greek Neoptolemus batters King Priam to death, using the body of his own grandson, Astyanax, as a weapon.

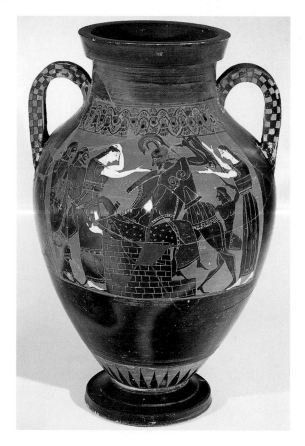

DECLINE AND FALL

An episode from Homer's *Odyssey*: Odysseus listens to the song of the Sirens; he has had himself tied to the ship's mast so that he can hear them but cannot be lured to his death; his men, their ears plugged, row on stolidly. Vase painting, c.490 BC.

If the Trojan War did take place in the 1230s, the Greeks' triumph must have been short-lived, for in the years that followed Mycenaean society went into rapid decline. The continuations of Trojan War legend hint at internal troubles in several states. After his victory Agamemnon returned to Mycenae, only to be murdered by his wife Clytemnestra and her lover; but Agamemnon was avenged soon afterwards by his son Orestes, even though this involved killing his own mother. In Homer's other great epic, the *Odyssey*, the hero is Odysseus, shrewdest of the Greek leaders at Troy; after years of war and wandering he returned to his palace at Ithaca to find it occupied by a gang of outsiders, each hoping to

take over Odysseus' wife and kingdom; Odysseus, more fortunate than Agamemnon, killed them all and reclaimed his own.

The archaeological record is less eloquent but still more sombre. From about 1200 onwards the great Mycenaean centres were devastated and fell into ruin; Mycenae seems to have made a temporary recovery, but a second catastrophe around 1150 BC ended its greatness for ever. The population of many areas fell sharply as refugees fled *en masse* to safer places such as the north-west corner of the Peloponnese and the Aegean islands. Several explanations have been put forward for this catastrophe. The decline in Mycenaean power, visible even in the 13th century, may have been the result of over-rapid population growth, which would have reduced the amount of surplus produce available for export. Trade with the eastern Mediterranean may have been disrupted by upheavals in the region. And the response of the Mycenaean kingdoms could well have been to make war on one another in a struggle to control such resources as there were. If this general account is correct, then the destruction of the Mycenaean centres may have been brought about by the Mycenaeans themselves rather than by the operation of outside forces.

However, this collapse does seem to have been related to a wider upheaval that sent peoples wandering over the entire eastern Mediterranean. Egyptian records in particular give a fairly clear picture of 'Peoples of the Sea' who twice descended on the Nile delta. They were beaten off by the Egyptians, but their incursions did bring down the mighty Hittite empire, and that alone must have destabilized the entire region. The Peoples of the Sea may have raided Greece, perhaps recruiting as well as doing mischief; at any rate there seem to have been Mycenaean Greeks in their ranks – and, coincidentally or otherwise, there are references in the *Odyssey* to raids on Egypt, which Helen's husband Menelaus is said to have visited before returning home from the war.

The Mycenaeans among the Peoples of the Sea may have been refugees, in flight from the invaders of their own territories. Was there an invasion of Greece, and if so did the invaders destroy the Mycenaean kingdoms or just move in after their destruction? Opinions differ sharply on

this. The 'invaders' have been identified as a new Greek-speaking people, the Dorians. They were the occupants of much of central and southern Greece, but this fact is known only through studies of the distribution of Greek dialects, which show that there was a large bloc of Doric speakers surrounded by, or interspersed with, others, including Greeks speaking a dialect that was much closer to the language of the Linear B tablets. The inference that the Dorians were newcomers is supported by ancient Greek traditions that identify them as invaders; but the archaeological evidence is sparse, and it is possible to doubt whether such an invasion ever took place. During subsequent migrations there seems to have been no hostility between the different dialect-speaking groups, and it may be significant that Greek legend pictures the Dorians as Heracleidae (children of Heracles) righteously returning from exile rather than entering Mycenaean Greece as strangers.

However it came about, the collapse of the Mycenaean order was shatteringly complete. Even the art of writing was lost – the only known example of such a cultural regression. For several hundred years, down to about 750 BC, the Greeks were illiterate and, with a few exceptions, unable to organize or build on any scale, although they preserved their farming and craft skills. Understandably, the period between 1100 and 750 has been called the Dark Age of Greece.

Dressed like a queen: photograph of Sophia Schliemann, the young Greek wife of the 19th-century German adventurer and archaeologist who discovered Troy. She is wearing some of the gold jewellery unearthed on the site.

2 THE GREAT AGE OF THE CITY-STATE

A NEW TYPE OF GREEK SOCIETY EMERGED FROM THE DARK AGE, IN THE FORM OF SMALL, INDEPENDENT CITY-STATES. THESE SPREAD BY TRADE AND MIGRATION UNTIL THERE WERE GREEK COLONIES FROM THE MEDITERRANEAN COAST OF SPAIN TO THE CRIMEA. IN THE GREEKS' AEGEAN HEARTLAND, POLITICAL SYSTEMS ROSE AND FELL UNTIL THE 5TH CENTURY BC, WHEN DEMOCRATIC ATHENS AND MILITARY-MINDED SPARTA TOOK THE LEAD AMONG THE CITY-STATES. THE ATTEMPTS OF THE MIGHTY PERSIAN EMPIRE TO CONQUER GREECE WERE DEFEATED ON LAND AND SEA, AND ATHENS ENJOYED A BRIEF POLITICAL PRE-EMINENCE AMONG THE CITY-STATES THAT ONLY INTENSIFIED HER RIVALRY WITH SPARTA. MEANWHILE, THE GREEKS CREATED WONDERFUL WORKS OF ART AND ARCHITECTURE, AND CREATED NEW VEHICLES OF THOUGHT AND EMOTION IN PHILOSOPHY, LITERATURE AND THE DRAMA. THE DEFEAT OF ATHENS BY SPARTA IN THE LONG PELOPONNESIAN WAR LEFT THE GREEK CITY-STATES AS DISUNITED AS EVER, AND BY THE 4TH CENTURY BC THEIR INDEPENDENCE WAS VISIBLY THREATENED BY THE RISING POWER OF MACEDON IN THE NORTH. CLEARLY THE GREAT AGE OF THE CITY-STATE WAS COMING TO AN END.

Out of the Dark Age: painted terracotta votive figures from Boeotia, a region in central Greece close to Attica. From the 7th century BC such figures were mass-produced in moulds; these date from about 600-550 BC.

OUT OF THE DARK AGE

Despite the Mycenaean collapse and the Dark Age, there were important continuities on the everyday level of Greek life. There were also positive aspects to disaster and impoverishment. Upheavals and migrations widened the area of Greek settlement, making the Aegean a Greek lake. Fleeing Mycenaeans established themselves on Cyprus. Others crossed from the eastern mainland to Lesbos, Chios and Samos, and on to the west coast of Asia Minor; the central section of the coast, Ionia, played a distinguished part in later Greek history, and its population was to remain predominantly Greek for almost three thousand years. The Dorians also broke out of the mainland; they reached Crete and Rhodes, and may even have taken some part in the settlement of Ionia.

Inability to import the copper and tin needed to manufacture bronze had the effect of forcing the Greeks back on local resources, and in the 11th century BC iron tools and weapons began to be widely used. The social consequences were important, since iron was a more democratic metal, because it was more widely available, than bronze. Kings and warrior castes could monopolize the use of bronze, but iron ore could be mined with relative ease in many places, so that tools and weapons became more widely distributed in a community. This made possible the emergence of the Greek city-state form that was to spread all over the Mediterranean world. By contrast with the militaristic and bureaucratic Mycenaean kingdoms, the city-states that emerged from the Dark Age were much simpler institutions: small, virtually self-sufficient agricultural communities, well able to support the city that served each as a meeting-place, market town and wartime refuge rather than a 'capital' in the modern sense. Such communities had little need for centralized organization, and they provided at least a basis for wide participation in public affairs. Their adaptable, unstructured nature made possible many of the Greeks' finest achievements.

Out of the Dark Age: this splendidly fashioned head of a griffin reflects the Eastern images that transformed Greek art; made late in the 7th century BC, as a decorated a bronze vessel.

AN EXPANDING WORLD

In the 8th century BC the Dark Age came to an end. It was probably never as dark as its name implies, and its later phases seem to have been relatively peaceful. As a result, in the 8th century population increase led to more extensive cultivation of the soil, and Greek traders were again seen in most parts of the Mediterranean. Writing was rediscovered, this time through contact with the Phoenicians, whose alphabet was an instrument far superior to the syllabic script of Linear B. By adapting the Phoenician alphabet to represent vowels as well as consonants, the Greeks created a flexible and expressive medium, capable of recording not just lists but the most subtle nuances of meaning. An early consequence was the writing-down of the *Iliad* and the *Odyssey*, perhaps after one or more 'Homers' had linked, shaped and polished a mass of traditional oral materials into two compendious epics.

Although new land was brought under cultivation, population increase continued over such a long period that the simple Greek economy could not cope. The soil was relatively poor and strictly limited to lowland areas that were hemmed in by the mountain ranges that dominated the Greek landscape. The Greeks tried several responses. As already noted, one was to increase trade, for example by exporting pottery and olive oil in return for the cereals produced in Egypt and the lands beyond the Black Sea. Another was to export men, relieving the pressure on resources at home. Many Greeks served as mercenary soldiers in Asia and Egypt; some of them scratched their names on one of the famous colossal statues at Abu Simbel, 1,000km (620 miles) up the Nile. A third response, combining the advantages of the first two, was to send out colonies from a mother-city to set up a new city-state on unoccupied or unconquered territory. With little room for further expansion in the Aegean, the Greeks looked further afield, beginning with a humble trading post in northern Syria around 800 BC and bursting out to the west by the mid-8th century. The Egyptians, Phoenicians and Etruscans effectively barred the way in many places, but Southern Italy and Sicily were so densely settled, and proved so

rich, that the area became known as 'Greater Greece'. Few mainland or Aegean Greek cities could match the wealth and power of ancient Syracuse; and the inhabitants of Sybaris were so renowned for luxury-loving that 'sybarite' is still used in English as a term of puritanical abuse. Ionian Greeks established a colony at Massilia, now Marseilles in France, which in turn gave birth to colonies on the Riviera (Nice, Antibes, Monaco) and the Spanish coast. Attracted by the trading possibilities offered by Scythian wheat, fish and timber, Greek cities also established colonies and trading posts along the north (Thracian) coast of the Aegean, on the Hellespont (modern Dardanelles), the Sea of Marmara and the Bosporus, and finally right round the shores of the Black Sea. Virtually all the Greek city-states played some part in the colonizing movement – even the little island of Thera, which was responsible for founding Cyrene, easily the most important Greek settlement on the North African coast. The colonizing impulse lasted for about two and a half centuries, petering out only after 500 BC.

There is no doubt about the urgency of the pressures that persuaded city-states to send out colonists. Surviving decrees make it clear that many colonists were unwilling to go, and that severe penalties were visited upon those who tried to return to their native city. Not surprisingly, relations between colony and mother-city were not particularly close. A colony was not a possession of the mother-city, and was not expected to look to it for help after the first few years of settlement. There was no shared citizenship; apart from a few short-lived exceptions the colony was completely independent; and although there was generally some kind of sentimental tie, war between mother-city and colony was not unthinkable. For this reason no individual state gained in political power from this mass-movement of the Greek people: the Greeks remained curiously small-scale, if not parochial, in their political thinking and political passions. But trade and colonization did enormously enrich the Greek world and made Greek society more complex, contributing to the achievements, and also to the turmoil, of the following centuries.

Opposite: beyond the Black Sea. This breastplate was made by a Greek craftsman for a Scythian client in the Crimea; it is decorated with a head of Medusa, the mythical creature whose serpent hair turned those who saw it to stone. 5th–4th century BC.

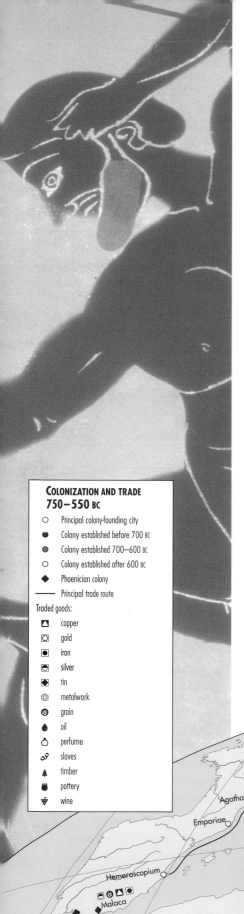

TURMOIL AND TYRANNY

The growth of wealth and trade upset the Greek social and political order. By the end of the 8th century kingship had long disappeared from most states, or had been reduced to a near-ceremonial role. Political power lay with the aristocracy (*aristoi*, 'best people'), and was based on its large landholdings, military prowess, and traditional prestige and clan following. The *aristoi* had encouraged the colonizing movement, since population growth threatened their power by increasing the numbers of the poor and discontented; but the long-term effects of colonization and trade proved to be at least as disruptive. As part of their far-flung trade the Greeks exported items such as oil and wine, pottery and metal-work; and this produced not only a few wealthy merchants but an entire class of non-aristocratic landowners and other men of substance. Later, coinage was introduced: that is, precious metal whose purity could be relied on because it was guaranteed by the state that minted it. This, the first true money, came to Greece at about the end of the 7th century from Lydia, a powerful non-Greek kingdom which had grown up to the south of Ionia. As well as facilitating trade, money made transfers of property easier, breaking up the older patterns of land-holding and the loyalties that went with them.

In this situation the aristocrats struggled to maintain their privileges and powers, but their

A surge of colonization and trade sent the ancient Greeks all over the Mediterranean and the Black Sea in the space of 200 years. Only the great Eastern kingdoms and the Phoenician colonies in the western Mediterranean restrained their expansion.

COLONIZATION AND TRADE 750–550 BC

- ○ Principal colony-founding city
- ◑ Colony established before 700 BC
- ● Colony established 700–600 BC
- ○ Colony established after 600 BC
- ◆ Phoenician colony
- — Principal trade route

Traded goods:
- ◭ copper
- ◙ gold
- ◨ iron
- ◙ silver
- ◙ tin
- ⚙ metalwork
- ◔ grain
- ◖ oil
- ◔ perfume
- ∽ slaves
- ⚑ timber
- ◙ pottery
- ▽ wine

Agatha · Massilia · Aleria · Emporiae · Hemeroscopium · Malaca · Carthage · Leptis · Ischia · Himera · Selinus · Gela · Sicily · Cumae · Gravisca · Sybaris · Locri · Syracuse · Euesperides · Cyrene · Naucratis · Spina · Epidamnus · Corcyra · Chalcis · Eretria · Corinth · Megara · Thera · Mesembria · Abdera · Byzantium · Phocaea · Miletus · Phaselis · Olbia · Tyras · Istria · Heraclaia · Sinope · Amisus · Panticapaeum · Phasis · Trapezus · Al Mina · Tanais · *Black Sea* · *Mediterranean Sea*

Hard currency; silver coin with the head of the goddess Athena; 6th century BC. The first true money appeared in the 7th-century kingdom of Lydia in Asia Minor; the Greeks soon followed suit.

position was fatally weakened by changes in military tactics and technology. Until about 700 BC the mounted man (and that meant the aristocrat, who could afford the heavy cost of a horse and equipment) was supreme. Then new tactics were devised, and the cavalryman went down before a moving wall of shields borne by armed and armoured infantrymen, known as hoplites. The aristocracy lost its military justification, and any man who could afford the new, far less expensive equipment, was of value to the state and a potential aspirant to political rights; in fact, the hoplites virtually constituted a separate social class, mainly drawn from the independent landowners with small or medium-sized holdings.

In the complicated struggles that ensued for control of the state, the most frequent victor was a general or maverick aristocrat who seized power with a greater or lesser degree of popular support and became a tyrant. 'Tyrant' was the term used by the Greeks for a ruler whose authority had no legal or constitutional basis; initially it did not imply moral disapproval, let alone blood-thirstiness on the part of the tyrant, although the experience of the 7th and 6th centuries left most Greeks in no doubt about the corrupting effects of absolute power when it was wielded by an individual.

Most tyrants tried to limit the influence of the aristocracy, if only because it was the main threat to their own authority. In quest of popularity most of them made more or less serious gestures towards the redistribution of land, a measure eagerly desired by the poor, to whom the new

The Charioteer of Delphi. The famous figure, holding the reins with one hand, survives from a bronze group that once included a chariot and a team of horses. It was sent to Delphi to commemorate a Sicilian tyrant's victory at the games held there in 478 or 474 BC.

money economy often meant no more than burdensome debts accumulating on inadequately profitable holdings. The shrewder tyrants signalled their devotion to the city by sponsoring programmes of public works while simultaneously seeking to form mutual-aid groups with fellow-tyrants in other states. Nevertheless tyrannies were generally short-lived, since they either failed to be useful or outlived their usefulness once they had carried out a 'popular' programme. One of the more important exceptions was Corinth, whose commercial prosperity made it the leading Greek city-state for much of the 7th century. There, a political adventurer named Cypselus became the first and one of the most successful of the tyrants. In about 657 BC, backed by a middle class excluded from political influence, he overthrew and exiled the aristocratic Bacchidae, of whom he is said to have been a poor relation. He created a vested interest in their non-return by distributing their lands, and effectively promoted Corinth's trade interests, remaining so popular that he was able to dispense with a bodyguard. In about 625 he was succeeded by his son Periander, whose 40-year reign can be regarded as the golden age of Corinth. The city's colonies were, most unusually, kept under close control, forwarding the booming trade with western Italy, Asia Minor and even Egypt. Among public works, Periander is credited with constructing a causeway across the Isthmus that enabled ships to cross it by portage instead of sailing right round the Peloponnese. Temple-building at home played its part in the creation of the first Greek architectural style, Doric, while the export market was dominated by Corinthian painted pottery of unequalled quality. Despite his achievements, Periander displayed the cruelty and excesses that have come to be associated with tyranny; he kept his grip on power to the end, but his nephew and successor Psammetichus was thrust aside after ruling for only three years.

Even Athens, later the doyen of democracies, underwent a period of turmoil and tyranny. Her crisis occurred later than those of most other states, perhaps because popular energy had been diverted by expansion into Attica, the relatively large area of countryside surrounding the city, where, as luck would have it, no rival settlements had survived the fall of the Mycenaean culture.

When tensions did begin to build up, two attempts were made to avoid faction-fighting and tyranny by appointing a universally respected man to mend the laws and the constitution. In 621 BC Draco devised Athens' first written code of laws: it was too favourable to the aristocracy to satisfy the citizenry, and the death penalty was prescribed for so many offences that the word 'draconian' has passed into English as a synonym for excessive severity. Rather better results were achieved in the late 590s, when Solon, an aristocrat who had also acquired experience as a merchant, was given full powers to reform the state. He cancelled all debts, abolished slavery for debt, and rescued as many as possible of those who had already been enslaved for that reason. He also gave the poorer citizens a greater role in public affairs, and took measures to protect their rights while leaving the old aristocracy the leading position in the state. Then, in a culminating high-minded gesture, he set out on his travels for ten years, putting to an immediate test the new laws' capacity for survival without the backing of his authority.

Solon's laws survived, but his liberal-conservative reforms failed to prevent party strife or economic discontents, and finally the state was taken over by Pisistratus. He might be described as a career-tyrant, since the successful coup of about 546 BC was his third attempt in 15 years; and once established he remained in power until his death in 527. Like Cypselus, Pisistratus was highly successful, observing legal forms and reconciling most of his opponents while immensely strengthening the state. He was one of the beneficiaries of Athens' increasing prosperity, which eased social tensions and swelled his tax revenues; but he used the revenues sensibly by giving long-term loans to poor farmers, probably to help them change over from cereal to vine and olive cultivation for the export market. Like other populist dictators he also impressed and employed the population by undertaking great public works and encouraging spectacular festivals, a policy that helped to make Athens the most splendid city in Greece over the next few generations.

Pisistratus' son Hippias inherited the tyranny and was initially popular. But tyrants were rapidly disappearing from late 6th-century Greece, and although Hippias survived a coup attempt in 514, he found few allies when the Spartans marched on Athens four years later to help his enemies. Surrounded, he held out on the Acropolis but agreed to surrender in return for a safe passage into exile. Soon afterwards Cleisthenes, one of the party leaders, took up the popular cause, greatly increased the number of Athenian citizens, and put through a series of reforms that committed Athens to democracy.

The Tyrannicides Harmodius and Aristogeiton, who killed Hipparchus in 514 BC before they perished in turn. Later Greeks looked back on them as heroes and their deed was commemorated c.470 BC by a bronze group of which this is a marble Roman copy.

OLIGARCHS AND DEMOCRATS

By the end of the 6th century, the age of Greek tyrants was over. But political conflict within the states merely assumed a different form – between the oligarchic party, which aimed to restrict political rights to an elite group, and the democrats, who favoured giving some voice in public affairs to all citizens. The oligarchs represented a fusion of the old aristocracy and new rich; the democrats were generally drawn from the poorer classes of citizens, although their leadership was often assumed by aristocrats and their followers,

Themistocles, the Athenian commander who planned the great naval victory over the Persians at Salamis. Despite his services he became a victim of political conflicts and died in exile.

who might champion the popular party from ambition, idealism or (as time went on, probably the most common reason) traditional alignment. At Athens, the Alcmaeonid family gave the democratic cause Megacles, leader of the 'party of the coast', who had both opposed and allied with Pisistratus; his son, the reformer Cleisthenes; the most famous of all Athenian leaders, Pericles, who was an Alcmaeonid on his mother's side; and a number of lesser figures. 'Democracy' in an ancient Greek context involved various degrees of popular participation, but even in the most democratic of city-states, Athens, it was never intended to apply to the non-citizen majority of foreign residents, women, children and slaves.

The 5th century BC was, like the 20th century AD, one in which ideology, patriotism and self-interest produced political confusion. A democratic state might intervene in the affairs of another state to help fellow-democrats, or might support an oligarchy which expediency made its ally; oligarchs might put loyalty to the state before party, or might conspire to hand over their city to an alien army; and so on, through all the possible permutations of interest and conviction. By any standards the Greeks were extraordinarily volatile and violent, and the 5th-century record is full of changes of regime, gross betrayals, broken oaths and harsh reprisals.

In this unstable world there appeared to be two fixed points: Athens and Sparta. They were the largest, strongest and most stable of Aegean Greek states, the one committed to democracy and the other to oligarchy; ironically, it was the Spartans who had rescued Athens from tyranny, only to see the Athenians adopt what they considered to be the equally intemperate democratic system. Both Sparta and Athens possessed an unusually large territorial base, having concentrated on expansion locally rather than on colonization. But whereas Athens had integrated Attica into the city-state, making Athenians of its inhabitants, the Spartans remained a kind of master-race holding down far more numerous peoples, many of them reduced to the status of serfs (helots). To maintain their fragile mastery the Spartans turned themselves into a people of full-time professional soldiers, living an austerely dedicated and largely communal life from which luxury, trade and culture had virtually been abolished. Sparta had the finest soldiers in Greece, and also the most conservative and unimaginative leaders. Ultimately hers was a sterile society, politically as well as culturally. By the 5th century she was easily the largest Greek state; but with no more than some 8,000 citizen-soldiers, further expansion by conquest without making partners of the conquered would have brought danger rather than security. In all her later wars, therefore, Sparta found it impossible to exploit her victories other than by setting up friendly oligarchic regimes in defeated cities. Spartan conquests were bound to be temporary, and much of her policy had the negative aim of stemming the growing influence of democratic Athens.

Although their constitutions were stable by comparison with those of their neighbours, neither Sparta nor Athens was entirely free of internal conflicts. The Spartans tended to fear the ambitions of their most successful kings and generals; Athenians, too, were often suspicious of the intentions of gifted and popular individuals, and they were also uneasily aware that a minority favourable to oligarchy existed in the background, ready to assume power if disaster overtook the state. However, for most of the 5th century BC Athens and Sparta represented opposing principles that might or might not prove able to co-exist. Whether or not conflict was inevitable, during the first half of the century it was deferred by the need to confront a greater threat that came from outside the Greek world.

Prisoners taken: their hands tied, the captives are being led away by two hoplites. There was constant warfare between the Greek city-states. 5th-century black-figure vase painting.

A foot soldier, or hoplite, running with his shield, helmet and spear. Athenian red-figure painting, skilfully designed to fit into the inside of a large drinking-cup; c.510 BC.

THE PERSIAN WARS

Hostility between Greek and Greek was so ingrained that it took the threat of being enslaved by an alien superpower to produce even a partial and temporary unity. The superpower was Persia, the latest and most formidable of the empires of Western Asia. In the 540s, under Cyrus the Great, the Persians swept through Asia Minor, destroyed the Lydian kingdom of Croesus – still a byword for fabulous wealth – and captured the Greek coastal cities in Ionia. Only a few years later Egypt was subdued, and the Persian empire stretched from India to Libya.

The Persian 'Great Kings' showed little interest in European Greece, an apparently insignificant region that could only be reached by land after a march right round the Black Sea. The situation changed when the Asiatic Greeks revolted in 499. Athens came to their aid, albeit briefly and rather half-heartedly; and when the revolt was crushed after a gruelling six-year struggle, the Persian king Darius turned his resentment against the Greeks. Athens and Sparta were particularly marked out for punishment, since they had responded to demands for submission by insolently executing the Persian messengers who carried them. In 490 a Persian force of some 20,000 men crossed the Aegean and landed on the Attic mainland at Marathon; with them was the aged ex-tyrant Hippias, who was to be

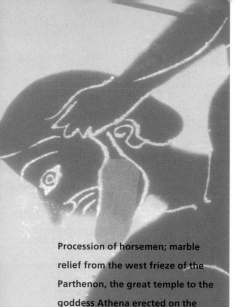

Procession of horsemen; marble relief from the west frieze of the Parthenon, the great temple to the goddess Athena erected on the Acropolis at Athens. Among other things, the Parthenon celebrated Athens' role in the Persian Wars and her imperial destiny.

reinstalled in Athens as a Persian puppet. But at Marathon the Athenian hoplites, led by Miltiades, attacked and enveloped an enemy that outnumbered them by two to one. The Persians were routed and slaughtered as they fled to their ships.

The battle of Marathon was the greatest feat of Athenian arms; but in Persian terms the expedition was a small-scale affair, no more than a raid that had gone wrong. Ten years later, when other distractions had been dealt with, Darius' son and successor, Xerxes, led a major Persian effort to break into Europe. He collected an enormous army, bridged the Hellespont with boats, and invaded Greece by land and sea. Some Greek states were bought off by the Persians, but Sparta, Athens and others had organized themselves even before the invasion into a defensive league; the Athenians tactfully yielded overall command on land and sea to the Spartans, though the Athenian leader Themistocles seems to have been the brains behind the subsequent campaign. The Greeks' hopes lay chiefly in the Spartan army and the Athenian navy, which had been much enlarged by the foresight of Themistocles. However, it seemed unlikely that the Greek forces could hold up against the sheer weight of the Persian onslaught.

Xerxes' army came down from the north through Thessaly, and the Spartan King Leonidas, commanding a hastily assembled mixed force, made a stand at Thermopylae where a narrow pass controlled the coastal route into central Greece. When the Persians discovered a mountain path that outflanked the Greeks, Leonidas and his personal guard of three hundred fought to the last man while the rest of the Greek forces made their escape. The episode is one of the most famous in history, though 'the 300 Spartans' are rather unfairly remembered in legend at the expense of the 1,100 Boeotians who also formed part of the rearguard, perhaps because Thebes and other Boeotian cities now made peace with the apparently irresistible Persians.

Meanwhile, the Greek navy was forced back at Artemisium, though the Persians and their Phoenician satellites suffered considerable losses from battle and weather. The way to central Greece now lay open. Athens was evacuated and the Spartans prepared to make a stand on the narrow

Isthmus of Corinth. But Themistocles persuaded the allies to fight the enemy at sea. The Persian and Phoenician fleets were lured into the straits at Salamis and destroyed in one of the decisive battles of world history. Xerxes returned to Asia; in the following year the army he left behind was wiped out at the battle of Plataea, while the remains of his navy were wiped out at Cape Mycale. European Greece was saved, the Asiatic Greeks again rose in revolt, and the initiative in the war changed hands.

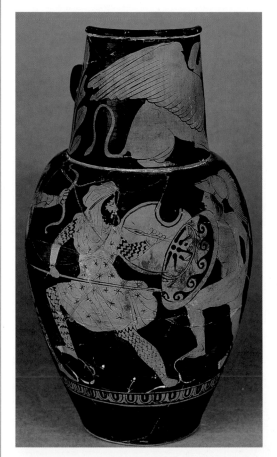

Greek and Persian locked in combat. During and after the Persian wars the Greeks showed their superiority as soldiers, and thousands of Greek mercenaries took service with the Persian emperors who sought to enslave their fellow-citizens. Mid-5th-century vase painting.

A duel played out before onlookers; two warriors are still engaged in combat, while a wounded man lies on the ground. All three are shown naked, an artistic convention that identifies them as Greeks. Black-figure painting on a water jug signed by the potter Kleimachos, c.560–550 BC.

THE ATHENIAN EMPIRE

Over the following decades the Greeks carried the war into Asia and even intervened against the Persians in rebellious Egypt. The Spartans, always careful of their limited manpower and reluctant to commit their forces far from home, soon began to hold back, leaving Athens effectively in charge of the war effort. The Greeks were less successful as aggressors, and the conflict eventually petered out in the mid-5th century. Its chief results were to restore Greek predominance in the Aegean and to increase greatly the power and prestige of Athens.

The political basis of Athenian power was the Delian League, founded in 478 to carry on the war. The members were Athens, her active allies, and the liberated Aegean islands and Asiatic Greek cities. All these essentially naval states contributed ships and money to the League's resources; the common treasury was kept at Delos, a small island sacred to Apollo. With her wealth from silver mines and trade and her dominating fleet, Athens led the League from the start;

Democrat and imperialist: as leader of Athens, Pericles combined the two roles. The bust, a Roman copy, is believed to be a good likeness, perhaps made not long before his death in 429 BC.

and it was not long before it began to turn into an Athenian empire. First Naxos, and later Thasos, Samos and others, found that resignation from the League was not permitted. Revolt was punished lightly but shrewdly – by dismantling the malcontents' navy and making their contribution to the League a purely monetary one, a policy that increased Athens' advantage and gave her funds for yet more ships. Member-states that contributed only money to the League gradually turned into dependants; and within 50 years this was the fate of virtually all of them. One by one local mints were closed, and Athenian silver coinage became the standard currency throughout the empire. The imperial reality was openly acknowledged in 454, when the treasury was transferred from Delos to Athens itself; and after peace was made with Persia in 449 it soon became clear that Athens contemplated no change in the situation. The wartime league was now an empire, 'protected' by her navy and paying annual tribute to her for the privilege.

Unlike Sparta, 5th-century Athens was brilliant as well as powerful. The flowering of the Greek genius was not confined to Athens in this, the Classical age, but it did find its most concentrated expression there. The first true dramas developed out of religious ritual under the hands of the Athenians Aeschylus, Sophocles, Euripides and Aristophanes. The first true historian, Herodotus of Halicarnassus, made Athens his home and inspiration; the next, Thucydides, was an Athenian general. Philosophy was transformed by Socrates and Plato. And sculptors developed the mature Classical style and used it to adorn the Parthenon and other great new buildings whose ruins are still among the wonders of the world; they were put up to replace the temples destroyed by the Persians in 480 – and, it must be said, were largely paid for by the tribute levied on Athens' subject-states.

Athenian democracy functioned remarkably well for most of the 5th century, until the strains of a protracted war began to tell on the citizens' nerves and temper. The guiding spirit of Athens for 30 years – from about 460 BC until his death in 429 – was Pericles, an aristocrat entirely convinced of the virtues of democracy. In his speeches he held up the ideal of a free and open society, and put for-

ward Athens as the fulfilment of the ideal; but he also supported a proposal to restrict citizenship to those who could show that *both* of their parents had been citizens: perhaps, like later democratic politicians, he sometimes had to bend with the wind rather than direct it. Whether he should be blamed for Athens' ultimately disastrous foreign policy is a matter of opinion; but he was certainly a convinced imperialist, and there is little indication that he tried to restrain Athenian bellicosity during his years of influence.

Despite some reverses, the Athenian empire was strengthened by the war of 460-445 against the Peloponnesians (supported rather unenthusiastically by the Spartans, who were still recovering from the effects of an earthquake and a helot revolt). At one moment Athens even succeeded in overrunning central Greece and conquering Boeotia; but long-term control of inland territory was beyond her resources, and the Boeotians liberated themselves without much difficulty. It is noteworthy that Athens felt strong enough to conduct this war while still engaged in the unfinished conflict with Persia. However, the Athenian intervention in Egypt proved disastrous, culminating in the destruction of an entire fleet; and in 449 the Persians, also war-weary, negotiated a peace that left the Athenians in effective control of the Aegean. The conflict with the Peloponnesians ended four years later in the signing of a Thirty Years' Peace.

On the sacred island of Delos: processional way with long-bodied lions (or lionesses), mid-7th century BC. The treasury of the Delian League was on the island until it was moved to Athens.

Chronicler of conflict. Thucydides took part in the Peloponnesian War, serving as an Athenian general. His account of it is the first known example of history carefully researched and objectively written.

THE PELOPONNESIAN WAR

The Thirty Years' Peace lasted less than half the appointed time. Athens helped Corcyra (Corfu) to fight off an attack by Corinth; Sparta sided with Corinth; and in 431 BC war broke out between the two over-helpful big powers. It may well have been inevitable, since Greece had been increas-ingly divided between two power blocs: the Spartan-dominated Peloponnesian League and the Athenian empire *alias* the Delian League. In general terms the struggle was also one between oligarchy and democracy, although Athens toler-ated oligarchies in her subject-states if they accepted her leadership. On the other hand, even the Athenian historian Thucydides admitted that Athenian imperialism had made all the Greeks uneasy, and that oligarchic Sparta was widely regarded as a potential liberator.

The war was long and exhausting because a decisive engagement was almost impossible to bring about. Athens, supreme at sea, could inflict only limited damage on the land mass of the Peloponnese and central Greece. The famous Spartan army could ravage Attica but could not take Athens, sheltered behind the impregnable Long Walls built in 461–456; these surrounded the city and stretched for 8km (5 miles) down to the Piraeus, the port of Athens, ensuring that unbroken contact was maintained with the fleet and supplies from abroad.

In 430 Athens was weakened by a devastating plague that carried off Pericles in the following year. Nevertheless the conflict dragged on until a truce was arranged in 421. When war broke out again in 414, Athens was already committed to an attack on Syracuse in Sicily, which was a major supplier of the Peloponnesian states. This proved to be the turning-point of the war: the Athenian besiegers were encircled, and in 413 the entire expeditionary force, ships and men, was wiped out. Still Athens fought on, building a new fleet and desperately trying to maintain her crumbling empire; despite everything that has been said about her methods, Athenian imperialism must have had its attractive side, since a surprising number of cities remained loyal to her in adversity. The end came when her grounded fleet was destroyed at Aegospotomi (405); unsupplied by sea, Athens was besieged, starved, and finally surrendered to the Spartans in 404.

The outcome of the Peloponnesian War was purely negative: the Athenian empire disappeared, and with it the relative political stability represented by the Delian League. The prospect of a united Greek state, transcending local rivalries, also vanished. Given the quarrelsome nature of the Greeks it may never have been a serious possibility; but if it was to happen during this period, only Athens could have achieved it, although a policy of shared citizenship would have been a more reliable basis for unity than

naval power and enforced payments of tribute. The Spartans, with their limited manpower and parochial outlook, never contemplated more than a loose hegemony over the other city-states, and in the event they even proved incapable of controlling fallen Athens, which soon expelled the Spartan-installed oligarchy, the 'Thirty Tyrants'. At once arrogant and politically incompetent, Sparta was soon at odds with Thebes, Corinth and a revived Athens. Too rigid to adapt to new military tactics, and weakened by a catastrophically declining birth rate, the Spartan army was smashed at the battle of Leuctra (371) by the Thebans under Epaminondas. Worse, Epaminondas invaded the Peloponnese and liberated the helots of Messenia on whom the Spartan economy depended; though still formidable, Sparta never fully recovered from the blow. Theban supremacy in Greece proved even more short lived, and later 4th-century Greece remained as fragmented as ever. Paradoxically, some Greeks were beginning to formulate ideals of 'Panhellenism' that cut across parochial loyalties; but it was now too late for such notions to influence political history, thanks to the appearance of a new power on the fringes of the Greek world. Macedon entered the arena and a new age began.

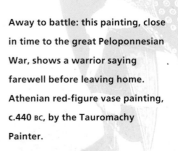

Away to battle: this painting, close in time to the great Peloponnesian War, shows a warrior saying farewell before leaving home. Athenian red-figure vase painting, c.440 BC, by the Tauromachy Painter.

3

ALEXANDER THE GREAT AND THE HELLENISTIC WORLD

WHILE SHIFTING ALLIANCES AND FRAGILE SUPREMACIES PREOCCUPIED THE CITY-STATES, IN THE MID-4TH CENTURY BC A NEW POWER AROSE ON THE NORTHERN MARCHES OF THE GREEK WORLD. MACEDON WAS LARGE AND POPULOUS, WITH A THOROUGHLY HELLENIZED COURT; BUT MOST GREEKS WERE RELUCTANT TO ACKNOWLEDGE THEIR KINSHIP WITH ITS TRIBES, A MIXED BAG OF ILLYRIANS, THRACIANS AND GREEKS WHOM THEY REGARDED AS SEMI-BARBARIANS – ALL THE MORE SO SINCE THEY STILL GAVE THEIR ALLEGIANCE TO A KING, JUST AS PERSIANS AND OTHER ALIEN PEOPLES DID. THE GREEKS OVERLOOKED OR UNDERESTI-MATED THE FACT THAT MACEDON WAS RICH IN RESOURCES, AND THAT ITS WARRIORS HAD BEEN HARDENED BY THEIR WARS AGAINST THE ILLYRIANS, THE THRACIANS, AND OTHER NON-GREEK PEOPLES. THEY WERE ALSO TO DISCOVER THAT MONARCHY, ALTHOUGH INCOMPATI-BLE WITH THE GOOD LIFE AS THEY UNDERSTOOD IT, HAD DISTINCT POLITICAL AND MILITARY ADVANTAGES WHEN THE RIGHT MAN OCCUPIED THE THRONE AND DIRECTED THE STATE.

King Philip of Macedon, shown on a contemporary coin. Philip's silver mines financed the ambitions which led to his domination of the Greek city-states and never-completed preparations for war with Persia.

THE RISE OF MACEDON

Macedon found the right man in King Philip II. He inherited a shaky throne in 359, efficiently disposed of his rivals, bought off and then fought off his barbarian neighbours, and only then turned his attention to a divided Greece. At a time when the city-states were beginning to prefer hiring mercenaries rather than fighting their own battles, Philip had distinct military advantages: a standing army of hard, disciplined, loot-hungry Macedonian soldiers, stiffened by the presence of permanently employed professionals. This military establishment was expensive to maintain, even with the proceeds from the gold and silver mines that Philip was lucky enough to possess; so the need for spoils gave the king an additional motive for aggression.

All the same, Philip moved slowly and carefully, combining devious diplomacy with ruthless use of force, and undertaking limited offensives that never alarmed enough of the Greek states for them to unite against him. His favourite tactic was to induce them to betray one another for short-term gains, confident that each state that did so would find itself friendless when the Macedonian army moved against it. Athens behaved no better than the rest, although Philip's aggressions were repeatedly denounced in the 'Philippics' delivered to the Assembly by Demosthenes, the greatest of all Greek orators; his speeches have often been likened to Winston Churchill's pre-war warnings against Hitler's Germany, which they also resembled in being heeded only at the last possible moment. After 20 years of skilfully managed expansion Philip had a firm grip on northern Greece. Then, belatedly, Athens and Thebes formed an alliance to resist further Macedonian encroachments. In the war that followed, the battle of Chaeronea (338) proved to be a turning-point in the history of Greece: the allies were defeated and the great age of the city-state effectively came to an end. Thebes and other cities were garrisoned by Macedonian troops; Athens was allowed to make a separate peace, though she and the other Greek

states had to join the new confederation organized by Philip, with himself as its 'elected' head.

The purpose of the confederation, the Corinthian League, was to march against the ancient enemy, Persia. Victory would crown Philip's efforts, and the loot of Asia would pay his mounting debts. Despite the enormous size of the Persian Empire and the overwhelming superiority of the Persian army in numbers, Philip's enterprise was less rash than it seems. Time and again in the past the Greeks had shown they were more than a match for the Persians, and the need for a war of liberation in Ionia – if not of wider conquest – was a commonplace of Greek political rhetoric; but its accomplishment had been indefinitely deferred by the Greeks' lack of unity.

Having imposed that unity, Philip was on the point of setting out when he was stabbed to death while taking part in a procession. The assassin was a man with a grievance, conveniently slain on the spot before he could implicate anyone else. The Persians may have been behind the murder, but it is equally possible that Philip's queen, Olympias, or his eldest son Alexander was responsible; Philip had put aside Olympias and had recently fathered a child by a new wife, making Alexander's position uncertain. Given Alexander's subsequent megalomaniacal career as a tireless conqueror, it is even possible that he had his father removed in order to make sure that Philip would not defeat the Persians and leave him no worlds to conquer.

A gold casket that held the remains of Philip II of Macedon, father of Alexander the Great. Decorated with the star-emblem of the dynasty, it comes from the king's tomb at Vergina.

The Lion of Chaeronea, a monument put up to commemorate those who fell in the battle, fought in 338 BC; Macedon's victory over the Greek city-states effectively ended their independence.

THE CONQUESTS OF ALEXANDER

If Philip's successor had been an ordinary man, the history of the world might have been different. But the 20-year-old Alexander was a military genius, audacious, inspired and inspiring, and utterly dedicated to his own glory. He had already distinguished himself as Philip's second-in-command at Chaeronea; now he demonstrated that he possessed the great general's ability to act more swiftly than his opponents believed to be humanly possible. Before the Greek cities finished celebrating the assassination of Philip, Alexander marched into their midst and over-

Marble head of Alexander the Great, found at Pergamum; mid-2nd century BC. The conqueror's image became known all over the Hellenistic world, and later kings imitated his flowing, centre-parted hair style and upward gaze.

awed them into electing him as his father's successor, authorized to lead them against Persia. Then, to secure his rear he undertook a campaign against Macedon's barbarian enemies. While he was away Thebes broke out in revolt, besieging the Macedonian garrison stationed in her citadel. When Alexander returned to Greece he stormed the city and, evidently determined to strike terror into his reluctant Greek allies, sold the Thebans into slavery and razed the city to the ground. While destroying one of the most sacred of cities, he indulged in the sort of cultural-sentimental gesture of which autocrats are fond by sparing the house in which the famous 5th-century poet Pindar had lived.

Still only 22, Alexander proceeded to embark for Asia to make war on Persia. After crossing the Hellespont with an army of some 40,000 men he was almost immediately confronted with a Persian host which he smashed at the battle of the Granicus river (334). The cities of Asiatic Greece were quickly liberated, and then the Macedonian army marched along the south coast of Asia Minor and on into the interior. Alexander had already shown himself to be a master of propaganda, making appropriately larger-than-life ges-

tures that evoked images of his supposed ancestor, Heracles, and of the Greek heroes who had vanquished Troy. Now, at Gordion, he visited the city's Acropolis to see a famous cart which was attached to its yoke by a complicated knot. According to legend, the man who untied the knot would become the lord of Asia. Alexander's response was to draw his sword and slash through the tangle (hence 'cutting the Gordian knot' is still used to describe ruthlessly decisive problem-solving).

Instead of pressing on into western Asia, Alexander marched south into Syria, intending to cut off the Persians from the Mediterranean and protect his rear against the powerful Phoenician fleet by occupying its Levantine bases. The Great King himself, Darius, arrived with a large army to intercept Alexander, unwisely drawing up his forces on a narrow coastal plain which prevented him from making his superior numbers tell. At the battle of Issus (333) Alexander led a breakthrough on the left wing, Darius fled, and the Persian rout was so complete that Alexander was able to capture the Great King's mother, wife and daughters; whether through foresight or chivalry he treated them with kindness and respect.

Alexander's conquests made Macedon, the Greek city-states and the mighty Persian empire, including Egypt, a single realm. Culturally, though not politically, this unification survived Alexander's death and became the basis of the subsequent Hellenistic age.

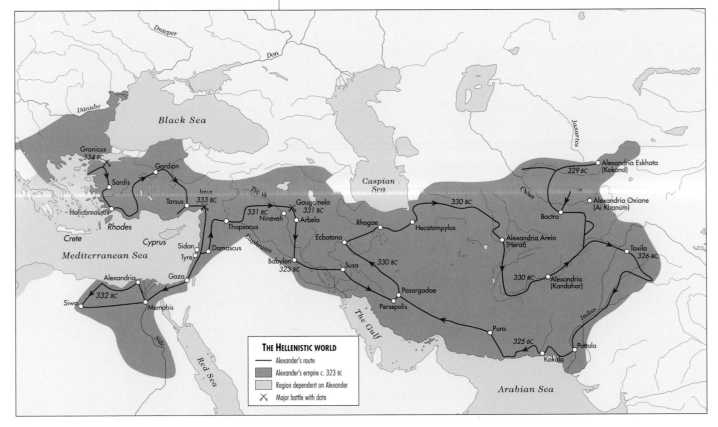

Having achieved as much as most other Greeks would have considered useful or feasible, Alexander refused Darius' offers of peace based on ceding all of Asia west of the Euphrates; clearly Alexander was no longer the rescuer of oppressed Greeks, but was set on carving out an empire for himself. He occupied Phoenicia and Palestine, and besieged the great port of Tyre, near-impregnable on its inshore island. The seven-month siege, persisted in while Sparta revolted and the Persians counter-attacked in Asia Minor, demonstrated that Alexander was more than just a brilliant cavalry commander; finally, with the help of Phoenician cities antagonized by Persian rule and jealous of Tyre, the port was stormed and destroyed. Alexander marched on into Egypt, where the Persians were unpopular and he was greeted as a liberator. He was also hailed as the new pharaoh by the famous oracle of Ammon at the oasis of Siwah. As pharaoh, and son of the god Ammon (whom, however, the Greeks equated with their own supreme god, Zeus), Alexander could himself be regarded as a god; and it seems possible that he took his promotion quite

seriously. His main achievement in Egypt was to found the city of Alexandria; it was the first of a series of foundations by Alexander, but whereas most of these were essentially military settlements, Egyptian Alexandria became one of the great cosmopolitan centres of the ancient world.

In 331 Alexander resumed the assault on Asia, crossing the Euphrates and the Tigris. At Gaugamela, faced with a huge Persian army under Darius, Alexander outmanoeuvred the enemy and broke the flower of the Persian infantry with a brilliantly timed cavalry attack closely supported by the pikemen who were a Macedonian speciality. Darius fled again, only to be murdered by his own lieutenants as Alexander's army moved inexorably from Babylon into Persia itself, taking the great cities of Susa, Persepolis and Ecbatana; at the ancient capital, Persepolis, Alexander captured the enormous gold reserves of Persia and burned the palace to commemorate his victory.

The burning seems to have been done as part of a drunken spree, though it is also possible that the episode was stage-managed by Alexander; if so,

A dramatic moment at the battle of Issus: Alexander seems about to hurl himself on the Persian king, who is visibly panic-stricken. The Alexander Mosaic, from the Roman city of Pompeii, is based on a 4th-century BC Greek painting.

he may have been taking revenge (as was later claimed) for the Persians' destruction of the Athenian Acropolis 150 years before; or he may have been serving notice on the Persians that they had a new master who was not to be trifled with. Here and in most other instances, Alexander's motives and intentions can be interpreted in widely different ways. However, most historians would probably agree that, once he had effectively replaced Darius as Great King, Alexander began to display signs of megalomania, easily flying into an ungovernable rage when faced with criticism or opposition, however well meant. When a conspiracy against Alexander was discovered, he put to death one of his commanders, Philotas, for failing to let him know of it. Then he ordered the death of Philotas' father, Parmenio, a veteran who had served Philip and Alexander faithfully. It may be significant that on several occasions the old general had tried to restrain Alexander's ambition; when Parmenio remarked that if he were Alexander he would seriously consider Darius' peace proposals, Alexander replied in manifest-destiny terms that he, too, would consider them – if he were Parmenio. Not long after

the deaths of Philotas and Parmenio, during a drinking bout at which Alexander was being grossly flattered, his friend Cleitus, who had saved the king's life at the battle of Issus, dared to scoff and was killed by Alexander's own hand. Another who suffered for crossing him was Callisthenes, the official historian of the expedition; he appeared to have emerged unscathed after refusing to take part in a Persian-style ceremony in which those present abased themselves before the king, but soon afterwards he was arrested on a charge of conspiracy and executed.

Despite his conquest of the Persian heartland, Alexander was not done with fighting. Bactria and other parts of the vast, mountainous eastern regions of the Persian Empire remained unsubdued, and the man most responsible for the murder of Darius, Bessus, the *satrap* (governor) of Bactria, had proclaimed himself Great King. Alexander pursued him relentlessly until his own lieutenants betrayed him; according to one account, Alexander handed him over to Darius' family, who took a terrible revenge on him. During a period of three years (330–327), the Macedonian army marched beyond the river Oxus

Greeks and Persians engaged in furious combat, with a mounted Alexander (far left) riding down the opposition: part of a frieze on the Alexander Sarcophagus (late 4th century BC), found in a royal cemetery at Sidon in Phoenicia.

(modern Amu Darya) into Central Asia and crossed and re-crossed the Hindu Kush, besieging and capturing one fortress after another; the Macedonians even pursued Alexander's enemies beyond the limits of civilization when they took refuge with Scythian barbarians.

Even when the entire empire had been pacified, Alexander pressed on into the Indian subcontinent, subduing cities and kingdoms and crossing one tributary of the Indus after another. The most serious opposition was provided in 326 by Porus, a Punjabi king whose large army and force of battle elephants tested Alexander's generalship to the limit. After his victory Alexander drove the army on, intent on invading the rich northern plain that lay beyond the Indus. It had become apparent that he was prepared to go on to the end of the world, wherever that might be. However, in 325, on the river Hyphasis, the most easterly tributary of the Indus, his troops, weary of fighting and 4,000km (2,500 miles) from their homes, simply refused to go on. Alexander's speeches and sulks failed to move them and he was forced to turn back, although under his

leadership even this return journey took the form of a hazardous land-sea exploration, along the Persian Gulf, which came close to disaster.

Back in Babylon, Alexander dealt ruthlessly with the governors who had got out of hand during his absence; many had never expected to see him again once he had disappeared beyond the Persian borders of the known world. He also pushed on with a plan to fuse Macedonians, Greeks and Persians into a single imperial race. After taking Persepolis he had arranged for some thirty thousand young Persians to begin military training under Macedonian instructors; he had appointed Persians as well as Macedonians to govern provinces while he was campaigning; and he himself had assumed the Persian title of Great King after the death of Darius, dressing in the Persian fashion and allowing his Eastern subjects to prostrate themselves when they came into his presence. Alexander's followers were dismayed by his policy towards the Persians, and many were disgusted by his adoption of a semi-divine monarchical style that was so alien to Greek tradition. During the wars only the circle around

The ruins of Persepolis, the capital of the Persian Empire. In 331 BC it was largely destroyed by Alexander the Great; during a drunken spree, or possibly as a calculated gesture, he burned down the royal palace, after which the city rapidly declined.

Alexander himself had been much affected (with unfortunate results for Cleitus and Callisthenes), and although there were mutterings among the troops Alexander had succeeded in keeping the loyalty of the army in the field, partly no doubt by the way in which he shared the hardships and dangers of his men and always led from the front. Once returned to Persia, however, the soldiers showed their opinion of Alexander's proposed integration of Macedonian and Persian units: 'Go fight your battles with your Persians and your father Ammon!' shouted the Macedonians. But this time it was the army, not Alexander, that capitulated after he threatened to discharge them all and began to replace his officers with Persians. The soldiers besieged Alexander's tent, begging for forgiveness and, for the time being at least, they put up with the new policy.

There followed the famous 'marriage of East and West' in which thousands of Macedonians took Persian wives, while Alexander himself, already possessed of one Persian spouse, wedded Darius' daughter. Alexander's policy has often been interpreted as an idealistic attempt to reconcile East and West – a view that, among other things, ignores all the peoples in the empire who were not invited to join in the Greco-Persian reconciliation. But the policy was a realistic and necessary one, implicit in Alexander's decision to pursue the war beyond the Tigris-Euphrates line: if he was to capture the Persian Empire and control its vast area permanently, he needed a larger master-race than Greece alone could provide. (The Persian kings had had the same problem: the major weakness of their empire had been the insufficient numbers of the Iranians available to run it; so the enlargement proposed by Alexander made good military and political sense.) He may also have thought that the Greeks and Persians were more likely to work well together if they were united in the worship of a god-king – or he may have suffered from delusions of grandeur; at any rate, already acknowledged as the son of the god Ammon by his Egyptian subjects, Alexander took the trouble to secure a recognition of his divinity from the Greek cities in 324 – and then died the following summer, aged 33.

Because of his youth, his invincibility, and his self-promotion through the diffusion of carved and painted images of himself, Alexander became a potently glamorous figure who has dazzled some historians while being execrated by others for making slaughter seem glorious. His ultimate aims can never be known, but it says little for the idealism sometimes attributed to him that he was preparing yet another warlike expedition, to southern Arabia, when he was carried off by a fever.

Divine image: a silver coin bearing the head of Alexander the Great, who wears the ram's horn that identifies him with the Egyptian god Ammon. This is the first true coin portrait, issued by Lysimachus, one of the Diadochi, in about 286 BC.

Ptolemy I, king of Egypt; portrait on a four-drachma coin. He was governor of Egypt when Alexander died in 323 BC. He made himself king and founded a dynasty that lasted for over 300 years.

THE HELLENISTIC WORLD

With the carelessness of one who believed himself immortal, Alexander had made no arrangements for the government of his empire in the event of his death, or for the safety of his posthumously born son. Held together by the centripetal force of one man's authority, the empire fell apart as soon as he disappeared. In the ensuing scramble for power among Alexander's generals and his relations, the relations perished and the generals emerged as kings, reigning over the giant fragments of his empire. All of the great new successor-states remained under the control of Macedonian Greeks, with a Greek-speaking elite and administrators and, for a long time, a mainly Greek army. The consequences were momentous. Alexander's dream of a Greco-Persian fusion failed to materialize, but Greek culture permeated the lands he had conquered; this was especially true of the many great cities that were founded on the Greek model all over the Near East and remoter parts of Asia. For this reason the age that followed the death of Alexander the Great, and the Greek-dominated societies of the eastern Mediterranean and the East, are described as 'Hellenistic': not Hellenic, but certainly Hellenized.

The late 4th century witnessed fierce struggles among the *Diadochi*, or Successors, who contended for Alexander's inheritance. Attempts were made to keep the empire intact, notably by his second-in-command, Perdiccas, his regent in Macedon, Antipas, and Antigonus, a general stationed in Asia Minor. They were opposed by three of Alexander's generals who were bent on transforming their commands into private domains: Ptolemy, governor of Egypt; Seleucus, who controlled large areas of Asia; and Lysimachus, ruler of Thrace and part of Asia Minor.

Decades of battles and shifting alliances followed. In 320 BC Perdiccas invaded Egypt in a bid to unseat Ptolemy, only to be murdered by his own officers. Antipas died in 319, and his son, Cassander, seized power for himself in Macedon and murdered Alexander's family. The remaining loyalist, Antigonus, was defeated and killed in 301 by a coalition of his enemies.

By this time each of the *Diadochi* had proclaimed himself king and the division of Alexander's empire was no longer in doubt. But political instability continued into the 3rd century, and the period produced some brilliant but erratic adventurers. Antigonus' son, Demetrius Poliorcetes, won and lost battles and kingdoms with apparent recklessness, ending as the pampered prisoner of Seleucus. Equally mercurial, Pyrrhus, king of Epirus (297–272 BC), moved from one military adventure to the next, at one time attempting to seize Macedon, at another

going to the aid of the Greeks in Southern Italy against the rising power of Rome. It was after two successes against the Romans, achieved at a very heavy cost, that he is said to have remarked: 'One more victory like this and I shall be ruined', which gave rise to the phrase 'pyrrhic victory'.

Pyrrhus' death in 272 BC left Antigonus II (grandson of the Antigonus who had tried to preserve Alexander's empire) secure on the throne of Macedon. Like Ptolemy in Egypt and Seleucus in western Asia, he founded a great dynasty; and since Seleucus had eliminated Lysippus in 281, the Antigonid, Ptolemaic and Seleucid kingdoms became the great powers of the Hellenistic world.

In this enlarged political theatre the small city-states of Greece no longer carried much weight, although their cultural prestige was high

The god Serapis. From the time of Alexander the Great, Egypt was ruled by Greeks. The cultural mix produced a composite Greco-Egyptian god, Serapis, who became widely popular.

ATHENA

Relief from the Great Altar at Pergamum, a wealthy kingdom that emerged in Asia Minor during the Hellenistic (post-Alexander) period. The goddess Athena defeats the giant Alcyoneus by lifting him away from his mother Gaia (Earth), the source of his strength.

among the upstart Hellenistic kingdoms. For long periods Macedon remained, in effect, the protecting power in Greece. Immediately after Alexander's death, Demosthenes led the Athenians and other Greeks in a new attempt to regain their independence, but the rising was premature; the Macedonians, victorious on sea and land, dismantled Athens' democracy and hunted down Demosthenes, who took poison to avoid capture. From about this time mainland Greece went into an economic decline that was bound to have political consequences. Exports fell as their small-scale production of wine and oil struggled to compete with the huge output of the Hellenistic kingdoms. Athens was the most prosperous mainland state, helped by the fluctuating production of its silver mines at Laureum; but international commerce was largely taken over by the eastern Hellenistic states, with Rhodes and Delos

providing carriers and staging points. Still in theory independent, the Greeks remained irritably inclined to revolt against the Macedonian hegemony and, rather late in the day, began to combine their efforts. In the 3rd century the Achaean and Aeolian leagues brought together many of the city-states in confederations that were (unlike the old Athenian- and Spartan-led leagues) genuine partnerships involving joint decision-making and a pooling of resources. They achieved some noteworthy feats of arms, but they were no longer strong enough to resist the Macedonians on their own; and their 'liberation' by the Romans in 197 proved to be a prelude to the absorption, in 146, of Greeks and Macedonians alike into the fast-growing empire of Rome.

The most stable of the Hellenistic kingdoms was Egypt. Ptolemy made the new city of Alexandria his capital, and the ruling-class culture and governmental apparatus remained Greek throughout the long history of the dynasty; but Ptolemy also inherited the semi-divine authority of the pharaoh and some of his successors adopted the Egyptian custom of brother-sister marriages, keeping royalty in the family. Ptolemy organized a system of administration that ensured an abundant yield in taxes, enriching the dynasty. The Ptolemies were munificent patrons of scholars and scientists, assembled the great library of Alexandria and built its famous lighthouse, the Pharos. Big-city culture had its dangerous side, and later and perhaps more decadent members of the dynasty were sometimes vulnerable to popular riots and revolts, especially when feuds arose within the ruling family. However, the dynasty survived until 30 BC, when a defeated Queen Cleopatra and her lover-ally Mark Antony committed suicide, and Egypt became part of the Roman Empire.

Ptolemy's ambitions outside Egypt were curtailed after he lost the famous naval battle of Cyprian Salamis against Demetrius Poliorcetes in 306 BC. Egypt's later foreign wars were mainly fought against the Seleucids for control of the Palestinian coast, with fluctuating results. Seleucus I was arguably the most successful of Hellenistic rulers, beginning as governor of Babylon and eventually recreating Alexander's entire Asian empire except for some regions ceded to Indian rulers in return for several hundred war elephants that were put to good use in the west. Still vigorous in his late seventies, Seleucus defeated Lysippus, took over Asia Minor, and seemed on the point of occupying Macedon when he was assassinated. Seleucus' vast empire had twin capitals, Seleucia in Mesopotamia and Antioch in Syria, which were centres of Greek culture. Its size made it hard to hold the empire together, and the Seleucids, like the Persians before them, relied on provincial governors and client kings who were liable to bid for independence as soon as the opportunity arose. The empire gradually shrank until it was reduced to (roughly) Syria; Antiochus III managed to reassert his authority for a time, until he was defeated by the Romans and driven from Asia Minor in 191–190. The remains of the Seleucid empire were extinguished by the Romans in 64 BC.

During the 3rd century a new power appeared in the Hellenistic world. The city of Pergamum, on the west coast of Asia Minor, revolted against the Seleucids and became the nucleus of a state that owed much of its power to the wealth provided by its silver mines, grain and textiles. It was also famous for its production of parchment and, appropriately, became a great centre of Greek learning and art, under a dynasty, the Attalids, that was notably eager to achieve cultural respectability; the Great Altar of Zeus, made for King Eumenes (197–159), is one of the masterpieces of Hellenistic art. The Attalids shrewdly cultivated close relations with the Romans, which saved them from Macedonian aggression, and Pergamum's independent existence came to a peaceful end in 133 when the dying Attalus III bequeathed his dominions to Rome.

During this period the Greeks made an extraordinary impact on the wider world. In Asia, the Iranian and Indian areas of the unwieldy Seleucid empire broke away but continued to use the Greek language and issue coins with Greek inscriptions. The Hellenizing process may have been confined to the cities and the cultural and political elites, but the effects could still be far-reaching: in north-west India, for example, Greek and native sculptural traditions were blended in the school of Gandhara, which produced the earliest statues of the Buddha, who therefore appears with features of 'Classical' handsomeness.

Antiochus III, ruler of the Seleucid empire in western Asia. During his long reign (223–187 BC) Antiochus restored the failing Seleucid empire to its former glory – until he came up against the Romans and was decisively beaten and driven from Asia Minor.

4 THE GREEK EXPERIENCE

THE GREEKS WERE AN ADVENTUROUS PEOPLE WHO SETTLED ALL OVER THE MEDITERRANEAN, LIVED BY FARMING, FISHING, TRADING OR SOLDIERING, AND BELONGED TO SOCIETIES AS DIVERSE AS MYCENAEAN WARRIOR KINGDOMS, BUSTLING LITTLE CITY-STATES, AND VAST HELLENISTIC MONARCHIES. NO ACCOUNT OF THEIR WAY OF LIFE CAN TAKE IN EVERY ASPECT OF THEIR EXPERIENCES OVER TIME AND SPACE, SO SUCH AN ACCOUNT WILL INEVITABLY CONCENTRATE ON THE 'CLASSICAL' CITY-STATE, OR *POLIS*, OF THE 5TH AND 4TH CENTURIES BC. THIS WAS THE SETTING FOR THE GREEKS' GREATEST ACHIEVEMENTS IN POLITICS, WAR, LITERATURE, DRAMA, ART AND PHILOSOPHY. SUPPORTED BY ITS AGRICULTURAL HINTERLAND, THE *POLIS* SERVED AS A MARKET-PLACE AND MEETING-PLACE, WHERE CITIZENS COULD TAKE A GREATER OR LESSER PART IN PUBLIC AND RELIGIOUS LIFE. AS IN OTHER ANCIENT SOCIETIES, WOMEN AND SLAVES WERE LARGELY EXCLUDED FROM PARTICIPATION; NEVERTHELESS, BY THE STANDARDS OF THE ERA GREEK SOCIETY WAS NOT ONLY HIGHLY CREATIVE BUT ALSO REMARKABLY OPEN AND OPEN-MINDED, AND THE EDUCATION, OCCUPATIONS AND LEISURE PURSUITS OF ITS CITIZENS REMAIN OF ABSORBING INTEREST.

The battle between the lapiths and the brutish, half-equine centaurs was an episode in Greek myth. By Classical times it had come to stand for the conflict between civilization and barbarism, as on this scene from the Parthenon.

THE POLIS AND THE GREEK WAY OF LIFE

Although they fought one another savagely, the Greeks thought of themselves as one people, the Hellenes, inhabiting a fragmented but distinct entity they called Hellas. They shared a common language and religion which brought them together, regardless of their city of origin, at the great Panhellenic festivals and games. Their name for a non-Greek was *barbaros*, a barbarian, though the word was originally no more than a mild expression of contempt for the unintelligible 'bar-bar-bar' of jabbering foreigners. The contempt intensified as the Greek came to consider his way of life superior to that of (for example) the Persian, who was dwarfed by the monstrous size of his state, powerless to influence events and an equal citizen only in so far as he shared the universal slavery. In other words, the city-state and the Hellenic concept of citizenship were central features of what it meant to be Greek.

Late in the 4th century, when the glories of Athens and Sparta had vanished, the philosopher Aristotle stated firmly 'Man is a political animal' – by which he meant an animal fitted by nature to live in a *polis*, the Greek word for a city-state and the way of life it embodied. The normal *polis* consisted of an area of countryside surrounding a single walled city with a dominating citadel, or *acropolis* ('the' Acropolis at Athens is simply the most famous example), and a market place or *agora*. With the exception of Sparta, the *polis* was very small; even at Athens, hardly any part of the countryside was more than 20km (32 miles) from the city and most of the population lived outside the walls, travelling in for social or civic purposes. The leading states seem to have had a citizen population of only 10-20,000. (Here Athens was the exception, as her commercial and maritime greatness might lead us to expect: just before the Peloponnesian War she is estimated to have had 40,000 citizens and a total population of about 300,000.) In the eyes of the philosophers even these modest figures were too high: Plato pro-

Jurors' ballots. Athenian citizenship was restricted, but those who held it played an important part in the state, casting their votes in the Assembly and the courts.

posed five thousand as the ideal number, while his one-time pupil Aristotle held that every citizen should have no trouble in recognizing every other citizen in the city.

Plato and Aristotle were writing after the disasters of the late 5th and 4th centuries and with more than a touch of nostalgia for the old self-sufficient *polis*, uncorrupted by trade, luxury and ideas. Still, as far as the normal Greek was concerned, smallness was certainly one of the virtues of the *polis*: he lived in a society whose workings he could understand, and which he as an individual could hope to influence. The 'failure' of the Greeks to unite, although undoubtedly disastrous in the long run, must be understood with this point of view in mind. The Greeks despised the Persians because the most powerful of them could be killed at the whim of their king, which made them rather worse off in practice than most Greek

Festival prize, late 6th century BC.
The Panathenaea was the greatest
Athenian festival, celebrated with
games. This amphora, a prize in
the boxing contest, is painted with
a graphic representation of its
subject.

slaves. In the *polis*, citizens lived under the law. It might be reactionary or excessively severe, like the late 7th-century Athenian code issued by Draco, but it was known to all and applied to all. That, at least, was how things were supposed to be; and although the reality was less than perfect (especially where political passions got the upper hand), reverence for the law was deeply ingrained among the Greeks. Few, however, would have gone as far as the philosopher Socrates, who refused several chances to escape after being sentenced to death on a politically motivated charge of impiety, arguing that the wrongness of the verdict was no excuse for disobeying the law.

The rule of law was common to all the main forms of government, operating in oligarchic Sparta at least as rigorously as in democratic Athens. The main differences between oligarchies and democracies lay in the balance of powers between the political institutions, and in how widely citizenship was extended. In most Greek states the basic political process was the same: a Council prepared and recommended laws and acts of state; an Assembly voted their approval or disapproval; and magistrates then carried out the decisions that had been arrived at. In oligarchies the Council tended to carry the greatest political weight, since it was necessarily a small body and could be kept a select one by attaching property or age qualifications to membership. By contrast, in the full democracy of Athens an Assembly consisting of all the citizens was the centre of power. Naturally there were all sorts of shades and variations of practice among the hundreds of Greek city-states, in this as in other aspects of life.

The situation was much the same with regard to citizenship. In oligarchies, those who owned less than a certain amount of land could not be citizens; or if they could, they enjoyed only limited rights (for example, the right to vote but not the right to hold office). At best, the Greek concept of citizenship was a narrow one: even the most radical democracy excluded women (they might technically be citizens, but never possessed political rights), children, slaves, and the often large population of *metics* (resident foreigners) created by the growth of trade. If the exclusion of women and slaves was inevitable in terms of the social order, the exclusion of foreigners and various other free men suggests that the Greeks never entirely shed the conviction that the state was fundamentally a collection of tribes and families, established since remote antiquity, in which 'strangers' were not welcome. The division of the *polis* into tribes probably originated with the Dorian settlements, and though they were much modified over the centuries, membership of a tribe remained a condition of citizenship and most civic activity was organized on a basis of tribal groupings. But citizenship was a matter of place as well as birth: a colonist could no longer remain a citizen of his old *polis* once he was unable to attend its public meetings or carry out any of his local religious duties. Only Athens in her high imperial phase experimented with a wider citizenship, sending out some colonies whose members remained Athenians. These were settled at strategic points or used to keep an eye on unreliable allies; they retained the rights and duties of citizens, and were exempt from the tribute paid by subject-cities. The idea of extending citizenship beyond this, to the subject-cities themselves, was never seriously considered.

It was, then, characteristic of Greek society that a man's loyalties were directed towards immediate and tangible objects; and for this people, who lived so much out-of-doors, the *polis* was a larger home and an extended family circle, evoking as such an intense but close-bounded piety. The obverse of this attractive particularism was the dangerously limited manpower of even the largest Greek state and the impossibility of turning its subjects or allies into fellow-citizens in a larger political association. The first factor hastened Sparta's decay, the second restricted the effectiveness of the Athenian empire; and divided Greece, which had only narrowly escaped Persian domination, eventually went down before the single-minded kings of Macedon.

The Acropolis at Athens. Every city had an acropolis, or citadel, though Athens' is now regarded as the Acropolis. Destroyed by the Persians, the Athenian Acropolis was rebuilt to dazzling effect in the late 5th century BC.

A Scythian archer. The Greeks had extensive contacts with this nomadic south Russian people. A curious feature of Athenian society was the employment of 300 slaves of Scythian origin as a kind of police force. Red-figure vase painting, c.520 BC.

CONTRAST IN SYSTEMS: ATHENS AND SPARTA

The development of Athenian democracy involved a gradual transformation of the institutions inherited from the Dark Age. Aristocratic Athens was ruled by a council, the Areopagus, and three magistrates or *archons*. These survived the age of Solon and Pisistratus as prestigious conservative institutions, and subsequent Athenian reformers shrewdly worked to render them innocuous rather than attempting to abolish them. Cleisthenes introduced a new, elected council (the Council of Five Hundred) which a later democrat, Ephialtes, made supreme by limiting the powers of the Areopagus to those of a court dealing with crimes of violence. Similarly, the *archons* were pushed into the background by the *strategoi*, ten military commanders elected annually by the Council of

Five Hundred. Their military function was genuine, but their growing importance in government can be gauged from the fact that both Themistocles and Pericles were *strategoi*; indeed Pericles was elected to the office almost continuously for a number of years before his death, and it was the basis of such formal executive power as he possessed.

The enhanced importance of the Five Hundred and the *strategoi* was not achieved for their sakes but to promote the supremacy of the Assembly – the full citizen body, which was as close as antiquity ever came to the concept of the Sovereign People in session. The Five Hundred were chosen annually by lot, which meant that bribery and influence could not be brought to bear on the selection; and since no member could serve on the council more than twice, there was no possibility of the membership developing an *esprit de corps* that might convert it into a vested-interest group. Rapid rotation had a further advantage from a democratic point of view, making it certain that a high percentage of the citizenry would hold public office at some point in their lives. All of this represented a thoroughgoing attempt to ensure that the council did its job – prepared legislation – and nothing else; the Athenians had thoroughly grasped the dangers of 'steering' committees which in practice run everything. All real power lay with the Assembly, which met about once every ten days; it could approve, modify or reject any suggestion, debate and decide as it chose – and, for better or worse, change its collective mind from day to day. The executive arm, the *strategoi*, was directly accountable to the Assembly – literally so, since the *strategoi* had to explain and justify their expenditure. Pericles was often accused of dictatorship by his enemies, but although he had immense authority, he had no institutionalized power: he led by virtue of persuasion, conviction, and the weight of his reputation. Even the courts were popular institutions, with juries of two hundred or more, making bribery or intimidation almost impossible. The state arm was virtually non-existent: prosecutions were initiated and conducted by private citizens, and the nearest thing to the police was a force of 'Scythian archers', who were actu-

ally slaves of foreign origin, mainly employed as heralds and chuckers-out for the Assembly: when the citizens were summoned to attend, the 'archers' literally roped them in, moving across the *agora* with a long rope, soaked in red paint, that left a tell-tale smear on the laggards.

How well did the system work in practice? The highest praise of Athens and her democracy was given by Pericles himself, in a speech delivered to commemorate the men who had fallen in the first year of the Peloponnesian War. According to the historian Thucydides he said:

We live under a form of government that is not copied from the institutions of our fellow men but rather provides a model for others. It is known as democracy because power is exercised in the interests of the many, not the few. But while the laws give all men equal rights in their private disputes, public honours are paid to an individual on the basis of his personal qualities, not his rank or family connections; nor does poverty disqualify a man of low birth if he is capable of useful public service. We conduct ourselves as free men in our private lives too, avoiding mutual jealousies and suspicion; if our neighbour chooses to live after his own fashion, we do not resent it, or scowl at him in a manner that may be ineffective but is still unpleasant . . . in public life we are chiefly restrained from lawlessness by feelings of awe and fear; we take heed of those who speak with authority, and we obey the laws – especially those enacted to assist the downtrodden, and those unwritten laws which all men regard it as shameful to break.

But there were other points of view, especially once war-weariness set in. Twenty years after Pericles' speech, the comic dramatist Aristophanes wrote a scene in which an earlier playwright, Aeschylus, returns from the dead and asks about those currently in charge of the city: presumably they are the kind of men they ought to be – honest, able, patriotic and so on? The assumption is enough to make everyone on stage fall about laughing, and was presumably intended to have the same effect on the audience. The political philosophers also tended to disapprove of democracy, which to them meant rule by the 'senseless

Demosthenes, the most famous of Athenian orators. He denounced the ambitions of Philip of Macedon. Later, following the death of Alexander, he led an unsuccessful attempt to throw off the Macedonian yoke; rather than be captured he took poison.

mob'. Then, as now, interpretations differed according to bias: sympathisers called democracy 'rule by the people', whereas those inclined to oligarchy preferred to talk of 'rule by the poor', whom they saw as plundering the rich. Near-contemporaries were harsh in their comments on the demagogues who swayed the Assembly, especially since their influence was thrown against peace on the several occasions when, even towards the fatal close of the Peloponnesian War, Athens might have had it. But retrospective criticism is always suspect: had the war taken a different turn, opinion would have promoted the demagogues to resolute statesmen.

A more telling accusation was that the Assembly was impulsive and unstable, too often taking wild decisions and then revoking them. This was particularly true as the war went on and hopes and fears intensified. One famous incident has an aura of grim farce. After a revolt at Mytilene, on Lesbos, the Assembly decreed that the male population should be executed and the women and children enslaved. Then tempers cooled, and the order was cancelled. The ship carrying the original decree had already left for Mytilene, so a second ship had to be despatched in break-neck pursuit; its exhausted crew arrived only just in time to prevent the massacre. Later, there were no cancellations: when Thrace was threatened by the Spartans and the city of Scione revolted, the population was put to the sword or sold into slavery; and in 416, as the Cold War intensified during the truce of 421–414, the same savage treatment was accorded to the island of Melos, which had never been in the Athenian sphere of influence. At home, the greatest injustice committed by the democracy was the trial and execution of the victorious commanders at the battle of Arginusae, who were charged with failure to rescue their shipwrecked men. Neither trial nor sentence was legal; they illustrated the perils of direct democracy, in which an inflamed sovereign people can all too easily override not only the laws but justice itself.

On the other hand Athenian democracy survived personal ambitions and party rivalries with remarkably little in the way of disturbances. The most violent single act in the great years of the

democracy was the assassination of Ephialtes, the democratic leader who had dared to strip the Areopagus of its power; and that was an isolated murder whose only effect was to substitute Pericles for Ephialtes as leader of the dominant democratic party. An institution peculiar to Athens may have played a part in reducing political tension: ostracism, devised by Cleisthenes, was a kind of unpopularity contest that painlessly reduced the numbers of faction leaders. Any year, if the Assembly so decided, every citizen wrote on a pottery sherd (in Greek, *ostracon*) the name of a man he wanted to see banished. If there were at least six thousand votes for a particular candidate, the 'winner' was exiled for ten years, but without dishonour and without forfeiting his property or his other rights.

Political decision-making has been a crude business in most societies: a particular point of view has generally prevailed after its adherents have murdered the people holding other points of view. So perhaps one should not be too critical of ostracism, while admitting that many of Athens' most distinguished men suffered by it. Themistocles, who masterminded the victory over the Persians at Salamis, was ostracized a few years afterwards; incredibly, he ended his life in Persian pay, as governor of the Asian Greek city of Magnesia. And at least one anecdote about ostracism indicates that human perversity has changed little over the millennia. Earlier in Themistocles' career, he and his chief political rival, known throughout the city as Aristides the Just, were rival candidates for ostracism; and one citizen who intended to vote against Aristides explained that he was doing so because he was sick and tired of hearing Aristides called 'the Just'. According to the story, this citizen was in

Three examples of the ostracon, a fragment of pottery on which an Athenian citizen could scratch the name of the man he was voting to 'ostracize' – that is, send into exile. One of the names is that of Aristides, exiled in 482 BC.

An appropriately martial image: a Spartan footsoldier marches behind a chariot. It comes from the frieze of the Vix Crater, a large bronze vessel found in France and believed to be Spartan; c.520 BC.

fact talking to Aristides himself, whom he had not recognized; and, being illiterate, he asked the stranger to scratch 'Aristides' on the *ostracon* for him. Which Aristides, as maddeningly just as ever, promptly did. He was ostracized, although not perhaps by one vote.

For all its shortcomings, democracy was the chosen political system of Athens in its greatest age. It withstood a century of almost continuous warfare before succumbing to the short-lived oligarchy of 411–410, set up in the mistaken belief that a more conservative system would bring Persia into the war on Athens' side. And even defeat and loss of empire failed to discredit democracy in the eyes of the Athenians themselves, who rapidly ejected the pro-Spartan Thirty Tyrants of 404–403. For Athenians democracy

had evidently become a way of life, and they adhered to it while Athenian independence remained a reality.

Sparta was an oligarchy, and the champion of oligarchy throughout Greece, but her constitution and way of life were unique. There were two kings who had very limited powers (presumably whittled away in the course of the Dark Age), but who still led the Spartan army into battle, as Leonidas did at Thermopylae. Five *ephors* exercised most of the executive powers. However, the oligarchic centre of power was the Council of Elders, consisting of the kings and 28 men over 60 years old who were elected from a limited number of noble families. Unlike the Athenian Council of Five Hundred, the members of the Spartan Council were permanent and prestigious, and no doubt developed a strong *esprit de corps*. The advice they gave the magistrates must have been compelling, and their influence over the Assembly (males over 30) must have been immeasurably strengthened by the fact that debates, amendments and counter-propositions were not permitted: the Council's proposals could only be accepted or rejected (and rejection, as those who hold referenda know, is psychologically difficult to contemplate where no certain alternative exists). Even the voting procedure at Sparta had an archaic flavour: every man in the assembly roared his Yes or No, and assessors stationed at a distance decided which side had the majority – or the louder voices.

Sparta's institutions were peculiar because they were partly archaic and partly adaptations to a special situation; legend attributed them to a law-giver called Lycurgus who was probably a composite or mythical figure. The institutions almost certainly reached their final form by the end of the 7th century, which had given the Spartans some bad moments. A serious defeat by Argos and a fierce, protracted revolt by the helots of conquered Messenia were evidently sufficient to convince the Spartans that permanent mobilization and constant vigilance were necessary if they were to hold down their large subject population and wide territories. Not only the institutions but most other aspects of life became fixed; change was unwanted, and so, since the world changed, the world had to be shut out. The entire content of Spartan life was determined by this fundamental decision: the 'Spartan' education in endurance; the militarization of the entire male citizen body; the fixed distribution of land; the prohibition of money, the exclusion of foreigners and contempt for trade; and the cultivation of an austere, taciturn, duty-conscious, unimaginative character-type in marked contrast to the more erratic, eloquent and creative Athenian.

Too much attention can be paid to political history and political institutions: most people in most societies have only a minimal contact with politics except as victims. But, as should now be apparent, this was not true of life in ancient Greece, where the mild climate and small scale of organization encouraged a wide and direct involvement that was quite different in quality from the kind of participation that occurs in a modern 'representative' democracy. There was no sharp distinction between public and 'everyday' life: indeed, the citizen idly shopping in the *agora* might find himself moments later swept along to the Assembly to discuss a military expedition in which he would have to serve, or the dispatch of a ship on which he would take an oar. When we turn to the subject of everyday life, in its normally accepted meaning, we find the same mingling of the public and the private, even in childhood.

'Leonidas': this marble figure has been fancifully named after the Spartan king whose forces held the Persians at Thermopylae. It is one of the few surviving pieces of Spartan sculpture.

PARENTS AND CHILDREN

References to children are common in Greek literature, and images of them appear in art. This is especially true of vase paintings, examples of which show a baby on its potty, an infant crawling, and children playing with pull-along toys and trying to ride on animals. There is every reason to suppose that parental affection was the norm, and it was if anything intensified by more selfish considerations: the child carried on the blood-line and could be expected to look after its parents when they were old and helpless. Consequently it was preferable to have male children, since they remained members of the family throughout their lives, whereas a girl married, left home for the house of a stranger, and acquired a new set of loyalties. In Greek literature maidens are apt to bemoan the prospect of leaving home, which may be a comment on married life but also suggests that girls, too, grew up in a happy atmosphere.

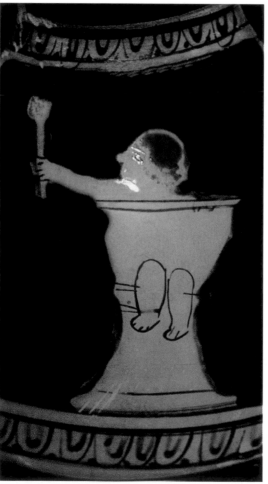

An infant on a potty, holding a rattle; Attic red-figure wine jug, c.440 BC. This ingenious potty has holes for the child's legs, so that it can settle and remain stable; surprisingly, an example of these ceramic objects has survived effectively intact.

The first few days of an infant's life were fraught with danger. Both the mother and her baby must often have died during childbirth; and if the child survived it might still be abandoned if it seemed too sickly or the family could not afford to feed an extra mouth. This was not hard-heartedness but obedience to necessity, and some form of infanticide has been common in most pre-industrial and some more advanced societies. Strictly speaking the Greeks did not practise infanticide (except for the Spartans, who are said to have flung weakly infants over a cliff), although exposing them in remote places virtually guaranteed that they would not survive. The alternative was to leave the child in a more-frequented spot where it was likely to be found by some affluent individual and raised as his slave. This may well have been more common than exposure on a mountainside – which, however, had more dramatic potential and therefore figures much in myth and literature, where the infant is often, like King Oedipus, the predicted agent of his parents' doom, left to perish in order to forestall the prophecy, but inevitably rescued and brought up in ignorance of his identity so that he will, in time, fulfil his destiny. Fiction aside, girls were much more likely to be exposed than boys.

About a week after a child's birth (time in which to decide whether or not to keep it), a naming ceremony was held and it was received into the family. At Athens children were swaddled; in Sparta their limbs were left free, but some of the benefits of this enlightened policy may have been counterbalanced by a preference for washing infants with cold water and clothing them lightly in all weathers. Mothers breast-fed their children, but wet-nurses were also employed, and pottery feeding bottles have survived.

In early infancy boys were enrolled in phratries (kin-based cult groups) at the Apaturia festival. Children of both sexes took part in another major festival, the Anthesteria, which was held to celebrate the new wine; during it they were presented with little wine jugs called *choes*, and the paintings on these are now an important visual source

A boy playing with his dog; red-figure vase painting, c.425 BC. Dogs were used for a number of purposes in ancient Greece, and some hunting breeds were elegant as well as efficient creatures. But the rather portly pet shown here seems unlikely to have had a distinguished pedigree.

of information about childhood in ancient Greece. Children were customarily given toys at a number of festivals, and most of the games and playthings devised before modern times were already known to the Greeks. Small children had pebble-filled rattles with which to make a satisfying din, while their elders played ball games, flung themselves about on swings and seesaws, or manipulated spinning tops and hoops. Dolls made of many materials have come to light, and fortunate children had dolls' houses complete with furniture. As far as it is possible to tell, childhood was a pleasant, carefree experience, at least until it was time for education to begin.

EDUCATION AND EXCELLENCE

The Greek idea of education was *arete*, 'excellence', but excellence of a particular sort, which would enable its possessor to live the good life within the framework of the city-state. Introspection and special skills were not included in it: what counted were the qualities of the socially effective all-rounder, as we should expect in this intensely sociable society. The product of a good education would be physically active but dignified, quick on the uptake, eloquent, and able to hold his own at drinking, performing on the lyre at a party, or scoring points in debate. The Greek tendency to identify physical, moral and intellectual qualities is revealingly shown in descriptions of Socrates, in which the philosopher's virtues and brilliance of intellect are made to sound all the more astonishing in view of his paunchy, satyr-like appearance and entire lack of physical grace.

There is no way of knowing how many Greeks received any formal education. The pasting up of laws and, in Athens, the practice of ostracism, imply that all the male citizens were literate; and Athenian law did in fact require that they should be so. But it seems unlikely that the children of the poor spent long at schools, which were all fee-paying. Their education, insofar as it existed at all, must have been education at work, as apprentices. In better-off homes the first teaching was imparted by a household slave, the *pedagogus*. Then, at about 6, the boy was taken to school by the *pedagogus* – or rather to schools, since he attended each of the three separate kinds in the course of a day: the grammar school for academic, and primarily literary, education; a music school; and a training school or gymnasium for dancing, exercises and sport. Some girls may have gone to school, but (if so) at separate establishments.

Boys learned to write, using a stylus and a tablet of soft wax on which letters and words could be incised and then rubbed out so that the tablet could be used again and again. But Greek culture still had a marked oral bias, and boys who stayed on at school were required to memorize long passages from the poets. Above all they were immersed in the works of Homer, so thoroughly that in later life his words would spring to their lips on all sorts of occasions, providing striking examples, apt comparisons and authoritative pieces of wisdom, which an opponent in debate would be expected to cap with equally striking examples on the other side of the argument.

The emphasis on musical education reflects the Greek conviction that it was a profound influence for good or evil. Bad music could corrupt: in his political Utopia, the *Republic*, Plato declares that effeminate music must be banned, and only sober, inspiring modes permitted. And singing and playing were important not only during leisure but on many civic and religious occasions. At school, therefore, a boy learned the flute or, more often, the lyre, a stringed instrument used as the accompaniment to a song; 'lyric' poetry originates in such songs. The importance of athletics in Greek life is well known; its various forms and its larger implications are discussed later on.

Formal education ended with two years of military training, begun when a youth reached the age of 18. Such young men, known as *ephebes*, were originally a select aristocratic band, but by the 4th century all male citizens were enrolled and the training came to include instruction in social and religious duties. There were no universities or equivalent institutions, but many roving teachers called sophists appeared in 5th-century Greece, offering to instruct paying pupils in the arts of success. Above all this meant the art of persuasion, so vital in the Assembly and courts of law: the art of marshalling evidence, drawing inferences, conducting arguments – and making the best of a bad argument by false reasoning, fine words and appeals to emotion; only this last aspect of their teaching survives in the English term 'sophistry'. Some 5th-century sophists taught other subjects including mnemonics and political theory, almost always with a view to practical application. In the 4th century a number of permanent teaching institutions were set up, notably Plato's Academy, named after the

A man seated, writing; terracotta figure from Boeotia, c.575 BC. Literacy was essential for many purposes: for administration, taxation and trade, as well as for the study and practice of literature and rhetoric. This little figure may represent a professional scribe.

gymnasium outside Athens where the school was founded. Though now remembered for breeding philosophers, this was intended to be a school for statesmen (philosophic statesmen, to be sure); and although the curriculum included geometry and other 'impractical' subjects, men did come from all over Greece to study at the Academy from careerist as well as intellectual motives.

As in most things, Sparta was different from the rest of Greece. Everything was sacrificed to the creation of a hardy military race. Spartans continued to dispose of sickly children. At seven, boys were taken from their parents and became part of a group that has aptly been compared to a boarding school – though few boarding schools would be happy about the comparison. The 'headmaster' and his assistants imposed savage discipline, assisted by chosen older boys for whom the younger 'fagged'. Boys wore a simple tunic in all weathers, and bathed in the cold rushing water of the River Eurotas.

Their bedding consisted of reeds, which the boys themselves tore from the river, and their food of variations on porridge, deliberately so meagre as to encourage stealing, which was only disgraceful if the thief was unskilful enough to be caught. According to one famous story – famous because it recorded an action that was held to be admirable – a young Spartan stole a fox, hid it under his tunic, and allowed it to gnaw away his vitals rather than own up. Athletics and brutal games seem to have dominated the syllabus, along with dancing – which was, however, the occasion for drilling. Such learning as they acquired seems to have been patriotic fare, including the laws of Sparta and militaristic verse; but even in Sparta a certain amount of Homer had to be committed to memory. Finally, Spartan education ended with the military training and militarized life for which it had always been intended as a preparation. One beneficial side-effect of the Spartan obsession

A music lesson: the pupil is playing the *aulos*, a flute with a double reed, while the master directs him with upraised hand. In ancient Greece, music and dancing were not regarded as optional refinements but as basic elements of an education. Attic red-figure vase, early 5th century BC.

Portrait of an *ephebe*, a young man between eighteen and twenty; he wears a cloak and is shown in an unusually reflective pose. During these years, young male citizens completed their education by undergoing a course of physical and military training; Hellenistic marble, 1st century BC.

with health and efficiency was that even girls were given a vigorous athletic education; and indeed women were rather freer in Sparta than in most Greek states. Other Greeks professed to be shocked by the girls' short tunics and occasional wrestling matches with the boys; the Athenian tragedian Euripides – admittedly writing at the height of the Peloponnesian War – asserted that their education led to unchastity, but they were portrayed in a rather different vein, by the comic playwright Aristophanes, as hopelessly provincial muscle-women.

THE CULT OF THE ATHLETE

The Greeks made a cult of the human body and were intensely conscious of its beauty when naked. This was especially true of the male form, which they felt no compunction about exposing to the view; by contrast, women were never seen naked in public; and even in the form of statues of goddesses, nude females were not acceptable until the mid-4th century BC. Male nakedness was mostly apparent in the closely related cult of athletics, which played a part in Greek life for which it is hard to find parallels in any other culture. Athletic exercises were a significant part of a youth's education and were maintained through adult life; and a large number of citizens attended the Olympic Games and other competitive festivals, where the winners were regarded as having won immortal fame.

Two athletic institutions, the *palaestra* and the *gymnasium*, were prominent in every Greek city. The *palaestra* was the centre of athletic schooling, where pupils performed gymnastic exercises to the accompaniment of music and practised running, jumping and other competitive sports; it was also used by adults for wrestling contests. The *palaestra* was a public institution, equipped with changing rooms, washing facilities and shops; it was open to all the children of citizens, but a small fee had to be paid to the instructor in charge, and it is difficult to be certain how widely it was actually used. At the same time there were also privately run *palaestrai*, patronized by the sons of the rich. *Gymnasia* were larger versions of the *palaestrai*, in effect sports grounds with even more facilities. They were set up in spots where there were springs and shady trees. Athens possessed three; one, celebrated for its beauty, was the Academy where Plato founded his famous school of philosophy.

The Greek passion for athletics almost certainly originated in training to ensure that the entire citizen body was sufficiently fit and skilled to fight for the *polis*; and an alternative use for *gymnasia* was as drilling grounds. But long before the Classical period athletics had acquired a separate personal and social significance. The *gymnasia*, open to all citizens, became probably the most important social centres in the city, in which exercise, relaxation and conversation served to promote male bonding and were conducted within a framework of pleasurable rituals – oiling and dusting the body before working out, washing it afterwards, and scraping it down (in the absence of soap) with a curved bronze implement known as a *strigil*.

Graceful victor. Wearing a wreath that attests to his prowess, the athlete strides on, in a pose that is at once dynamic and relaxed. Among other things, a life-size bronze figure of this kind embodies the Greek tendency to identify excellence with physical beauty; 1st century BC.

The Greeks were intensely competitive and thirsty for glory. Athletic prowess was regarded as one of the highest forms of achievement, worthy to be immortalized in poetry, and sporting events were a notable feature of the Greek year. Most of the many festivals on the calendar had athletic competitions attached, but the most prestigious were Panhellenic (that is, open to and watched by individuals from all over the Greek world). The oldest of these was the Olympic Games, founded in 776 BC and held every four years until AD 396; as is well known, these were the inspiration for the present-day Olympics, begun (or revived) in 1896. By the early 6th century BC there were also Panhellenic Isthmean Games at Corinth and Nemean Games at Nemea in the north-eastern Peloponnese, each held every two years, as well as Pythian Games held at Delphi every four years. These festivals were arranged so that the year of the Nemean Games alternated with a year in which both Isthmean and Olympic, or Isthmean and Pythian, Games were held. All of these events were religious festivals, accompanied by sacrifices and solemn rituals; but they were also jamborees, drawing spectators and tourists from all over the Greek world; among those who turned up in the hope of exploiting the occasion were vendors of food, trinkets and prophecies, along with philosophers and

historians bent on declaiming their works to anyone who would listen.

The Olympic Games set the pattern for later athletic festivals. Olympia, in the north-west Peloponnese, was a cult centre dedicated to Zeus, the king of the gods. The festival was held in mid-summer and lasted for five days. Weeks before it began, the city of Elis sent messengers all over Greece inviting participants and spectators to come. This also served to remind the city-states that they must observe a sacred truce for several weeks; in practice this did not prevent inter-city warfare, but it did mean that anyone travelling to and from the games could pass freely through 'enemy' territory or battle zones without fear of being detained or harmed.

At Olympia and the other Panhellenic games, the contests took place in a stadium for track-and-field events and a hippodrome for horse- and chariot-racing. Essentially these were areas marked out for the competitions; apart from a few honoured delegates, spectators were not provided with seats but took up their places on banks and hillsides from which they could view the action. As always, the athletes were naked, except for one foot-race in which they had to wear armour. The athletic events consisted of four foot-races and the pentathlon, a five-event competition consisting

Young men playing a game resembling hockey; the players about to vie for possession of the ball appear to be concentrating intensely. The scene is unusual, since most Greeks had only a limited interest in team games. Athenian marble relief from the base of a statue, c.510 BC.

of javelin- and discus-throwing, the long jump, a foot-race, and wrestling; the winner was the athlete who was victorious in three of these events. Athletes trained hard for the Olympics, but for a long time the track-and-field events were reasonably open to talent. By contrast, horse- and chariot-racing were only possible for the affluent, and so contests in the hippodrome were in part displays of conspicuous expenditure; one of the most glamorous and erratic figures in Athenian history, Alcibiades, entered no less than seven chariots in one of the Olympic races and, as he later boasted, carried off the first, second and fourth prizes.

At Olympia a footrace was also held for women in honour of the goddess Hera, although it was not part of the official Olympics; not much is known about it except that the competitors ran in tunics and the event was dominated by Spartans, the only Greek women who received physical training.

No financial rewards were on offer at the Olympic Games and other festivals: the prizes for a champion were an olive wreath, cut from a sacred tree in the sanctuary of the god, and the imperishable fame that he had won through his speed, skill or stamina. Athletes participated in the games as individuals, not as representatives of their cities; but a man's success did cast a reflected glory on his

A scene from the *palaestra*, the athletic training ground and sports centre where the young received their physical education. It was also used for wrestling contests between adults, like the one shown here; marble relief, c.500 BC.

A young man prepares for a javelin throw. Most Greek sports probably originated as forms of military training; in the case of the spear-like javelin the link between martial and athletic skill remained obvious. Red-figure painting, c.470 BC, on a cup found at Vulci in Italy.

Below: a young athlete cleans his body by scraping himself down. Before taking part in athletics, men oiled their bodies and covered them with a fine dust; later they would bathe, oil themselves, and then use the scraper, or strigil. Attic red-figure vase painting, late 6th century BC.

birthplace (especially if it was a city of Greater Greece, wealthy and yet still struggling with feelings of inferiority *vis-à-vis* the famous states on the Greek mainland), and material benefits could result. By the end of the 5th century BC such incentives, combined with rising standards and more and more protracted and intensive training, had produced a class of professional athletes who toured the circuit of festival competitions and expected to carry off most of the prizes. Although the Olympics maintained something of their austere integrity, during the Hellenistic period *palaestrai, gymnasia* and festivals grew larger and were more splendidly appointed than ever, but we also hear of turbulent, abusive crowds of spectators and familiar charges of cheating and result-fixing. In modern terms, amateurism (or 'shamateurism') had been replaced by spectator sports that served as a branch of the entertainment business.

WOMEN, MARRIAGE AND SEX ·

The Greek woman was emphatically inferior in status to men, both in custom and law. As a girl she owed perfect obedience to her father; he decided whom she would marry, and after the wedding she found not independence but merely a change of masters. In most states she could not own property, let alone take part officially in any but the most trivial commercial transactions (Sparta was one of the exceptions); her husband could do what he liked with her dowry unless he decided to divorce her, in which case her father could claim it back. Greek men married late, and the age-gap between an oldish man (say 30) and a teenager must have reinforced the authority of the male. A wife was expected to spend most of her time at home, supervising the domestics if the family was well off and in any event making sure that the necessary housework was done, the food cooked, and the family clothes and other fabrics spun and woven. Wives of poor men might have to work – keeping a market stall or acting as wet-nurses – but that only reinforced the low status of the entire family. Among rich and poor, when friends (who would always be male friends) came to dinner, the wife had to retire to the women's quarters, which were as inviolable as a harem; no respectable woman ate with anybody but members of her family. Apart from attending certain festivals, she would make no significant public appearances except for shopping expeditions to the *agora*. By contrast, her husband might be sociable and mobile; and if his mobility took in more or less serious sexual adventures she was expected to put up with them, although any adventures on her part were liable to attract severe punishment.

Put in these legal and social terms, the Greek woman's lot was an unhappy one; and many writers have so described it. But if so it was an unhappiness shared by most women in the West down to the 20th century, and even now by many women in Southern Europe and the Islamic world. This is not to defend inequality, but to point out that the position of the Greek woman was much the same as that of civilized women at most times and places. And that means that married life was probably much the same too – that there were sly wives and domineering wives as well as downtrodden and submissive ones; and that people valued domestic happiness but, if that was not available, settled for comfort and compromise. There is little evidence in Greek literature

Queenly housewife. This ivory figure appears to represent a wealthy woman, for she wears pearls on her headdress and round her neck. All the same, she carries the symbols of domestic duty, a distaff in one hand and a spindle in the other; late 7th century BC, from Ephesus.

Seated woman opening a wicker box; relief on a clay plaque from Locri in Southern Italy; 5th century BC. Despite its quiet domestic air, the interior is by Greek standards luxurious, with beautifully carved furniture decorated with rosettes; the elegantly clad woman may well represent a goddess.

that women were despised. Homer can sympathize with a noble and touching woman like Hector's wife Andromache, doomed to widowhood and slavery, and also with a charming girl whose mind is beginning to dwell on men, like Nausicaa, the princess in the *Odyssey* who discovers the shipwrecked Odysseus salt-caked and fascinatingly naked, and would clearly be willing to take him, properly cleaned up, for her husband. Greek drama has its heroines, too, including Queen Alcestis, who in Euripides' play gives her life so that her husband may live. It also has a number of fatal women: Queen Phaedra, who enacts the story of Joseph and Potiphar's wife with her stepson; Medea, abandoned by Jason, who murders her children by him and poisons her rival; the vengeful Clytemnestra, who despatches her husband Agamemnon; and the female devotees of Dionysus, who tear their king apart when he tries to calm their frenzy.

In the great age of Athens there seems to have been more interest in the ordinary life of women and the home. Tender domestic groups appear as memorials on tombstones, and women and household scenes are frequently the subjects of vase paintings. Literature, too, makes more of women. But the conventional ideal remained the submissive housewife: in his funeral oration, Pericles lays it down that 'the greatest glory of a woman is to be talked about as little as possible by men, whether the talk is complimentary or critical'. And the tragedian Euripides, who created a splendid gallery of women characters, was widely regarded as a misogynist, apparently on the grounds that he showed women as capable of passion and action. The strongest indication that Athenian women were far from nonentities comes from the comedies of Aristophanes, the chief source of all our information about the less formal side of Greek life. In *Lysistrata*, the women of Greece withdraw their sexual favours to force their husbands to end the war. The men are consistently outwitted and eventually capitulate, but it is clear that abstinence is as difficult for the women as for the men — especially for those couples who love each other. It would be unwise to draw too many conclusions from Aristophanes' mixture of farce and fantasy, but it at least suggests that the mutual satisfactions of family life

were as important in the 5th century BC as at any other time — and, incidentally, that most men cannot have got their main satisfactions from homosexual relationships or the services of courtesans, as has often been asserted. Aristophanes' *Thesmophoriazusae* is an even wilder farce in which Euripides' father-in-law disguises himself as a woman and spies on a festival from which men are excluded in order to find out what they are up to. The women are furious with Euripides — the 'misogynist' — but mainly, it seems, because he has found them out: thanks to his revelations, Athenian husbands now lock the doors of the women's quarters, keep guard dogs to scare off other men, and even lock up the larder (presumably to stop their women tippling and subsidizing their boyfriends). The women are such bold hussies, Euripides' father-in-law implies, that they will commit adultery under their spouses' noses, and may even do away with them if their presence becomes too inconvenient!

Prostitution flourished in ancient Greece, though probably no more so than in other societies. There were streetwalkers of both genders, and flute-girls and dancers who entertained at banquets were expected to provide sexual services. The most interesting practitioners were the *hetairai*, who closely resembled the traditional Japanese geisha girls or the poetically named *grandes horizontales* of Parisian society in the 1890s. *Hetairai* were skilled musicians, good conversationalists (who could, not being respectable, dine with the men) and also, presumably, stimulating lovers. Whether they were quite as cultivated, shrewd or golden-hearted as they were reputed to be must remain an open question, although by the 4th century BC Greek writers were already glamorizing the oldest profession. *Hetairai* were emancipated slaves or foreigners; the most famous, Pericles' mistress Aspasia, came from the city of Miletus in Ionia. She, at least, seems to have lived up to the legend, since she was a friend of Socrates as well as a 'friend' of Pericles, who divorced his wife and went to live with her. Having sponsored the law which restricted citizenship to those whose parents were both Athenian citizens, he later had to get round it so that his own son by Aspasia could be admitted as a citizen. As Aristophanes' plays — and common sense — suggest, prostitution can hardly

Lovers, painted on the inside of a drinking vessel so that the scene would come into view as it was emptied by the drinker. Both tender emotion and erotic excitement are represented in Greek art. Red-figure vase painting by Makron, beginning of the 5th century BC.

Women at play. Images of ordinary Greek women (as opposed to figures from myth) most often show them washing and beautifying themselves or engaged in their household tasks. But here the two terracotta figures are absorbed in playing the dice-like game of knucklebones; c.340–330 BC.

have been more than an occasional substitute for marital relations; and the famous *hetairai* must have been purely upper-class luxuries.

The situation is less clear in the case of male homosexuality, despite the popular reputation of the ancient Greeks. All-male gatherings at *gymnasia* and dinner parties are thought to have promoted a homoerotic atmosphere, and although not officially condoned everywhere, in practice homosexuality was widely accepted, as lyric poems, inscriptions and other references testify; and there were writers prepared to argue that the love of man and boy was on a higher plane than love between man and woman. In this idealized version of homosexual relationships the older man stood *in loco parentis*, lovingly guiding his young friend towards spiritual and intellectual maturity. (The elite corps of the Theban army, the Sacred Band, is said to have been made up of just such lovers.) In this situation there seems to have been some doubt whether full sexual relations ought to take place, and it has been suggested that a prejudice existed against imposing or adopting sexually passive roles; but given the gap that exists in most societies between how people are supposed to behave and how they actually do behave, we may guess that many relationships were less elevated and more varied than convention prescribed. Surviving paintings on pottery appear to support this view, but inevitably the exact nature and proportions of different sexual preferences cannot be known. The situation in regard to lesbianism is even more obscure, despite the fact that the term was suggested by the passionate verses of the poet Sappho of Lesbos. The wealth of Athenian references to *hetairai*, female prostitutes, adultery and other heterosexual matters has probably been under-advertised; they suggest that homosexuality and bisexuality were more openly recognized, but not necessarily more common, than they are in present-day society.

Guest at a banquet listening in a state of rapture, or perhaps singing, while a youth plays on the flute. The atmosphere seems charged; such entertainers were frequently expected to provide sexual as well as aesthetic pleasure. Red-figure painted cup, 460–450 BC.

HOUSE, HOME AND MARKET

At Athens and other leading cities, the houses in which people lived must have looked mean and insignificant by comparison with the splendid public buildings on the Acropolis and elsewhere. At the very height of Athenian power there seem to have been some six thousand houses in the city proper, chaotically huddled together in crooked streets and holding about 36,000 people. Many more must have lived within the walls at the Piraeus, or close to the city; and during the long periods in the Peloponnesian War when the Spartans were ravaging Attica the population of the city was swollen by rustic refugees and their livestock. In normal times a majority of the people probably lived in the country; and in less commercially oriented places than Athens even the city-dwellers may often have gone to work in the countryside every morning, reversing present-day commuting habits.

The contrast between public and private building extended to materials: the temples were built of stone, a durable but expensive material, whereas houses (even wealthy men's houses) consisted of sun-dried or baked clay bricks, topped with terracotta tile roofs. As a result, some trace remains of many temples, but Greek houses have vanished except for occasional hints of outlines in the soil. However, archaeologists and historians have managed to create a general picture of Greek dwellings. The walls were lime-washed on the outside and plastered inside. Furniture was sparse and holes in the roof served as chimneys; on a cold night when the wind was in the wrong direction, the inhabitants of a Greek house must have been faced with an unpleasant choice between freezing and choking. In houses of any size the basic layout was one that has often been seen in Mediterranean lands: an uninviting, small-windowed facade looked on to the street, while the true centre of the dwelling lay at the back, where rooms clustered round an inner courtyard in which an altar stood. The layout could be adapted to every kind of private and commercial purpose, accommodating workshops, shops and offices in the ground-floor street front. Most of the private rooms served the functions we should expect, but in addition there were one or more rooms set aside for the womenfolk, right at the back of the house, where they probably did their spinning and weaving and to which they retired when there was male company. As a corollary, the dining room (*andron*) to which the head of the family invited his friends for

A busy household on the eve of a wedding: gifts arrive for the bride, including a box of jewels. Red-figure vase painting, mid-5th century BC; the vase itself is a type of nuptial amphora (the bride is holding another), used to contain lustral water.

casual conversation or a formal dinner party (*symposium*) was at the very front of the house, where there was little likelihood that male guests would accidentally encounter any of the resident females.

Many Greek households must have been nearly self-sufficient, making clothes from wool supplied by the master's farm outside the city and bringing in food from the same source. However, the market or *agora* was thronged and seems to have had something for everyone – scent and probably cosmetics, fine fabrics and other ladies' luxuries, as well as fish, cheese, oil, corn and so on; taverns and stalls selling drinks provided a cheap and cheerful counterpart to the upper-class dinner party; and there were even money-lenders doing business at 12 per cent interest with optimistic or desperate clients. At Athens the *agora* ran into the *ceramicos*, where potters made and sold vases and terracotta statuettes intended for votive offerings. Officials were appointed to fix prices and ensure that the market remained unobstructed, but the clusters of shops, tables, stalls and booths must have made their tasks onerous. As so often, it is the comic dramatist Aristophanes who has given the liveliest picture of the proceedings, including a snapshot of a vainglorious army officer clanking about in his armour between the vegetable and crockery stalls before going home with an omelette carefully packed into his helmet.

Fair dealing in the marketplace: men weighing bales at Athens, or just possibly at some smaller centre in Attica. The market place was economically important as well as serving as a social centre. Black-figure vase painting, mid-6th century BC.

A huntsman on his way home after a successful outing; a catch of small game could make a difference to a diet that was, for most people, not rich in meat. Black-figure painting in a cup, c.500 BC; the figures are cleverly, almost wittily fitted into the circular frame.

LIFE ON THE LAND

Greek literature and art tell us relatively little about farmers, and even now not a great deal is known about the ownership and distribution of agricultural holdings. Yet farmers made up the majority of the population, and it was their work, in the countryside beyond the city walls, that made possible the brilliant culture of the *polis*. Mountain barriers and poor communications ensured that Greek states aimed at self-sufficiency (although Athens, a heavy importer of food, was a notable exception), and by the Classical period farming had become specialized and intensive in order to take advantage of every type of soil and variation in the climate.

This was all the more necessary as the population increased, since most Greek soil was poor and the weather (and therefore the harvest) was highly unpredictable.

The staple crops were cereals, which in most places meant barley; less palatable than wheat, it was more reliable except in a few areas such as the western Peloponnese, where rainfall was heavier. Also very widely cultivated were olives and vines. Olives were wonderfully multi-purpose crops, providing (among other things) food, oil for lighting and a skin cleanser; vines produced grapes and wine, which was often a lucrative export.

Beans, figs and other plants supplemented the Greeks' diet, providing carbohydrates and calories. Meat was rarely eaten and consequently had such prestige that stories of Greek heroes dwell on high-roast feasts, thereby giving a false impression of everyday life; in reality the townsman was most likely to taste flesh after the sacrifice of a beast during a public festival, when portions were distributed to the celebrants. Cattle, sheep, goats and pigs were raised, but horses were not farm animals, remaining the preserve of the aristocracy; wagons and ploughs were pulled by oxen. Cattle and goats were also important as a source of milk and cheese, while sheep provided wool for clothing, more commonly worn than linen made from flax.

Fish played a larger part in the average person's diet than meat, and it was widely available thanks to the fact that hardly any place in Greece is more than 65km (40 miles) from the sea. Some fish were salted and dried to preserve them, but most were eaten fresh from the water; and in the markets cheap cuts and fish-cakes were on sale to the poor.

The busiest times in the agricultural year were early summer and autumn. Cereals were harvested between late May and early July; in September it was the turn of the grapes to be gathered; and the period from October to mid-December was the busiest of all, a time of ploughing and sowing, pruning, harvesting olives and performing many other tasks before the onset of winter. In compensation, spring and high summer were seasons of relative leisure, and it was then that the major festivals and athletic games were held. This was also when much building was done, since oxen were free to haul marble and labour was available for public projects. Such was the commanding importance of the agricultural cycle that even the frequent wars between Greek and Greek could only be fought when there was no work to be done on the land.

Gathering olives, one of the great staple products of the Mediterranean; they were valued for their oil as well as for their nutritional value. Here they are being shaken from the trees so that they can be gathered on the ground; Athenian black-figure vase painting, c.520 BC.

SOCIETY, WORK AND SLAVERY

On this subject, as on so many others, 5th-century Athens is easily the best-documented of the Greek states, and is therefore taken to represent them all. There is an unavoidable element of distortion in this, if only because Athens is known to have been more articulate and prosperous and imperial than the rest: most of the city-states must in fact have been simpler and more 'old-fashioned' and rural in organization and outlook. Still, other Greeks may have complained of Athens' tyranny, but they never referred to her as a freak; so the distortions are perhaps no worse than those of most city-biased descriptions of how societies function.

The influence of the aristocracy on Athenian life never entirely disappeared; as we have seen, for most of the 5th century aristocrats led the rival factions in the democratic state. But the wealthy businessman had no trouble in being accepted as a member of the upper class, and was not necessarily expected to give up his business interests in order to make a public career; Nicias, chief commander of the disastrous Sicilian expedition, was an immensely wealthy man who hired out a thousand slaves to work in the Athenian silver mines at Laureum. However, there was some feeling that – as in 19th-century Britain – the unemployed gentleman of private means was the most suitable person to run a state in which many of the highest official positions were unpaid. Aristophanes was a typical conservative in his attitude towards the radical democrats who exercised most influence at Athens during the last years of the war. He always refers to them as lining their pockets at the expense of the state, with how much justification it is now impossible to say. By contrast, the richest thousand or so citizens were expected to help the community by

The peasant behind a plough, driving a span of oxen. As in all settled ancient societies, working the soil was the basic activity on which the entire structure of civilization rested. In this terracotta group, man and beasts exude weariness; from Thebes in Boeotia, earlier 6th century BC.

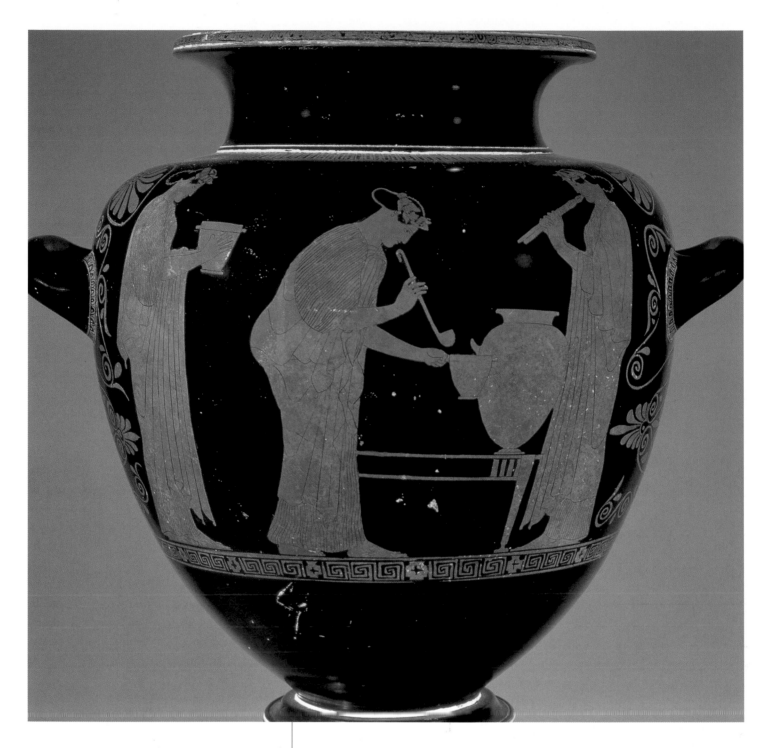

paying for certain important items, notably the fitting out of state shipping and the production of festival plays.

Below this level, 5th-century Athenian citizens fell into two social groups: hoplites and thetes. The hoplite group was defined in military terms: it comprised all the male citizens, whether farmers, traders, or craftsmen, who could afford the armour and weapons needed to serve as a hoplite (heavy infantryman). The thetes were the poorer classes – mostly small farmers and the poorest craftsmen who hired themselves out by the day; they served in the army as auxiliaries or manned the fleet. From the meagre information provided by local government registers and army and religious fraternity lists, it looks as though hoplites and thetes were very roughly equal in numbers; the size of the hoplite class confirms the general impression that at Athens wealth was quite widely distributed among the citizenry.

Drinking as a Dionysiac ritual. A woman ladles wine into a cup while her companion partakes and another stands by playing on the flute. The object shown here (and also in the painting) is a *stamnos*, the main Dionysiac cult vessel. Attic red-figure scene, by the Villa Giulia Painter, 460 BC.

The staff of life: just as the man laboured in the field to grow grain, the woman laboured to turn it into bread, kneading dough. Like the ploughman on page 78, she may be a family slave or servant. Clay figure with traces of pigment from Aulis, c.500–475 BC.

The military classification persisted, thanks to Athens' many wars and imperial commitments, and at times formed the basis for political groupings. As the strength and survival of Athens came to depend increasingly on the navy, the thetes gained previously denied political rights; eventually, though there was no change in the law, they were tacitly allowed to hold most offices, including membership of the Council of Five Hundred, and small daily payments made regular attendance at the Assembly and the law courts a practical possibility for the less well-off. (However, the payment was never so generous as to encourage thetes to devote themselves to politics rather than work for a living, although conservatives inevitably claimed that it was.) Significantly, the destruction of the Athenian fleet in Sicily, which was a blow to the prestige of the navy, and therefore to the influence of the thetes, was followed by the oligarchic reaction of 411, apparently supported by the hoplites; one of the first actions of

the new regime was to disfranchise the thetes and abolish payments for civic attendance. The oligarchy fell mainly because the Athenian navy based on Samos remained adamantly pro-democratic; and after the great naval victory over the Spartans at Cyzicus, the pre-eminence of the navy was fully re-established and all the rights of the thetes were restored.

The *metics* (foreign residents) lived and worked outside this socio-political hurly-burly. As non citizens they could not vote and were not allowed to own land, so they could never put down roots in the community. They were liable to military service, though it seems unlikely that they were called upon except in emergencies, or perhaps for material contributions. In communities like the Greek city-states, where kinship, ownership of land, political activity and membership of religious associations were so large a part of life, the *metic* was an anomaly: a free-floating individual in a closely bonded world. On the other hand there seems to have been no social discrimination against *metics*, who appear on an equal footing with citizen guests at banquets and on other social and business occasions. A great many of them must have been merchants, and they may well have formed substantial colonies in only a few of the busier commercial cities such as Athens and Corinth.

The proportion of slaves to the rest of the population was probably higher in such cities too. In the Dark Age, and later still in many places, slave-owning on any scale was not particularly attractive: an extra worker also meant an extra mouth to feed in hard times, while in a good year there was not much to be done with a surplus. The introduction of money and the growth of trade transformed the situation. This was true above all at Athens, where farming for the market and a booming foreign trade created a demand for cheap labour. Most estimates put the slave population of Athens in 431 BC at 80–100,000, that is, between a quarter and a third of the population as a whole.

At first sight the attitude of the ancients towards slavery is puzzling. In the *Iliad*, the Trojan hero Hector tells his wife Andromache that his own inevitable death in battle troubles him less than the knowledge that she and her children will pass into bondage in a stranger's land; and there are many similarly heart-rending passages in Homer, Aeschylus and other authors, lamenting the chances and changes of life that lead to enslavement. There is, in other words, just the imaginative sympathy we expect to find in great literature; but there is no note of outrage and no expression of protest. There can only be one explanation: to a Greek or Roman it would have been as pointless to condemn slavery as to condemn death: both were simply in the nature of things. Few writers thought it necessary to attempt a defence of slavery, though the philosopher Aristotle did something of the sort by equating slaves with barbarians who, unlike the Greeks, were slaves by nature – a feeble enough argument since, as Aristotle knew very well, many Greek prisoners of war had been enslaved, while perhaps an even larger number of Greek women and children from captured cities had been sold into bondage by the Athenians and other inflamed belligerents.

Many of the slaves at Athens were probably non-Greeks: Thracian victims of the Greek colonists who had established themselves along the coast, or Asians specially purchased in the great slave markets of the East. It is not possible to be more precise: only slaves, perhaps, would have been interested in discriminating between their places of origin, and the contemporary records were not compiled for their benefit. Bearing this qualification in mind, it seems that the slave's lot was a relatively happy one in 5th-century Athens. He had some legal rights: he could not be killed, or violently assaulted without provocation – though all experience in similar situations indicates that such rights were hard to enforce in a world run by property owners. Of more practical importance was the mild tone of Athenian society, created by its small-scale, domestic nature. Very few men seem to have owned large numbers of slaves: the norm was the family unit with two or three slaves – a man or two to help the master in the fields or workshop, and a nurse or maid working in the house. In this kind of atmosphere a certain degree of affection and companionship flourished, and there is cer-

tainly no evidence that the Athenians feared the slaves all around them as the Spartans feared their own helots. In so far as slaves appear in Athenian literature it is as amiable rogues – pretty much the standard ruling-class literary version of serfs and workers for the next two-and-a-half millennia. The atmosphere was so relaxed that slaves were hired out by the day to other people, and even allowed to set up in business on their own, in separate premises from their masters'. Under this remarkable arrangement the slave merely paid over one-sixth of his income to his owner; the rest belonged to him, and if he was successful he might save enough to buy his freedom. How often this happened – and how often a master gratuitously gave a slave his freedom – is not known; freedmen certainly played no notable part in the

A shoemaker cutting leather. The boy who is to be shod stands on the workbench while the craftsman uses his foot as a template; the boy's father looks on. The furnishings are shown in interesting detail. Athenian black-figure vase painting by the Eucharides Painter, c.500–475 BC.

Opposite: the artist at work. A youth sits painting a type of vase known as a bell crater. The painting is itself a detail from a bell crater showing figures in a pottery workshop. As so often, 'the Komaris Painter' is known only by a name made up by experts; Attic red-figure, c.430–425 BC.

Youth carrying a couch and a three-legged table on his back: he is probably going to set in place the furniture needed for a symposium (banquet). This is an unusual glimpse of a commonplace type of domestic task. Red-figure vase painting by the Pan Painter, c.480 BC.

public history of Greece, in marked contrast with the freedmen of Rome.

Greek slavery was relatively mild; but only relatively. The well-treated slave might be cuffed when his master was bad-tempered, sold when his master got into debt, and tortured (to make sure his evidence was not biased by loyalty) when his master got into trouble; and if he was really unlucky he was sent to work in the Athenian silver mines. On one occasion, at least, the slaves voted with their feet. In 413, during the Peloponnesian War, when the Spartans took more or less permanent control of the Attic countryside by setting up a fortified camp outside besieged Athens, 20,000 slaves fled to join them. The details of the incident are obscure, but the slaves' sentiments are clear enough.

The small scale of production was not incompatible with vigorous activity and rapidly expanding trade. Although the evidence is sketchy, it seems likely that much of the fertile land in Attica consisted of small plots, owned or leased by fami-

lies, although larger estates existed and may have been the dominant type before the reforms of Solon and Pisistratus (who also seem to have suppressed the demoralizing practice of sharecropping). Much of the land was turned over from cereals to olive trees and vines; the oil and wine produced could be sold in the city for local consumption or export, while the shortfall in grain production could be made good by imports from the Hellespont and Black Sea regions.

As we have seen, this imbalance between cereal and olive and vine production was a distinctively Athenian phenomenon. The need for thousands of storage jars for oil and wine caused pottery to become a thriving trade, and the 5th-century Attic masterpieces of vase painting were the superb side-effects of a craft largely devoted to producing sound but commonplace jars in great quantities. The existence of an export trade must have given opportunities to develop all sorts of new lines with which to impress barbarians or the less sophisticated 'colonial' Greeks. Athenian metalwork has been found as far away from Hellas as central Europe and southern Russia, and there may have been other, perishable export goods that have left no visible traces. The most active merchants had agents in several ports, but even so their business was a high-risk, high-profit one (as, for that matter, most international trade remained down to quite recent times).

Manufacturers in Athens itself were also small; the largest workshop in the city, owned by a *metic* from Syracuse, employed some 1,200 slaves making shields. Even a very wealthy man like the father of the orator Demosthenes owned a variety of small properties and concerns rather than one large one; and the great buildings on the Acropolis were not the work of teams but of a host of independent craftsmen and small contractors.

We know of only one really large industrial enterprise in the whole of Greece: the silver mines at Laureum, on the southernmost coast of Attica. These mines, productive from the 6th century, played a decisive role in Athenian history. They made it possible for the city to mint its own coinage without indebtedness to other states, and even to export silver to places where oil and wine were not sufficiently in demand. But even more

crucial was the rich new vein struck in 483 and used on Themistocles' advice to build a great fleet of triremes; it was this fleet that smashed the Persians and effectively created Athens' seaborne empire. The mines were state-owned, but the working was contracted out; the hiring prices of slaves – hardly more than the purchase price – suggest that the working conditions must have been appalling, and that being sent to Laureum may have been a punishment meted out to fractious slaves, equivalent to a death sentence. However, anything up to 30,000 of them worked in the mines, so that is not likely to be the whole story.

The economics of everyday life are hard to make sense of because the evidence is so fragmentary. The silver drachma was the main unit of currency, but there was a smaller silver coin, the obol, six of which were equal in value to a drachma. Athenian coins were stamped with the head of Athena, patron goddess of the city and goddess of wisdom; her special bird, the owl, appeared on the reverse side. In the 5th century an unskilled manual worker could earn two or three obols in a day, a skilled man perhaps twice as much. There were some extremely wealthy individuals who left 80,000 drachmai or more on their deaths, but most 'middle-class' Athenians were not grotesquely better off than the poorer citizens; one convincing estimate puts 90 per cent of the population in an annual income group of 180–480 drachmai. Prices are even harder to set out usefully, and a sample must do. A decent workaday pot could be purchased for less than an obol; a decent workaday slave cost around 150 drachmai (the price would vary enormously, depending on the age, health and skills of the slave, who might, for example, be a labourer, a mason, a goldsmith, a clerical worker or a schoolmaster); a good upper-middle-class town house could be bought for 3,000 drachmai. For ease of calculation, 100 drachmai were called a mina, and 60 mina a talent. These terms were mostly used in trade or government finance; Athens, for example, had an emergency fund of 100 talents that was spent on building a new fleet after the Sicilian disaster. But at least one example from a somewhat later period indicates that the inflated values of show business are nothing new: the famous 4th-century actor Polus is said to have received no less than a talent for only two appearances.

Opposite: a girl playing the flute; her nakedness indicates that she is a slave or hired performer. This is one of the reliefs from the famous 'Ludovisi Throne' of c.470 BC, found in Rome.

Women at a fountain, which has been given a substantial architectural setting. Vase painters were fond of this subject, which suggests that fountains were an important amenity of city life. Black-figure Athenian vase, c.525 BC.

SPARTAN LIVING

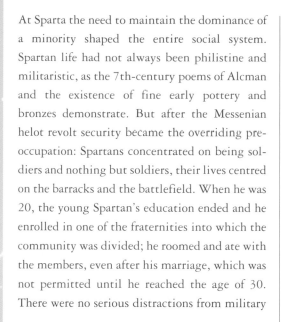

The Vix Crater. This splendid bronze vessel, 1.64 m (5.38 ft) high was found at Vix in eastern France and is an example of export ware, probably from Sparta. A frieze of warriors and chariots runs round the neck, and each handle takes the form of a scroll and a Gorgon head. 6th century BC.

At Sparta the need to maintain the dominance of a minority shaped the entire social system. Spartan life had not always been philistine and militaristic, as the 7th-century poems of Alcman and the existence of fine early pottery and bronzes demonstrate. But after the Messenian helot revolt security became the overriding pre-occupation: Spartans concentrated on being soldiers and nothing but soldiers, their lives centred on the barracks and the battlefield. When he was 20, the young Spartan's education ended and he enrolled in one of the fraternities into which the community was divided; he roomed and ate with the members, even after his marriage, which was not permitted until he reached the age of 30. There were no serious distractions from military life. No Spartan farmed his estates; they were worked by helots who gave up a fixed proportion of their produce, which the owner contributed in turn to the mess of his fraternity. Every effort was made to fix the social order and protect citizens against temptations. Each man inherited a portion of land that was inalienable, helots could not be gambled away, given away or emancipated, since they belonged to the state, not the individual whose land they cultivated; money was prohibited (iron was the closest thing that existed to currency); and since luxury was frowned upon, trade remained a fringe activity that was undertaken by a few licensed non-Spartans. For at least 250 years the system produced a high degree of social cohesion; despite the oligarchic functioning of their political machinery, the Spartans happily called themselves 'the Equals', not without social justification.

The helot was the economic basis of the Spartan system – far more so than the slave in democratic states. This form of serfdom occurred in some other places – in Thessaly, Argos and Crete, for example – but the only information about it of any substance comes from Sparta. On the face of it there was not much to choose between being a slave and being a helot. The slave could be bought, sold and moved about at will, whereas the helot was at least secure on his land; but on the other hand a slave, unlike a helot, might hope to buy or win his freedom. In reality, helots seem to have been worse off: we hear of revolts by helots, not by slaves, and many stories describe the ill-treatment meted out to the helots by their Spartan masters. On one occasion the Spartans are said to have encouraged those helots who believed they had served Sparta well to claim their freedom; those who did so were formed into a triumphal procession which filed into a temple... and was never seen again. By this kind of ruse the Spartans made sure that they thinned the ranks of the boldest, and therefore potentially the most dangerous, helots.

Other sources claim that the Spartans privately but officially declared war on the helots at the

beginning of each year, thereby justifying their excesses to themselves; and young Spartans are even said to have gone in for helot-hunting as part of their training. Not being a literary people, the Spartans left no account of their way of life, but most of the stories about their treatment of helots come from sources that are reasonably sympathetic towards them; though possibly exaggerated, they must represent the essential attitudes of the Spartans. However, there must have been helots and helots, since large contingents served with the Spartan army and seem to have been conspicuously loyal to their masters; some, for example, fell with

the Three Hundred at Thermopylae. The explanation of this apparent contradiction may be that the loyal helots came from the Spartan 'home' territories in Laconia, which seem to have been more docile. The Messenians, to the west, had been a free people whom the Spartans had conquered and among whom they had no roots; and on two occasions the Messenians were the mainspring of revolts that almost overthrew the Spartan system. This was finally accomplished from outside by the Thebans, who not only defeated the Spartans in battle but subsequently destroyed their economic base by liberating Messenia.

Weighing and transporting a cargo under the supervision of King Arkesilas: this action-packed scene is a rare example of Spartan vase-painting, picturing a scene set in the North African Greek colony of Cyrene; black-figure painting on a white ground, second half of the 6th century BC.

The pleasures of the banquet. The revellers lie on their sides on couches, drinking wine; one of their number is expertly serving himself. Low tables are piled with food and a naked female entertainer is on hand to play the flute. Attic red-figure vase painting, 4th century BC.

LEISURE AND PLEASURE

The Greeks were as sociable in their leisure hours as they were in their public and working lives. Eating and drinking and bathing were most fully enjoyed in company; and so were piety, literature and philosophizing, activities that are looked at in later chapters.

The Greeks ate three meals a day which corresponded fairly closely to our breakfast, lunch and dinner. Breakfast was 'continental' – a hunk of bread soaked in wine – and lunch, though more substantial, was equally functional. Dinner, however, was a festive and luxurious occasion for those who could afford it: men invited their friends home and were invited in turn, or they joined dining clubs which used the subscriptions to hire premises and pay for meals. (Such dining facilities, provided by emancipated slaves, were the nearest thing Greece offered to restaurants in this period; otherwise there were only vendors of snacks and wine in the market-place, reputedly all cheats or poisoners.) In some circles the guests brought their own food and the host simply

Unlovely amusement: young Athenians engaged in setting a dog on to a cat. The cruelty of the proceedings evidently went unperceived, for the relief is one of a group of sporting scenes on the base of a statue, dating from about 570 BC, in the Dipylon cemetery in Athens.

provided the drink. On his arrival, a guest removed his sandals and a slave washed his feet. Then tables laden with food were brought in and the diners were arranged around them on couches; like the Romans later on, they lay on their sides, leaving one hand free to pick at the food; knives and forks were not used, though there were spoons for consuming liquids. At Athens meals became more elaborate in the course of the 5th century, but oriental imports, like many other refinements, became common only later on, in the Hellenistic age.

In a well-ordered banquet, serious drinking began after the meal: libations were poured, a hymn was sung, and the company got down to business. Often there was a Master of the Banquet who laid down the proportion of water to wine: the thick, sweet Greek wine was always watered but, as pottery paintings show, had all the usual effects in the long run. Most of the main pottery types were developed as part of the ritual of sociable drinking. Wine was stored and transported in a two-handled jar, the *amphora*, and water likewise in a *hydria*. But at a banquet wine and water were mixed in a large, wide-topped bowl, the *krater*; a jug, the *oinochoe*, was dipped into the *krater* to serve up the wine, and it was drunk from cups of various types, the most popular being the wide, shallow *kylix*.

The other pleasures of the banquet took a number of forms. Sometimes the company provided its own entertainment; and here the ability to sing to a lyre was an asset. Riddles were propounded, jokes told, verses recited; and on occasion – perhaps not so often as the literature

suggests – the occasion turned into an earnest exchange of views. The Greek word for a banquet or drinking party was *symposium*. One of the most famous dialogues written by the philosopher Plato is called *The Symposium* and features Socrates, Aristophanes and other leading Athenians of intellectual ability debating the nature of love; and it was the title and occasion chosen by Plato that eventually gave rise to the modern, intendedly non-alcoholic application of the word 'symposium' to joint scholarly productions. During the ancient Greek versions professional entertainment could be laid on too, usually by specially trained troupes of slaves hired out for the evening; these included musicians, dancers, jugglers and acrobats who might later be called on to provide the company with more intimate services.

A number of daytime social centres existed where a man could meet more casual acquaintances to exchange news and gossip. One was the barber's shop – or rather the hairdresser's, since styling rather than shaving was the professional service the customers looked for. Athletic and conversational pleasures could be combined at the *gymnasium*, and the public baths lent themselves even more to relaxation and sociability. The baths were, by Greek standards, luxurious places, offering facilities for cooking, steaming and cooling the body in a leisurely progression, although even the grandest Hellenistic baths were to be surpassed in scale and sophistication by the great Roman establishments. The Spartans, predictably, bathed in river water.

Greeks also enjoyed a variety of non-athletic games. The most popular involved simple, easily replaced equipment: marbles, five-stones (now a children's game, involving throwing the 'stones' into the air and catching them on the back of the hand), and various dice and ball games. Board games included a chequerboard contest that resembled draughts (checkers) in appearance, although its rules are not known. Bets were laid on cock-fights and other animal combats. And the popularity of wine ensured that *cottabos* became a national late-night sport, since it involved flinging wine-dregs at a target. Significantly, none of these were team games: at play, as in most things, the Greek had an obsessive desire to shine.

Nevertheless there were collective pleasures and entertainments. Most of these were religious, or at least religious in origin, like the dramatic performances that evolved from rituals in honour of the god Dionysus. The many festivals in the Greek calendar offered the pleasures of spectacle, including processions and sacrifices, as well as opportunities for participation in choral singing and dancing. Athletic contests were a feature of the four great games at Olympia, Corinth, Delos and Nemea; and there were also displays linked with other festivals, notably the Panathenaea at Athens, where armoured men gave exhibitions of chariot control which involved leaping on and off and stopping and starting their vehicles with great rapidity, rather in the fashion of a modern military tattoo.

The words 'Nothing in excess' were carved on the temple wall at Delphi. The Greek attitude towards pleasures of all kind – sensual, physical or intellectual – favoured a degree of self-control and consequently moderation in indulgence; along with these went a sense of decorum that restrained the individual from choosing inappropriate times and places for his activities. Any excess that led to the neglect of family duties or citizenship was to be deplored, even if it was harmless in itself. In matters such as sex and gambling, these considerations, rather than moral prohibitions, seem to have determined Greek attitudes.

Like ethical codes at other times and places, a sense of moderation was widely disregarded in practice, especially by the young and wealthy. Cases of men running through their inheritance were cited – usually, it is true, by opponents in the law courts or the Assembly, but with plausible details that can sometimes be independently verified. The playboy might gamble away his substance on cock-fights and dicing, or become a hopeless drunkard, but the commonest objects of mad extravagance were *symposia* and sex. Lavish party-giving could become addictive and, if the fare was luxurious and the guest-list long enough, could dissipate a fortune in a surprisingly short time. But the most dangerous of passions were for women and boys, and it comes as a surprise to find accounts of the reputedly temperate and rational Greeks behaving like the heroes of 19th-century

Revel and intimacy: a fluent and expressive western-Greek view of male bonding and banqueting. The large gestures suggest a sustained drinking session, and one couple are evidently in the grip of debate or desire. Wall painting from the Tomb of the Diver at Paestum, Southern Italy; 480 BC.

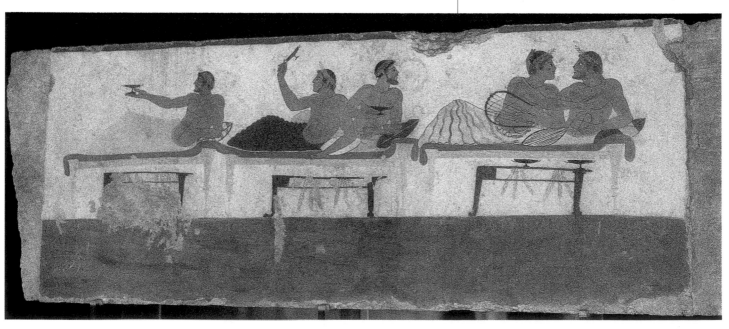

French novels, ruining themselves for the sake of a grand passion. Whether this involved buying the love-object out of slavery or showering gifts on a calculating *hetaira*, the consequences were likely to be disastrous. Immoderate and indecorous, the lover's behaviour also exhibited a dependency that was, in Greek eyes, humiliating; so it is not surprising that in antiquity an uncontrollable passion was portrayed, from Paris and Helen onwards, as a kind of madness and certainly a supreme misfortune. Such episodes warn us that it would be a mistake to think of Greek life purely in terms of the 'calm grandeur and noble simplicity' pictured by some earlier commentators.

At play, but fully armed: two Trojan war heroes, Achilles and Ajax, are intent upon dice, or possibly a board game. Amphora with a painting by Exekias, probably the greatest master of the black-figure style; he signed his works as both potter and painter. Athenian, 540–530 BC.

COSTUME AND FASHION

Both men and women were intensely conscious of their physical appearance, and in spite of their relatively limited equipment and attire, they created and competed with one another in following fashions. As a rule men wore beards during the Classical period, but they patronized hairdressers who trimmed, styled and perfumed their locks. In the Hellenistic period the example of the clean-shaven and thick-maned Alexander the Great provided the model for the entire political elite. The generation gap appeared still earlier. Even before the Persian wars, aristocratic young men were adopting a style that doubtless outraged their elders: wearing their hair very long, dressing in prettily decorated linens, sporting jewellery, and even carrying flowers. Women, too, could be very elegant: in Aristophanes' comedies, references to their saffron robes, perfumes and dainty shoes are frequent and disapproving, in a tone that suggests that the writer enjoys mocking follies but has not the faintest hope (or perhaps intention) of reforming them.

The costume and materials worn by most Greeks did not lend itself to much in the way of fashionable variation, although some degree of distinctiveness could be achieved by using patterned borders and dyes. The most common material was wool, woven on the household loom, although in Classical Athens those who could afford it bought imported linen. But the main garment for both men and women consisted essentially of an oblong of material, folded and wrapped round the body and held in place by pins or, sometimes, simple sewing. The result was a tunic that could be long, like the full-length *peplos*, fastened at the shoulders, which was worn by women in early times (and even later by Peloponnesian women), or short and sometimes sleeved, like the linen *chiton* adopted by both men and women during the Classical period. In cold weather or on formal occasions a man might put on a cloak, or *himation*, over the tunic, and at times it was fashionable to wear only a *himation*, the material wound round the body and flung over one shoulder. Respectable women always appeared in public with a *himation* over the *peplos* or *chiton*. They did not go bare-breasted, let alone nude: in this respect the artistic record can be misleading. The same applies to men: the Greeks do seem to have been completely unselfconscious about nudity, and their appreciation of male beauty led them, for example, to dispense with the wearing of loin cloths for certain kinds of athletic contest; but most of the time they wore clothes for obvious practical reasons. (An interesting example of artistic licence is the convention observed in vase paintings, which represent the Greek soldier as fighting naked, whereas in reality he was of course clad in armour; pictorially his nudity served as a uniform, distinguishing him from any foreign soldier in the same scene.)

If clothes were relatively unexciting, women could and did wear their hair pinned up in a wide range of styles; only slaves (male and female) had short hair, but women in mourning were expected to cut theirs. The wealthy Athenian lady also used as many accessories and beauty aids as most modern women: jewellery, wigs, hair-dyes, curlers, perfumes and cosmetics could all be bought in the *agora*. A pale complexion was particularly admired and sought-after, since it was interpreted as the look appropriate to ladies who belonged to an affluent household: they spent most of their time indoors, by contrast with lower-class women who had to go out to work and became tanned or weather-beaten. Those who were naturally dark or wished to ape their betters could (and did) use white lead as a cosmetic preparation that created the fashionable pallor at considerable cost to the health.

Apart from the 'dainty shoes' of the women – perhaps reserved for festivals – Greeks wore sandals, and sometimes leather boots, if they wore anything on their feet; much of the time, especially in the house, they went barefoot. Walking sticks were standard equipment outdoors, but hats were rarely worn except as protection against the elements, especially when travelling; made of felt or leather, they were appropriately large and broad-brimmed, though some workmen and travellers favoured a distinctive conical cap, the *pilos*.

Opposite: mirror with a handle in the form of a naked male figure. In antiquity mirrors were, like this one, made of bronze, given a high polish so that it reflected the user's image; 5th century BC, from one of the Greek colonies in Southern Italy.

Below: perfume pots in fanciful shapes from the eastern Greek territories of Asia Minor. The containers represent a crouching monkey, the helmeted head of a warrior, and a foot in a sandal. These rather winsome objects were made in the 7th century BC.

Left: trying to look her best: a young woman examines her appearance in a mirror while holding a jewel or make-up box in her other hand. She wears an elegant pleated gown and her hair has been done in a fashionable style. Red-figure vase painting, c.420–410 BC.

OVERSEAS SETTLEMENTS

During the Dark Age the Greeks spread out over the mainland and occupied the islands of the Aegean and the west coast of Asia Minor. These territories became the centre of the Greek world, associated with its most prestigious cities and its most hallowed religious and athletic sites and festivals. But Greeks were also soon to be found all over the Mediterranean and around the Black Sea coasts, as they were set moving by population pressures at home and the lure of profit abroad.

From about 750 BC, city-states sent out groups of citizens to found colonies; despite the modern, empire-building associations of the word, these were independent settlements, endowed with the same laws and religious cults as the mother-city but bound to her only by ties of sentiment. The motives of the mother-city are far from clear, but the most plausible explanation is that in most cases there were too many mouths to feed. The only written record of arrangements for colonization comes from the island of Thera, which in about 630 BC sent out a party to found the city of Cyrene in Libya. One son from every family was chosen to go, and the members of the party were forbidden to return on pain of death. When a leader had been chosen, the approval of the oracle at Delphi was sought; we do not know just what had to be done to make sure that this was forth-

The birth of Aphrodite, goddess of love, washed up on the shore by the waves; relief on the back of the Ludovisi Throne (in fact possibly an altar), c.470 BC. Female nudity and transparent drapery appeared earlier in Greater Greece (Southern Italy) than in the Aegean homelands.

coming, but the cities evidently did know, since hundreds of colonies were founded during the two centuries or so when the movement was at its height.

Colonies were normally founded on the coast, at sites with a good harbour. This enabled the colonists to keep in touch with the mother-city and to trade with both the Greek states and the hinterland of the colony, which was occupied by less sophisticated tribes who were prepared to exchange raw materials or slaves for Greek manufactures. (There was no attempt to plant colonies in more politically advanced regions such as Egypt, although the establishment of Greek trading posts might well be encouraged.) If a colony prospered, more settlers from the mother-country were often sent out, and the colony might go on to found further colonies of its own. Initially the local tribes often welcomed Greek colonists and their wares, but even where Greek cultural influence was at its strongest there was no integration, and in the long run conflicts between the two played a large part in undermining the colonies and bringing about their eventual extinction.

The first wave of colonization, in the late 8th century BC, was directed at Southern Italy and Sicily. It was followed in the 7th century by foundations along the Bosporus and Hellespont and around the Black Sea, where colonists from Miletus were particularly active. Cyrene was the only direct foundation in North Africa, but the colony was able to establish a number of new settlements along the Libyan coast. Expansion in North Africa and the western Mediterranean was limited by opposition from the Etruscans of central Italy and the Carthaginians, a Phoenician people based in the North African city of Carthage, who had built up a formidable maritime trading empire. Of the handful of Greek colonies in the western Mediterranean, the most important was Massilia (modern Marseilles), founded in about 600 BC after a naval victory had given the Greeks a temporary advantage over the Carthaginians. The geographical reach of the Greeks is shown by the fact that Massilia was founded by colonists from Phocaea in Asia Minor, and that despite its distance from Hellas it followed tradition by main-

taining a treasury (a small building filled with offerings) on the sacred island of Delphi.

The densest and wealthiest of Greek settlements were in Southern Italy and Sicily, which the ancients called Greater Greece. Its prosperity was based on the surpluses of wheat produced by its fertile soil. The Sicilian city of Syracuse emerged as the most powerful Greek state, and for several hundred years it was in the forefront of a struggle for control of the island between Greeks and Carthaginians. Under Hiero, Dionysus and other tyrants, Syracuse attracted writers and philosophers such as Aeschylus, Pindar, Simonides and Plato, while its military achievements included the annihilation of the Athenian expedition of 415–13, the turning point of the Peloponnesian War. Ironically, Syracuse lost its independence by allying with its old Carthaginian enemies against the Romans, who besieged the city and took it in 211 BC.

Colonization had petered out by the early 5th century, although colony-like garrisons were established on the territory of unreliable allies by Athens at the height of the city's power; and later Alexander the Great and his successors established garrison-colonies throughout the East, some of which became flourishing cities and centres of Greek influence.

The Temple of Concord at Acragas (modern Agrigento) in Sicily. The tyrants who ruled the Italian Greek colonies built on a grandiose scale; this impressive Doric temple is the best preserved, though not the largest, at Agrigento; 5th century BC.

TRADE, TRAVEL AND EXPLORATION

A cargo vessel being attacked by a warship, perhaps as an act of piracy. Robbery was a possibility on both sea and land, but water was the most dangerous element; experienced sailors though they were, the Greeks stayed in sight of land where they could. Black-figure vase painting, c.500 BC.

Travel was a slow business in the ancient world; but surprisingly large numbers of people did take to the high- or sea-road, and they covered long distances. The Greeks outdid even the Phoenicians in their mobility, travelling as colonists, traders, pilgrims, diplomats and soldiers (mercenary and otherwise); the most spectacular examples were of course Alexander the Great and his army, who ventured over the greater part of the known world on foot or on horseback.

These were the main ways in which individuals travelled in Greece itself, where the terrain was difficult and roads were generally little more than tracks. Wagons and carts were useful only over short distances, but donkeys and mules made reliable pack animals. However, it was almost always preferable to travel by water, and the Greeks' early experience as seafarers is preserved in the mythical travels of Jason and the Argonauts and the wily Odysseus. Greek merchant vessels, unlike warships, were essentially sailing ships, broad-beamed, single-masted and decked. The individual traveller had to find a merchant ship bound for the right port and persuade (and pay) its captain to take him along.

Apart from colonization, trade was the most common motive for travel. Colonies were themselves part of a Greek trading network, established after traders had pioneered the sea routes. There were also trading posts on territories where colonization was unwise. One, at Al Mina, in what is now southern Turkey, dated back to about 800 BC and must have been one of the earliest overseas ventures undertaken by the Greeks as they emerged from the Dark Age. Probably vital as a channel for Eastern influences, it has left no trace in surviving written records, and its existence would be unknown if 20th-century archaeologists had not uncovered the site. By contrast, Greek dealings with Egypt are well-documented. They became so important that in about 620 BC they were allocated a trading centre, Naucratis, on the westernmost branch of the Nile Delta; unlike a colony, it was not under Greek sovereignty, and it contained the offices of all the city-states involved in Greco-Egyptian trade.

Cereals were a major Greek import, brought from Egypt, Greater Greece and the Black Sea region. These supplies made good the harvest shortfall in bad years, and in prosperous times made wheat available rather than the more commonly home-produced barley. With its exceptionally large population, Athens was more dependent on regular supplies than most Greek states, taking pains to control the vital routes to the Black Sea. The Greeks also imported a wide range of foodstuffs and unworked stone and metal, paid for by exports of olive oil, wine, and manufactures such as quality painted pottery and metal cauldrons, ornaments and weapons. The reach – and the cultural influence – of Greek trade has been shown by a variety of archaeological finds, from wrought bronze objects in the Paris area to armour and silver and ivory work placed in Scythian tombs in the Ukraine.

Some Greeks travelled purely to satisfy their curiosity. In the 6th century BC one Hecateus visited Egypt and the Near East and published a *Journey Round the World*. Most of it is lost, along with the map that accompanied it. Unfortunately, not a single ancient Greek map has survived, although it is likely that they showed Eurasia and Northern Africa fairly accurately, grouped round the Mediterranean and themselves surrounded by 'Ocean'; in such a map Greece naturally took a central position, justifying the belief that sacred Delphi was the navel (*omphalos*) of the world.

Other travellers included the historian Herodotus, who gathered materials for his great work in Egypt and the Near East, and military men such as Xenophon and Alexander the Great. None of these were, strictly speaking, explorers, although Alexander's expedition across the Oxus might be considered as venturing beyond the known world. But around 130 BC the Hellenistic pharaoh Ptolemy Euergetes sent Eudoxus of Cyzicus on two voyages from the Red Sea to India, and later Eudoxus tried to reach India by sailing west round Africa (he was never heard of again).

Greek mariners rarely ventured beyond the Pillars of Hercules (the Straits of Gibraltar) into the Atlantic. But about 340 BC Pytheas of Massilia sailed round the coast of Spain, along the French coastline and across to Cornwall, in the far south-west of England; his motive for the voyage is not known, but he may have been seeking to trade for Cornish tin. Then, instead of returning, he sailed north to a land he called Thule, where the night lasted only two or three hours (perhaps Iceland). Prevented from going further by ice, he turned east, discovered an amber-rich island (which fits the fact that the Baltic was the great source of amber), and then made his way back to the Mediterranean. Pytheas' exploits are known only from somewhat later accounts, but they are geographically convincing and entitle him to be called the greatest of ancient Greek explorers.

A Greek woman wearing the kind of tall hat used by travellers and well wrapped up against bad weather. The poor state of the roads made journeying on foot more reliable than using animals or wagons. Terracotta figure from Tanagra, c.300–250 BC.

BIG-CITY LIFE

Though Greek in culture and outlook, the large Hellenistic states that emerged after the death of Alexander the Great were very different from the city-states of the Classical period. Hellenistic cities were different too, becoming larger and more populous, and also more impersonal and cosmopolitan. In Greece and elsewhere the city remained an important expression of municipal life, but it no longer acted as the focus of an individual's existence; even Athens turned into something between a tourist centre and a university town. The citizen ceased to be a member of a small, visible community, and became an isolated individual in a superstate. In some respects this situation resembled that of 20th-century mass society, and the results were similarly paradoxical: individualism in philosophy and art, gigantic public works glorifying a state arm more powerful than anything imaginable in the Classical age, and an increasing nostalgia for that age. Big-city life in great imperial centres such as Alexandria and Antioch was more irresponsible, more consciously 'cultured', and far more comfortable for the better-off. Palaces rivalled temples in size, and although the houses of the rich still followed the old Greek pattern, clustered round a courtyard that was now invariably colonnaded, the scale of the buildings and the quality of the furnishings indicated that luxury was no longer considered the prerogative of the gods.

The city of cities in the Hellenistic age was Alexandria, the Egyptian port founded by Alexander the Great and turned into an opulent cosmopolitan capital by Ptolemy and his successors. Unlike the old city-state, it housed an enormous mixed population – at the height of its prosperity perhaps as many as a million Greeks, Jews, Egyptians and others. Its prosperity was firmly based on Egypt's superabundant wheat harvests, which fed the city masses and ensured Alexandria's livelihood as an exporter. Papyrus for writing, fine fabrics, glass, perfumes, drugs and a great variety of craft and luxury objects were also traded through the port, which benefited in one way or another from almost every commercial transaction involving Egypt and the outside world.

Alexandria's advantages as a port were improved by human effort. The city was laid out on a stretch of coast with the island of Pharos immediately in front of it, sheltering the harbour. This was turned into a double harbour by the construction of a mole linking Pharos with Alexandria; and ships entering the great eastern harbour were guided in by one of the Seven Wonders of the World, the Pharos, a lighthouse high enough for its fire to be visible at a distance of 50km (30 miles).

The Ptolemies' choice of Alexandria as the capital of Egypt doubled its glory. A whole series of magnificent palaces grew up alongside the eastern port, since it became a tradition that each Ptolemy should build a new one for himself. The body of Alexander the Great, 'kidnapped' by Ptolemy I, was entombed alongside those of the new Greek pharaohs. All the standard amenities of Greek urban life were present at Alexandria: an *agora*, a theatre, an amphitheatre and a *gymnasium*; also an artificial hill in the centre of the city, devoted to the cult of the god Pan; and also the Serapeum, the temple of the god Serapis, whom the Ptolemies introduced into the Greek world.

The royal palace complex included the Museum (that is, a place dedicated to the Muses), where scholars, scientists and writers worked

Opposite: the abundance of Egypt, celebrated in Greek fashion. The symbolic figures, including Isis and the Nile, are Egyptian, but the style is adapted to the taste of the land's Hellenistic rulers. Cameo bowl, known at the Tazza Farnese, cut from sardonyx; probably 1st century BC.

A rare image of one of the Seven Wonders of the World, made at a time when it was still standing. The Pharos, the great lighthouse on an island in the harbour at Alexandria, appears on this Roman bronze coin alongside a ship and a Triton (a kind of merman) who is blowing a conch.

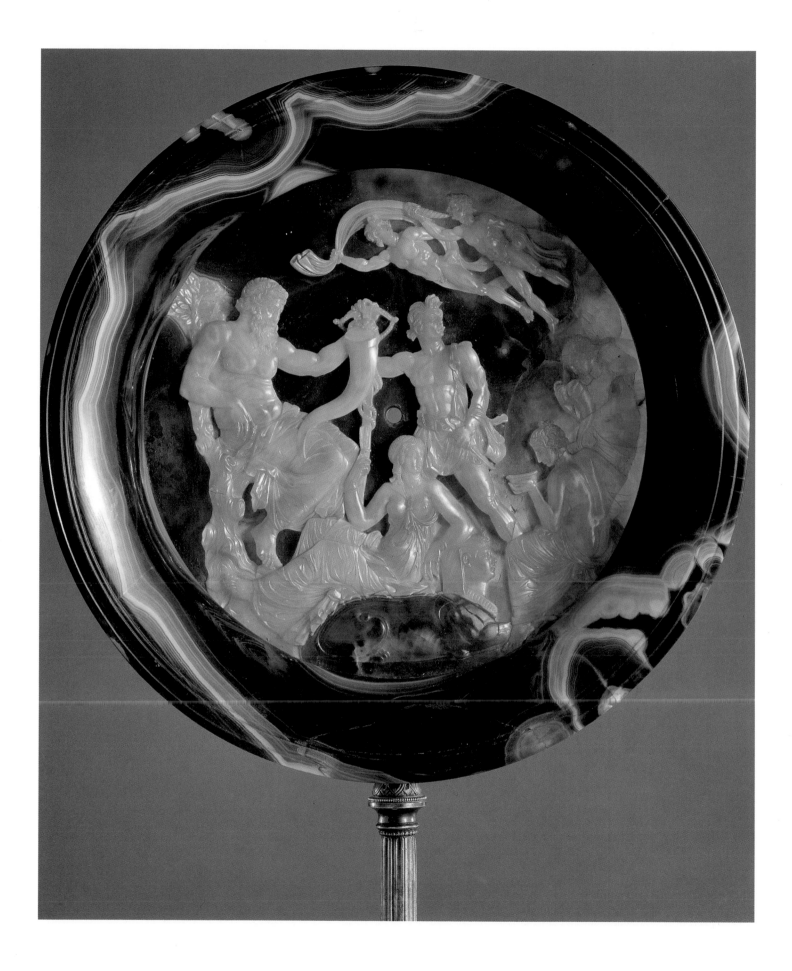

under royal patronage. Although to some extent foreshadowed by Plato's Academy, this was unique in being a self-regulating, tax-exempt corporation – not a museum in the modern sense, but something more like an endowed research institution. The most splendid of its facilities was the famous Library of Alexandria, which was built up in an astonishingly modern spirit. All the important works ever written in Greek were assembled in the most accurate texts available; with the royal blessing, librarians pursued original manuscripts all over the Greek world, often paying very high prices and, inevitably, often being swindled.

The Asclepion, a large complex at Pergamum with a hospital, a theatre and other facilities. Sited on the west coast of Turkey, the kingdom of Pergamum was famous for its silver mines and for parchment, which became widely known as *charta pergamena*.

Ptolemy II had other records made in (or translated into) Greek, including the history of his own kingdom by the Egyptian high priest Manetho. He is also credited with arranging for the Greek translation of the Old Testament, called the Septuagint after the 72 scholars Ptolemy is supposed to have summoned from Jerusalem and set to work on the island of Pharos; however, textual analysis has shown that the Septuagint could not have been compiled at a single time and place, though it is almost certainly the work of Egyptian Jews.

Original creative work was also done at Alexandria. In literature most of it was minor, but then the Hellenistic age was not one of great literary creativity anywhere, so far as it is possible to judge from surviving works. The benefits of enlightened patronage are demonstrated by the career of the greatest Alexandrian poet, Theocritus, actually a native of Syracuse who failed to find a patron until Ptolemy II took him up. Most of the poet's life seems to have been spent in Alexandria or on the island of Cos, at that time part of the Ptolemaic empire. Alexandria's role as a centre of scientific and mathematical research was even more impressive. The city became the home of Euclid, who systematized geometry, of the inventor Ctesibius, of the mathematician and astronomer Apollonius of Perge, and of Eratosthenes of Cyrene, who became chief librarian and measured the circumference of the earth with surprising near-accuracy. Alexandrian science, like Alexandrian commerce, continued to flourish in the Roman period, and the 2nd-century AD geographer Ptolemy (not a member of the royal house) produced a map of the universe, with the earth majestic and unmoving in the centre, which exercised an unfortunate authority over the European mind until it was discredited by the Copernican revolution of the 16th century.

Apart from Syracuse in Sicily, the great Hellenistic cities were all in the eastern Mediterranean and owed much of their wealth to the profits of trade with Asia. The Seleucid empire was the main political adversary of Ptolemaic Egypt, and it too had a splendid capital. Antioch soon surpassed its eastern twin, Selencia, and became a cosmopolitan city, con-

trolling important trade and strategic routes from west to east and south to north. It boasted a royal library and even a school of poets of whom the best known was Meleager; but it never rivalled Alexandria in cultural prestige. In that respect Pergamum, capital of a very much smaller kingdom in Asia Minor, was more successful. Her rulers maintained their independence in a world of great powers, and lavished the wealth of the state silver mines on beautifying the city and advertising themselves. All these great Hellenistic capitals had rational grid-design town plans, quite unlike the huddled accumulations that had gone to make up the city-state; Pergamum was an outstanding example, skilfully laid out on the terraces of a hillside and culminating in the theatre, the acropolis and royal palace. The grandest Pergamene monument was the Altar of Zeus and Athena, erected around 180 BC to commemorate the victory of Pergamum over Gaulish tribesmen who had ravaged Asia Minor. The culture-conscious Pergamene kings made much of their devotion to Athens, and did in fact lavish gifts on the city; the most splendid was the Stoa of Attalus, a long colonnaded walk-cum-shopping area that has been restored in modern times and now serves as a museum.

The island of Rhodes was also a small but flourishing Hellenistic state. It became a wealthy maritime society with the opening up of the East by Alexander and, like Pergamum, maintained its independence of the great powers and produced a flourishing art. The famous Colossus of Rhodes – another of the Seven Wonders – was actually a bronze statue of the sun god Helios, 32 or 33m (105 or 108 ft) high; made between 292 and 280 BC, it probably stood beside the harbour of Rhodes city, although legend has it straddling two rocks in the harbour mouth, far enough apart for a boat to pass between its legs. The Colossus broke and fell during a severe earthquake in about 226 BC, but its remains could be seen down to the 7th century AD, when Arabs collected them and melted them down for re-use. Rhodes' prosperity lasted until the mid-2nd century BC, when Rome became the paramount power in the Mediterranean and decided to divert much of the island's trade to Delos.

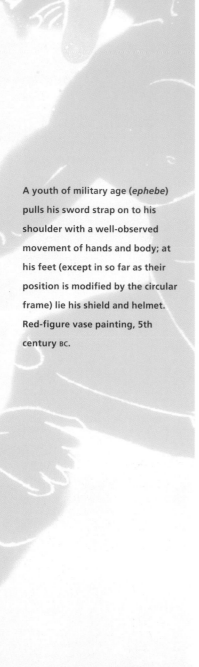

A youth of military age (*ephebe*) pulls his sword strap on to his shoulder with a well-observed movement of hands and body; at his feet (except in so far as their position is modified by the circular frame) lie his shield and helmet. Red-figure vase painting, 5th century BC.

GREEKS AT WAR

The earliest accounts of Greek warriors are found in Homer's epic poem the *Iliad*, where the battle-field is dominated by individual heroes who fight what are, in effect, a series of duels with other heroes. Mycenaean warfare may have had some resemblance to this picture, though it is hard to believe that the efforts of the chief or aristocratic leader did not need to be backed up by bravery or skill on the part of his kin or retainers. The pre-eminence of the hero was no doubt ensured by his access to horses, whether he fought mounted or used a chariot to deliver him to the crucial spot in the fray; chariots would have been too light, because Greek horses were too small, to be used aggressively in tank-fashion. They disappeared altogether after Mycenaean times, and in the 7th century BC the city-states produced a new kind of citizen army based on heavy infantrymen known as hoplites. Each of these was protected by a bronze helmet, breastplate and greaves (leg guards) and armed with a long thrusting (not throwing) spear, a sword, and a large round shield; the hoplite was named after his shield (the *hoplon*), a concave object with arm and thumb holds that was wider than the soldier's body, so that a line of hoplites presented a wall of shields to the foe. In battle they were drawn up in a phalanx, a bloc of men in rows eight or more deep, with spears resting on their shoulders. Success depended on a high degree of discipline, enabling the phalanx to respond to orders as one man; maintaining formation and often breaking into a trot just before the moment of impact, the spear-bristling mass attempted to shatter the enemy line at once, although the struggle between two hoplite phalanxes often developed into a more protracted and bloody pushing match.

The formidable qualities of the Greek fighting man are beyond doubt. Apart from their spectacular, against-the-odds victories over the Persians, Greeks were much sought-after as mercenaries; many thousands served Egyptian and Persian masters, where necessary doing battle with their fellow-Greeks. In Greece itself, armies were small and conflicts between the city-states were regulated by unwritten conventions. The hoplites' equipment was so heavy (about 27kg/60lb) that it was not put on until battle was imminent; and in defeat the Greek soldier had to discard his large shield to give himself a chance of running away fast enough to escape pursuit. Massed on a flat, open site, hoplites could crash into the enemy line with tremendous force; but the price of their weight was a loss of speed and flexibility. Even with some protection on the wings by cavalry or more lightly-armed infantrymen, they would have been vulnerable to skirmishers, bowmen or other forces employing guerrilla tactics, for which the rugged terrain of Greece was near-ideal. But this was not how the city-states fought battles

between themselves: instead, the invading and defending armies met, as if by appointment, on the nearest convenient plain, where the two phalanxes pushed, thrust and hacked at each other until one yielded.

New tactics were slow to evolve. During the Peloponnesian War, Pericles avoided the normal head-on land battle with the Spartans, relying on the strength of Athens' Long Walls and her maritime supremacy to protect the city. The Spartans, usually the most conservative of Greeks, eventually responded by establishing a permanent base at Decelea in Athenian territory instead of retiring in autumn, at the end of the campaigning season. It was a logical step, since campaigns came to an end because citizen-soldiers were also farmers who went home in October to plough and sow; but Sparta's soldiers were professionals, supported by helot farmers and able to take the field at any season. Their full-time commitment was the basis of Sparta's military reputation; their weakness was a dwindling manpower so acute that in 421 BC they were prepared to make peace with Athens in order to recover a hundred men who had been taken prisoner.

During the Peloponnesian War the Greeks at last began to experiment with the use of lighter-armed infantry, known as peltasts. But the crucial encounters were still decided by phalanxes of hoplites, and this remained true for most of the

A warrior continues to hold up his shield even as he sinks into death; a moving pediment sculpture from the Temple of Aphaea on the island of Aegina, c.500 BC. This life-size figure is a bearded older man; like the *ephebe* on the opposite page he is shown naked, indicating that he is a Greek.

A young helmet-maker at work. As in most other cultures, manufacturing the equipment, weapons and materials of war became a significant element in the economies of Greek city-states. Attic red-figure vase painting by the Antiphon Painter, c.480 BC.

The phalanx continued to be the main infantry arm, but divided into a number of battalions in the interests of manoeuvrability; and the thrusting spear was replaced by the longer, pike-like *sarissa*, which enabled its users to strike at a distance before the traditional phalanx could come to grips with them. Peltasts and other auxiliaries created a more balanced force. Above all, the fact that Macedon (unlike Greece) had an adequate supply of horses made it possible to develop an effective cavalry arm. Led by Alexander and his elite 'Companions', this was decisive in breaking through the weak point in the Athenian-Theban line at Chaeronea (338 BC), and similar feats were performed again and again during Alexander's campaigns in Asia.

Large armies were characteristic of the Hellenistic period, when new weapons included war elephants. At the same time, siege techniques and defensive countermeasures became more sophisticated. The unsuccessful Athenian assault on Syracuse during the Peloponnesian War was the first Greek effort that went much beyond a blockade intended to starve out the enemy, and Alexander the Great employed mobile siege towers and catapults in besieging Tyre. Hellenistic efforts were impressively more elaborate, although the Romans proved to be the most efficient of all siegecraft practitioners.

Naval warfare was a relatively late development. In the Homeric epics, ships are used solely to transport forces to and from combat areas, and are rowed by the warriors themselves. Though sails might be used, oar-power was more reliable during this early period and became increasingly important when true warships began to be built and speed and manoeuvrability counted most. Fifty rowers were the maximum it was possible to fit lengthwise into a ship, but in about the 8th century BC speeds were doubled by inserting a second bank of oars; this type of vessel is known as a bireme. From the 7th century the three-banked trireme was developed, and triremes were the warships that defeated the Persians at Salamis and upheld Athens' maritime 'empire'; thanks to the fleet-building policies of Themistocles and Pericles, the Athenians had a 200-trireme fleet at their disposal in the late 5th century.

4th century. The most important tactical innovation was made by the Theban commander Epaminondas, who reorganized the phalanx so that the left wing was 50 men deep, leaving minimal forces in the centre and on the right; at Leuctra, in 371 BC, the Theban line approached the 12-deep Spartans at a slant, so that the powerful left wing would engage with, and begin to demolish, the Spartan right (the best Spartan troops) before serious fighting began in the other sectors. The result was a decisive victory that changed the balance of power within Greece.

Later 4th-century city-states sought to strengthen their armies by recruiting increasingly large numbers of mercenary soldiers; but these did not save them from domination by the new power of Macedon. Philip II and his son Alexander the Great introduced a series of reforms that made the Macedonians, and the Greeks who were incorporated into their forces, world-beaters. The troops were full-time recruits, paid from the revenues of Philip's gold mines and drilled and disciplined with great thoroughness.

A nice nautical contrast between ancient and modern: contemporary Argonauts cleaning the keel of their vessel. This 1985 photograph shows the *Argo*, a reconstruction of a Greek trireme built by adventurer Tim Severin in order to re-enact the legendary voyages of ancient mariners.

According to the historian Thucydides, the earliest sea battle on record took place in 664 BC between Corinthian and Corcyran vessels. Tactics during this phase were probably an extension of land warfare, involving grappling and boarding the enemy vessel, followed by a hand-to-hand fight between the soldiers on board each ship. Later on, trireme were fitted with bronze-plated wooden rams which became the main offensive weapon. Ramming rather than being rammed required superior seamanship, and tactics differed according to the size of the fleets and the sea-room. At Salamis the overconfident Persian armada was lured into straits where its superior numbers could not be made to tell; the Greek ships, in crescent formation, closed in on all sides and not only rammed their overcrowded enemies but had room enough to draw back and acquire the impetus for repeated attacks.

Accounts of changes in ship design during the Hellenistic period are obscurely described. The dominant type of warship was the quinquireme, which seems to have retained three banks of oars but accommodated more rowers to each oar. In 306 BC, at Cyprian Salamis, Demetrius Poliorcetes' 108 warships won the most famous victory of the age against Ptolemy I's fleet of 140 vessels, only 20 of which escaped sinking.

A warship cleaving the waves; black-figure vase painting, c.500 BC. It conveys a sense of strenuous activity and movement but, like other images of ancient vessels, is short on technically useful details. Artistic convention shows the ship far too high in the water.

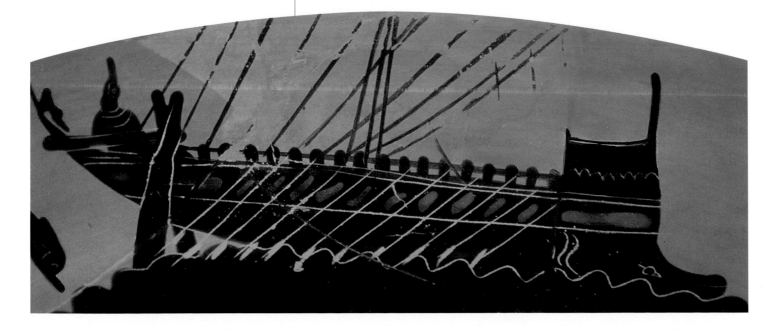

MEDICINE, DISEASE AND DEATH

A physician bleeding a patient; from a red-figure vase painting, 5th century BC. A belief in the efficacy of this treatment lasted right down to the 19th century.

The Greek attitude towards illness was part-superstitious and part-scientific. The average countryman had his store of herbs and remedies which were the familiar mixture of useful and useless, magic, common sense and common nonsense. But those who could do so, sought advice – from a doctor, or from a doctor-priest and the god he served.

The god was Asclepius, now better known by the Roman form of his name, Aesculapius. This

From a grateful patient. This votive relief was donated to the shrine of the healer-hero Amphiaraos by the cured Archinus; in the scene, a snake, symbol of healing, is licking the shoulder of a young man on a couch. The plaque was found among the remains of the Amphiaraion at Oropos; first half of the 4th century BC.

son of Apollo was widely venerated and had temples and shrines all over the Greek (and later the Greco-Roman) world; the most famous were at Epidaurus in the Peloponnese and on the island of Cos. At such places the afflicted gathered in large numbers to consult the priests and implore the god for assistance. The most favoured way of securing this was to sleep within the precincts of the temple, in the hope that one of the snakes sacred to Asclepius would come out during the night and bring about a cure by licking the affected part; or that the god would send his answer to the sick person's prayers in a dream. (As a matter of fact the 'temple dream' was a widely used method of eliciting advice and information from the gods on a range of topics from the fate of empires to the location of a missing ring.) Like their modern equivalents, a good many devotees of Asclepius claimed to have experienced miraculous cures, and left grateful inscriptions to proclaim the fact.

The earliest physicians in independent practice may have learned their art from the temple priests; the reputed 'founder' of scientific medicine, whose oath is still sworn by practitioners at the beginning of their careers, was Hippocrates, who came from the Asclepian centre of Cos. He seems to have lived in the second half of the 5th century, but despite his relatively late date almost nothing is known about him. The large collection of documents associated with his name originates from various periods of the 5th and 4th centuries, and does not even represent a single point of view or tradition; like the Spartan legislator Lycurgus, 'Hippocrates' may represent an historical phase rather than an individual, and if so 'he' is an example of the Greek tendency to personify the past. The Hippocratic collection of writings reveals that the medical profession had by this time shed any idea that illness was a form of divine retribution, and it concerns itself chiefly with the search for natural causes and cures. It includes a large number of carefully recorded case histories which, however, make rather depressing reading, since most of the patients died. There is also plenty of practical career advice. The physician must appear well-set-up and healthy, for people are prejudiced against doctors who seem unwell ('Physician, heal thyself!'); and he must look thoughtful but not gloomy. 'Hippocrates' also lays great emphasis on cultivating the ability to predict the course of a disease, which a cynic might describe as substituting omniscience for success.

In most cases the general practitioner seems to have prescribed the medicines that have become the standbys of his profession: rest, quiet, harmless herbal remedies and a sensible diet. The doctrine that nature is the best healer was already known, though not universally held. However, since operations were obviously dangerous and horribly painful (there were no anaesthetics), even the more 'active' practitioners generally confined themselves to cupping and bleeding – a cure-all which was almost universally accepted right down to recent times.

Before the Hellenistic period the physician seems to have had about the same status as a superior craftsman; he set up shop in a town, employed assistants and solicited for business; he was not licensed or otherwise subject to social control. By the 5th century there also seem to have been municipal surgeries in some towns, but little is known about them. As always, the spectacularly successful attracted most attention. In the late 6th century the outstanding physician of his time was (according to the historian Herodotus) Democedes of Crotona in Southern Italy. The tyrant Polycrates of Samos paid Democedes the huge salary of two talents a year; and he was even more lavishly rewarded after curing the Persian king and queen of serious illnesses. But Darius would not allow him to leave the country, so Democedes, being a Greek, preferred to abandon his barbarian gilded cage and flee back to his native city.

When the patient died, custom and the gods took charge. The corpse was washed, perfumed, dressed in white, and laid out on a herb-strewn couch at the front of the house, where it was visible from the street. An obol was placed in the dead man's mouth so that, once in the underworld, he could pay the ferryman Charon to take him across the River Styx to the land of the dead. A flask of oil was placed beside the corpse and accompanied it to the grave. Relatives and friends visited the house during the day to lament the death and console the family; as they left they purified themselves from the taint of mortality, using water from a jar placed at the entrance.

The funeral took place on the following day, beginning with a procession. The corpse was

Sleep and Death, Hypnos and Thanatos, carry a dead man; his warrior's helmet is prominently displayed. The interestingly wild, sketchy drawing style is mainly seen (as here) on *lekythoi*, vases used for funerary purposes whose white ground enabled the artist to work with great freedom; c.450 BC.

either carried on a litter or drawn along in a carriage, depending on the wealth of the bereaved family. The immediate members of the family and their close relatives dressed in dark clothes, lamenting loudly, weeping, beating their breasts and clutching their heads. The volume and intensity of the performance were increased by the practised efforts of old women who had been hired to make the display of grief more impressive; from legal prohibitions at Athens and elsewhere it is clear that no great encouragement would have been needed for enthusiastic mourners to gash their faces and arms and tear their clothes to shreds. At the rear of the procession walked a flautist, playing a melancholy dirge.

In Mycenaean times the dead had been buried, but cremation was the rule from about 1200 BC to the 5th century, after which both methods were practised. (Strictly speaking the difference was between inhumation – burial of the corpse – and cremation, which involved burning the body on a pyre and burying the bones.) In all cases it was important that at least a token handful of earth should be sprinkled over the remains so that the shades of the dead would not remain in the upper world but could go down into the underworld. Neglect of such rites constituted a terrible impiety, and one of the most profound of all Greek tragedies, Sophocles' *Antigone*, concerns the eponymous principal character's decision to give her traitor brother a proper burial in defiance of the king's orders; inevitably this brings about her own death. The play is, in effect, the first known dramatization of the conflict between duty to the state and private conscience.

The cemetery was normally outside the city, but the coffins of children, who were always buried, were interred within the walls. The dead person was entombed with coin and flask, and also with a range of grave-goods. With the underworld, the Elysian Fields and the Isles of the Blessed all mentioned in literature as possible destinations, Greek ideas about what followed death seem to have been rather incoherent and even contradictory. Moreover, the presence in the tomb of cups, plates, lamps and other items seems to indicate some kind of popular belief in an afterlife that would be not dissimilar to life on earth and lived in and around the tomb, as in ancient Egypt; at any rate the family of the deceased continued to make offerings of food and drink to placate or honour him or her. After the funeral a wake was held, and days of sacrifices and mourning followed. All of which takes us into the world of specifically religious beliefs and practices – a most important area of Greek life, as both a spiritual and a civic phenomenon.

Charon the ferryman receiving one of the souls of the dead. His duty is to carry them over to the underworld; his eagerness is perhaps explained by the fact that every passenger paid him an obol as his fare. Vase painting by the Thymbos Painter on a *lekythos*, c.475–450 BC.

A double commemoration. The amphora pictures, and so preserves the memory of, a *stele* (stone slab), whose function is itself commemorative (recording a burial). The *stele* is decorated and is flanked by actual or symbolic mourning figures. The amphora comes from Southern Italy.

5 MYTH AND RELIGION

Appropriately cloud-capped, Mount Olympus was the home of Zeus and the other gods, often described as Olympians. There were also a host of other supernatural beings, from Hades in the underworld to the spirits of groves and streams.

MANY PEOPLE FIND IT HARD TO TAKE GREEK RELIGION VERY SERIOUSLY. THE FIRST BARRIER IS THE SHEER NUMBER OF GREEK DIVINITIES: ZEUS, 'FATHER OF GODS AND MEN'; HIS WIFE HERA; HIS BROTHERS POSEIDON, THE SEA GOD, AND HADES, KING OF THE UNDERWORLD; HIS DAUGHTER ATHENA, PATRON GODDESS OF ARTS AND CRAFTS AND OF ATHENS; ARTEMIS, VIRGIN GODDESS OF THE CHASE; APHRODITE, GODDESS OF LOVE; APOLLO, GOD OF LIGHT, MEDICINE AND MUSIC; DIONYSUS, GOD OF INTOXICATION, BOTH MYSTICAL AND VINOUS; ARES, GOD OF WAR; HERMES, THE TRAVELLERS' GOD; AND MANY MORE, OFTEN WITH CONFLICTING OR OVERLAPPING ROLES.

GODS AND MYTHS

The gods themselves stand at the centre of a great body of myths, some of which have a beauty and archetypal resonance that has led writers and artists to re-use and reinterpret them for century after century. There are also rather primitive stories of the creation of the world and the genealogies of the gods: while Uranus (the Heavens) is having intercourse with Ge (the Earth), their son Cronus becomes supreme by cutting off Uranus' genitals and flinging them in the sea; later still, his son, Zeus, overthrows and imprisons him to become king of the gods. An even larger group of stories involves the gods' quarrels and intrigues with one another, often displaying them in a ludicrous or discreditable light: Zeus setting a vulture to tear eternally at the eternally self-renewing liver of the demi-god Prometheus, who had stolen fire from the gods to give to man; the lame blacksmith-god Hephaestus catching his wife Aphrodite making love with Ares, and hauling the guilty couple up to the ceiling in a net; and so on. Finally, there are the interventions of the gods in the world of men, which are almost always erotic or arbitrary: Zeus, lustfully intent on a suc-

Zeus, king of the gods, sits enthroned. A majestic miniature (14 cm, 5 ½ in high), the figure is solid cast bronze; it once held Zeus' favourite weapon, a thunderbolt, in the right hand and a sceptre in the left.

cession of human loves, changes himself into a bull, a swan, a shower of gold; and in Homer's account of the Trojan War the gods take sides and join in the slaughter like spiteful schoolboys, motivated by their own rivalries or by petty resentments against their human victims.

Below the gods in the hierarchy of myth come a group of heroes (human or superhuman) who were the objects of cults, notably Theseus, king of Athens and slayer of the Minotaur, and the mighty Heracles (called by the Romans Hercules), whose 12 Labours included cleaning the Augean stables. Myth shades off into history of a sort with the Trojan War, and perhaps with the Theban cycle of Oedipus and his children and the story of Jason, the Argonauts and the Golden Fleece. In addition to gods and heroes there are nymphs and satyrs; half-human, half-animal creatures such as centaurs; giants; and a whole gallery of monsters from the Furies (dog-headed women who plague and pursue the guilty) to the Sirens whose voices lure mariners on to the rocks.

There are several probable reasons for this fascinating confusion. Greek religion had no Bible, no prophet or lawgiver, no dogmas, and no church in the institutional sense. Myths were at

Aphrodite, goddess of love; Hellenistic bronze statuette. Though aspiring to moderation and self-mastery, the Greeks were keenly aware of love as a source of beauty, pleasure and trouble.

the mercy of popular imagination and the poets, who could vary their details or invent or reinterpret them at will. Indeed the earliest coherent information about gods and myths comes from Homer (written down in the late 8th century) and from Hesiod, a Boeotian poet whose *Theogony* of about 700 BC relates the genealogy of the gods.

The sheer antiquity of the gods and myths must have increased the likelihood of changes and accretions: many of the gods' names occur on the Linear B tablets of the Mycenaean age, at least five hundred years before Hesiod. The Olympians (the chief gods were supposed to live together on Mount Olympus) probably represent a fusion of two religions, after Zeus and other sky gods – perhaps brought by the Dorians – took over from an older earth-goddess and fertility-cult religion but absorbed some of its features. There is plenty of evidence that Athena, for example, was a pre-Dorian goddess; and, significantly, Athenians claimed that their city had never been occupied by the Dorians. According to one myth, Athena

A touching scene between Orpheus and his wife Euridyce. The god Hermes looks on; Euridyce is tied to him and he is about to carry her into the underworld. Orpheus' attempt to rescue her is a famous episode from Greek myth.

The goddess Artemis, whom the Romans called Diana. She manifested herself in a number of ways, notably as a huntress, as an upholder of chastity, and as goddess of the moon. Statue from Cyprus, 2nd century BC.

and Poseidon engaged in a contest to see which should be Athens' patron; Athena won, but in historical times Athenians in fact paid exceptional attention to Poseidon too. The obvious conclusion is that in this instance the old goddess held her own against the new god – but that ever afterwards the citizens hedged some of their bets. Many quarrels between the gods must have a similar explanation.

Other myths – perhaps the ones we find most satisfactory – are more obviously attempts to explain the world; in such cases, however, the story often represents a later, rationalized version of a less obviously 'meaningful' myth. At a very basic level are the geographical explanations: rivers run dry in summer because Poseidon became angry with the river-gods and never quite got over it; volcanic islands are the prisons of giants overthrown by the gods and still struggling to escape; and so on. At the highest level explanation and poetic symbolism combine, as in the story of Persephone. Hades kidnapped her and carried her off to his underground kingdom; only after her mother Demeter, the corn goddess, had brought famine to the earth by refusing to let crops grow, did Zeus relent and force Hades to release her. But Persephone has to spend a third of the year in the Underworld, during which time the crops do not grow. During her Underworld sojourn it is, of course, winter time in the world above.

The Greeks anticipated most of the moral and logical criticisms we can direct at their religious beliefs. Having no theologians to blame, critics like Xenophanes blamed Homer and Hesiod for portraying the gods as indulging themselves in all the pastimes that were condemned in men – theft, adultery and treacherous dealings. Xenocrates, an Ionian writing in the late 6th century, is already contemptuous of gods created in the image of man: not only do the Greeks make their gods resemble themselves, he observed, but Ethiopians worship black gods and red-haired Thracians worship red-haired ones. For Xenocrates there was only a single god, which he seems to have identified with the universe itself. Many Greeks in fact spoke of experiencing the presence or inspiration of 'God' or 'the God', often without

specifying further. By the 5th century some writers felt it necessary to apologize for the gods. The great lyric poet Pindar indignantly denies that the scandalous tales about them are true. Aeschylus, the father of tragedy, ignores the tales in his trilogy on the death of Agamemnon and Orestes' vengeance: in this, Apollo insists on righteous revenge, while Athena ensures that justice is done – significantly, against the opposition of older deities, the Furies (sprung from the blood of castrated Uranus), who represent superseded notions both of religion and of justice done by recourse to blood-feuds.

Other thinkers were more radical in their rejections. One, for example, propounded a version of the very modern notion that religion was 'the opium of the masses' – a set of fictions devised to keep the people in order. By contrast, the philosopher Plato recommended the deliberate creation of myths in order to shape the minds and emotions of citizens in his ideal society. And there were those, too, who sought to grapple with the problem that has puzzled all serious religious thinkers: the problem of how to reconcile a good and just god (or gods) with the existence of a manifestly unjust and often wicked world. From one point of view, the whole effort of Greek philosophy (examined in a later chapter) was to make natural and ethical sense of a world that was inadequately explained by the existing gods, myths and rituals.

Apollo and Artemis sacrifice at the altar of Zeus; like ordinary Greeks they seek to demonstrate their piety and perhaps to find favour in the eyes of the king of gods and men. Attic red-figure vase painting, c.490–480 BC.

THE AGE OF HEROES

The Argonaut's escape: Jason is regurgitated after being swallowed by a snake. The story of Jason, the *Argo* and Medea seems to be one of the oldest Greek myths, mentioned by Homer as though it was already familiar to everybody.

The primary meaning of *mythos* is 'story', and Greek mythology is outstanding for its many compelling narratives. Unlike the myths of most other cultures, a large proportion of the Greek stories are about human beings and their passions, are set against a recognizable landscape, and, for all their magical and fabulous elements, deal in adventures and intrigues that have a timeless appeal. Although nymphs, satyrs, naiads, centaurs and other unearthly beings pass through the landscape, the principal actors in the stories are most often heroes – that is, the children of gods and goddesses who have mated with men and women; they are stronger or more beautiful than

ordinary mortals, but share their passions and are doomed to die unless some special favour or achievement moves the gods to grant them immortality.

Most of the hero-stories consist of cycles or series of adventures or family histories, often relating to dynasties supposed to have ruled Greek cities in some earlier time. The Greeks themselves had a rough idea of when that time was, since the cycles interlocked and most of the events in them could be 'dated' to just before, during, or just after the Trojan War. The traditional Greek date for the end of the war (in terms of the present calendar) was 1184 BC; so that in

Heracles performs the first of his twelve Labours, slaying the Nemean lion. Invulnerable to the hero's club and arrows, the beast is vanquished when Heracles exerts his strength and strangles it himself. Vase painting, c.500 BC.

the mind of (for example) a 5th-century Athenian the age of semi-divine heroes lay in the not so very distant past.

Of course no true chronology of the hero-stories can be compiled, if only because they are fictional, exist in many variations, and do not interlock consistently. But the links between the stories are interesting nonetheless, and a kind of historical overview helps to bring out the sweep and complexity of the heroic myths.

References in Homer confirm that the tale of Jason and the Argonauts is particularly old. Peleus, king of Iolcos in Thessaly (eastern Greece), had seized the throne from his half-brother Aeson. When Aeson's son, Jason, arrived to assert his claim, he was tricked by Peleus into undertaking a voyage to recover the golden fleece, which hung in a dragon-protected grove at Colchis, a city at the furthest point of the Greek world on the Black Sea. A ship of 50 oars, the

Argo, was built for Jason, whose invitation to accompany him was answered by many of the great Greek heroes; they became known as Argonauts ('sailors of the *Argo*'). Aided by the goddess Athena, they survived a series of perilous encounters and arrived safely at Colchis, where the king agreed to give Jason the golden fleece if the hero could perform a number of superhuman feats: he must harness two fire-breathing oxen, sow the ground with dragons' teeth, and defeat the warriors who sprang from the ground as a result. Fortunately for Jason, the king's daughter, Medea, fell in love with him and used her magical powers to help him pass the test. Since the king had no intention of keeping his promise, Medea put the dragon to sleep and the lovers and the Argonauts slipped away with the golden fleece. The voyage was successfully completed, but the later adventures of Jason and Medea ended badly when Jason abandoned his wife and Medea murdered not only the other woman but also her own children by Jason.

Several of the Argonauts were important figures in their own right. Among them was Orpheus, the Thracian poet and musician who received his lyre from Apollo and sang and played so wonderfully that he was able to enchant wild beasts and even the denizens of the underworld when he visited Hades in a bid to bring back his dead wife Eurydice. She was allowed to go back with him to the upper world provided that he did not look back at her during the journey; at the last moment he succumbed to temptation and lost her for ever. Other Argonauts included the twin sons of Zeus, Castor and Pollux, the Dioscuri, who were widely worshipped as symbols of brotherly love, and Peleus, husband of the immortal Thetis and father of Achilles; a child when the Argonauts set out, Achilles became the greatest of all the warriors in the Trojan War.

The most celebrated of all Jason's companions was Heracles, whose adventures were even more numerous; in fact he played only a brief part as an Argonaut, being left behind on the coast of Mysia

Medusa head; relief from the Temple of Apollo at Didyma, Turkey. Anyone who caught sight of the snake-haired Medusa was turned to stone; she was killed by Perseus, who tracked her by watching her reflection in his shield, then struck her down without looking at her.

(in Asia Minor) on the outward voyage while he searched in vain for his beloved squire Hylas, who had been carried off by naiads. Superhumanly strong, Heracles was the son of Zeus and Alcmene; Zeus made love to her by assuming the appearance of her husband, Amphitryon. (Both Amphitryon and Alcmene, incidentally, were grandchildren of another son of Zeus, Perseus, who slew the Medusa, became the master of the winged horse Pegasus, and rescued Andromeda from a sea-monster.) The resentful Hera, wife of Zeus, showered Heracles with misfortunes, including fits of madness during one of which he killed his own wife and children. In expiation he was set to perform the 12 Labours of Heracles, seemingly impossible tasks such as fighting the nine-headed hydra, which grew two more heads every time one was cut off, and bringing the three-headed dog Cerberus, guardian of Hades, into the upper world. After an action-packed career Heracles was reconciled with Hera and at his death became a god; as Greek Heracles and Roman Hercules his cult was popular all over the ancient world.

Several heroes took part in the Calydonian boar hunt, held to stop a wild boar, sent by Artemis to avenge a slight, from ravaging the country. Jason and the Dioscuri were there, along with Nestor, who as an old man was to be one of the leaders of the Greek expedition against Troy. Meleager, the Calydonian king's son, took part; at his birth one of the Fates had told his mother that he would not die until a brand in the fire was totally consumed, and she had snatched it out, doused the flame and hidden the brand away. The hunt was a confused affair, and when the boar was killed there were disputes as to who deserved the prize of its tusks and hide. Meleager gave them to the Amazon warrior Atalanta, with whom he had fallen in love. His uncles, who were among the claimants, were so enraged that they attacked Meleager, but he killed them both. When his mother heard of her brothers' death she took the brand from its hiding place and burned it, destroying Meleager.

Atalanta, though a virgin vowed to Artemis, was much sought-after by suitors. She insisted that the man who married her would have to defeat her in a race; losers would forfeit their lives.

Despite a high casualty rate suitors continued to try their luck, and eventually Aphrodite helped a young man named Hippomenes by giving him three of the precious golden apples of the Hesperides. He challenged Atalanta, and at critical points in the race dropped an apple; three times she stopped to pick one up, so Hippomenes won the race and the woman.

The events of the Trojan War have been outlined in an earlier chapter, but these form only the core of a large cluster of episodes dealing with the causes, shifting fortunes and remote consequences of the conflict. Its direct cause, Helen, was one of the children of Tyndareus, King of Sparta, and his

Achilles slays the Amazon queen Penthesilea; the Amazons, warrior-women, were allies of the Trojans. In one version of the story, Achilles and Penthesilea fell in love during their mortal combat. This image, by Exekias, is one of the masterpieces of the black-figure painting style; 540-530 BC.

An unkempt Odysseus, washed up on the shores of Phaeacia, encounters his protector, the goddess Athena; his ten years of wandering since the end of the Trojan War are soon to be over. Athenian red-figure vase painting, c.450–440 BC.

queen, Leda – except that Helen was conceived after Zeus disguised himself as a swan and took advantage of Leda when she held him in her arms to protect him from an eagle. Thanks to her divine parent, Helen was superhumanly beautiful; she and her brother Pollux were Zeus' children, while her brother Castor and sister Clytemnestra were the offspring of Tyndareus.

Before a husband was chosen for Helen, her suitors agreed that they would accept the verdict and, if anyone tried to abduct her, would band together to return her to her husband. This explained why so many Greeks were prepared to fight the Trojans; but when war was imminent there were also reluctant recruits who tried to

avoid their prophesied fate. Odysseus, told that he would return late to his Ithacan home as a beggar, feigned madness but gave himself away when he stopped ploughing the moment his son was thrown in front of the horse. Achilles' mother, Thetis, dressed the hero in female clothing and hid him among a group of women; but as soon as there was an alarm, only one of the 'ladies' came out fighting and so revealed his true identity.

The war provided the setting for conflicts between a large cast of heroic figures. To name only a few: on the Greek side, Agamemnon and his brother Menelaus, the great warrior Achilles and his boastful rival Ajax, the wily Odysseus and wise Nestor; among the Trojans, the aged King

Priam, his wife Hecuba, his sons Hector and Paris, Hector's wife Andromache and his sister Cassandra, a prophetess who was fated to predict the future correctly but never to be believed.

There were also a number of subsidiary episodes, including the story of the great archer Philoctetes. He had lit the funeral pyre which ended Heracles' mortal life, and in return the hero bequeathed him his bow and poisoned arrows. As one of Helen's suitors he was honour bound to join the expedition against Troy, but during an island stopover he was bitten on the foot by a snake. The wound would not heal and gave off such a foul smell that the Greeks put Philoctetes ashore on the island of Lemnos. But in the tenth year of the war an oracle announced that they could only take Troy if they possessed the arrows of Heracles, so Odysseus and Diomedes travelled to Lemnos and persuaded Philoctetes to return with them. His wound was healed in a temple dedicated to Apollo, and Philoctetes went on to slay Paris, Helen's abductor.

After the war Philoctetes is said to have settled in Italy. Many other Greek participants came to a less happy end, returning home to find themselves supplanted or driven by contrary winds (or contrary gods) to distant places, like Menelaus and Helen or Odysseus; Odysseus' voyages and adventures (which seem to owe something to those of the Argonauts) culminated in his return, as predicted, in the guise of a beggar, and in a one-man massacre of the suitors who had been pursuing his wife and wasting his substance.

The most fatal and bloody homecoming was that of Agamemnon, king of Mycenae, who had led the Greeks to victory over Troy, only to be murdered on his return by his wife Clytemnestra and her lover Aegisthus. However, this was no ordinary crime of power or passion, but part of a cycle of dynastic mayhem. From the time when Agamemnon's great-grandfather, Tantalus, served his son Pelops as a meal for the gods, a curse lay on his house that doomed each generation. Agamemnon earned Clytemnestra's hatred by consenting to the sacrifice of his daughter, Iphigenia, in order to raise the wind needed to carry the Greek fleet to Troy. Aegisthus wanted revenge for the murders committed by Agamemnon's father, Atreus, who had kept up the cannibalistic tradition of the house by deceiving his brother Thyestes into eating the cooked flesh of his own children. Aegisthus, Thyestes' surviving son, struck down Agamemnon while Clytemnestra entangled the king in a net. The curse continued into the next generation when Agamemnon's son Orestes did his duty by avenging his father, although in killing the guilty Clytemnestra he also committed matricide. Pursued by the Furies, he eventually fled to Athens where, thanks to the goddess Athena, the curse was lifted at last.

A similar doom hung over the royal house of Thebes. The impossibility of cheating fate, one of the principal themes of Greek myth, becomes the

Odysseus, back home on the island of Ithaca, has found his house occupied by suitors who are pestering his wife and consuming his substance. When the opportunity arises he takes up his mighty bow and kills them all.

Oedipus and the Sphinx; he answered her riddle and she destroyed herself. Oedipus' triumph led to his acceptance as king of Thebes, and the fulfilment of his tragic destiny.

The Athenian hero Theseus slays the Minotaur, the man-bull who dwelt in the heart of the Cretan labyrinth. Theseus rivalled Heracles in the number and variety of his adventures.

basis of terrible ironies in the story of Oedipus, of whom it was prophesied that he would kill his father and marry his mother. As in so many similar stories, his father Laius tried to escape his fate by having the child killed, but Oedipus survived and was brought up by the king and queen of Corinth. When he learned of the prophecy he fled from his supposed parents, killed an old man (Laius) in a crossroads brawl and, having solved the riddle of the Sphinx, married the widowed Queen Jocasta (actually his mother) and became king of Thebes. When, later, the land was ravaged by plague, Oedipus' patient detective work uncovered his own guilt, with terrible consequences for himself, Jocasta, his children, and ultimately the city of Thebes.

The other major cycle of hero stories concerns Theseus, who found his way through the Cretan labyrinth and slew the Minotaur, subsequently becoming king of Athens. According to some accounts he was also one of the Argonauts and took part in the Calydonian boar hunt. He cer-

tainly seems to have been a younger contemporary of Heracles, living before the Trojan War (in which, mysteriously, Athens took no part). Many other adventures were attributed to Theseus (like Heracles he was subject to fits of madness), but he was also the dupe when, in old age, he made the youthful Phaedra his queen. She fell in love with his son Hippolytus, a great horseman, and when Hippolytus rejected her advances she claimed that he had raped her. Theseus prayed for his son's destruction and Poseidon obliged him by sending a bull from the water that frightened Hippolytus' horses; the young man became entangled in the reins and was dragged to his death; Phaedra, her crime discovered, and hanged herself; but there were still more adventures in store for Theseus.

EVERYDAY RELIGION

We can be quite certain that the ordinary Greek took religion seriously and derived psychological and emotional satisfaction from it, since there is plenty of evidence that it was an intimate part of his, and her, everyday life and thoughts. There were altars in the home, herms (bronze or marble figures of the gods) set up outside the houses in the street, and shrines here and there in the city in addition to the temples on the acropolis, which were filled with votive offerings from those who hoped for divine favours or forgiveness. Every feast began with a sacrifice, every drinking-session with a libation. Great decisions were influenced by omens, portents and oracles; ordinary events, such as starting a journey or setting up shop, were prefaced with a prayer. The gods might respond to appeals for help, but they were also easily offended and needed to be approached with care. Above all, it was necessary to avoid hubris – arrogance or over-confidence, which would provoke the Olympians to bring down even the greatest and most secure. The lesson was taught repeatedly in literature; for literature and art were also largely inspired by religion, mainly in the form of myth, or answered religious needs.

A host of annual festivals – great and small, solemn and verging on the frivolous – gave a religious turn to every aspect of an individual's life, as a private person, a worker, and a citizen. As usual, it is Athens we know most about. There, at least 50 festivals were celebrated every year. The virgin goddess Athena presided over rites in which phallic and other sexually powerful objects were paraded about to ensure the fertility of men and women, beasts and fields. By contrast (or as a result of the fertility rites), the Apaturia was a family event – a great three-day gathering of the kinship groups (phratries) into which the whole citizen body was divided; children born since the previous year were introduced into the group, young men who had reached the age of 18 were registered as adults, and men who had married since the previous Apaturia put the fact on record. Women had their own festival, the

Thesmophoria, held at the time of the autumn sowing to honour Demeter and Persephone. During the three days it lasted the sexes were separated – or at any rate its married members were, for the festival was restricted to wives, who left their homes and lived in a separate sanctuary. The proceedings involved sacrificing piglets and also digging up the remains of previous sacrifices, presumably as a ritual of renewal. Although the participants fasted for periods during the festival, some kind of antimale gesture seems to have been involved in the Thesmophoria that made the menfolk a little uneasy. Among others who celebrated festivals of their own were each of the important crafts and each of the city's parishes (*demes*).

Not all festivals were restricted to groups of citizens. At Athens the two major events were holidays for all – *metic*, freedman and slave as well as citizen. In March the City Dionysia was held (there was also a separate Rural Dionysia); the festival was introduced quite late by the tyrant Pisistratus, who doubtless wished to maintain his popularity as well as to proclaim the greatness of Athens. Although it developed into Athens' main dramatic festival, the Dionysia was essentially a fertility ritual, whereas the Panathenaea in July was a harvest festival dedicated to Athena and held at night. It was even grander once every four years, when a Great Panathenaea was held. Then, an endless procession of chariots, sacrificial animals and celebrants wound through the *agora* and up to the Acropolis, bringing the goddess a new robe draped on the mast of a ship that rumbled along on wheels: the scene has become immortal, recorded in stone on the famous frieze of the Parthenon. The Dionysia and the Panathenaea, like many other festivals, were celebrated with displays of lyric choral singing, dancing, athletics, recitations of Homer, and (in the case of the Dionysia) performances of comedies, tragedies and satyr plays; almost all were organized, in typical Greek fashion, as competitions, engaged in with intense rivalry.

Opposite: a couple pour a libation at an altar. Libations and sacrifices (offerings of drink and food) accompanied many events, although the economical Greeks convinced themselves that the gods most enjoyed the less appetizing cuts of meat. Vase painting from the early 5th century BC.

MYSTERIES AND ORACLES

The sentiment that seems to be absent from Greek religious emotion is the longing for immortality: virtually the whole of Greek religion is a celebration of the here and now, an expression of desire or gratitude for good fortune, an effort to avert calamities, an aspiration to approach the godlike in power and beauty while time and light remain. Such an attitude explains why the Greek conceived his gods as superhumans, addicted to human pleasures and vices, and liable to punish too-fortunate mortals; their real advantage over man lay in the fact that they could enjoy eternal life – on earth. If there was any sort of life after death, it was out of the light of the sun, in Hades' underground kingdom where the twittering souls of the dead were no more than bat-like wraiths. The intensity of the Greek love of life is perfectly expressed in a scene from

Homer's *Odyssey* in which the slain hero Achilles tells his old comrade-in-arms, Odysseus, that he would rather be the vilest beast-of-burden labourer alive than lord it as king of the dead.

We know of only one important exception to this attitude – that of participants in the Eleusinian Mysteries, who do seem to have experienced and treasured some ecstatic intimation of immortality. The Mysteries took place at Eleusis, a town about 20km (12 miles) from Athens, but they attracted devotees from far beyond Attica; these gathered at Athens and, white-robed, set out at dusk with flaring torches along the Sacred Way to the Eleusinian sanctuary of Demeter and Persephone, patrons of the mysteries. But despite this impressive public spectacle, the ritual involved esoteric knowledge that was confined to initiates; and only second-degree initiates were admitted to

Delphi, to Greeks 'the navel of the world' and one of the holiest of places. It was the site of the famous oracle, and the Greek city-states vied with one another in building treasuries and raising statues there. The photograph shows the remains of a circular monument, the *tholos*.

the very heart of the mystery. The ultimate nature of the revelation remains what it was intended to be – a mystery. It evidently involved the contemplation of a sacred ear-of-wheat, with all its obvious connotations of rebirth; but whether the ecstatic experiences undergone by initiates were produced by intoxication, illusionism or faith remains in question.

Greek festivals and cults were local in origin, but a number of them, such as the Panathenaea, became more widely celebrated and attracted participants from outside. Two centres, and the festivals associated with them, were revered by all Hellenes and accessible to all, even in wartime. Delphi and Olympia became in effect sacred cities – complexes of splendid temples, treasuries erected by the various states to house their offerings to the god, and votive statuary, with a tiny permanent population periodically swollen by devotees and supplicants. Delphi, situated in a high valley on the slopes of sacred Mount Parnassus, had been a holy place long before the god Apollo became its patron; in legend it was the centre or navel (*omphalos*) of the earth. Here dwelt the famous oracle that men came from all over the Greek world to consult. Individuals brought their problems to the oracle, and it was the ultimate authority on religious affairs. But the most astonishing fact about it (to the modern mind) is that Greek states regularly sent deputations to Delphi for prophecies and advice. The questions were put by a priest to a priestess, the Pythia, seated on a tripod. She answered in some kind of ecstatic trance whose exact nature remains unknown; it may have been induced by fasting or by drugs, or (an older but less plausible suggestion) caused by intoxicating fumes rising from a cleft in the ledge on which the ceremony took place. The priest then interpreted the wild words of the Pythia, often versifying his response – an impressive if somewhat suspect performance. Yet the Greeks had such faith in the oracle that when it seemed to prophesy wrongly they blamed themselves for misinterpreting its answers. Indeed, these were often prudently ambiguous. In the most notorious instance Croesus, King of Lydia, is supposed to have asked the oracle whether he should go to war with Persia. The

oracle told him that if he did so a great empire would be destroyed. He did, and it was: his own empire. The story is almost certainly apocryphal, but it exemplifies the Greeks' attitude towards the oracle as well as their characteristic delight in sheer cleverness.

The other major religious centre was Olympia in the Peloponnese. (This was far away, and quite distinct, from Mount Olympus, the highest mountain in Greece, which was the home of the gods, 'the Olympians'.) Olympia, the site of the Olympic Games, was the main cult-centre of Zeus himself, reaching a climax of magnificence in the 5th century with the building of the great temple of Zeus, which held a colossal seated gold-and-ivory statue of the god.

Demeter, Triptolemus and Persephone. Triptolemus, son of the king of Eleusis, helped Demeter to find her daughter Persephone; she rewarded him with the knowledge of agriculture, and his native Eleusis became the centre of the famous Mysteries. Votive relief, c.430 BC.

6 ART AND ARCHITECTURE

REGARDED IN MANY PERIODS AS THE ACME OF BEAUTY AND NOBILITY, GREEK ART AND ARCHITECTURE HAVE HAD AN IMPACT OVER THE MILLENNIA THAT CAN HARDLY BE OVER-STATED. THIS IS ALL THE MORE REMARKABLE BECAUSE ONLY A SMALL PART OF THE GREEK ACHIEVEMENT REMAINS, AND THAT PART IN GENERALLY POOR CONDITION AND INCOMPLETE. THE GREAT TEMPLES ARE ROOFLESS AND HAVE BEEN STRIPPED OF THEIR SCULPTURES. PAINTING, REGARDED BY THE GREEKS AS A MAJOR ART, IS VIRTUALLY NON-EXISTENT EXCEPT ON POTTERY, AND MOST OF THE MASTERPIECES OF STATUARY IN BRONZE AND MARBLE ARE KNOWN ONLY THROUGH ROMAN COPIES OF VARYING COMPETENCE. IN SPITE OF THESE CALAMITIES, THE GREEK ARTS CONTINUE TO ASTONISH, AND THEIR HISTORY CAN BE TRACED. IN FACT, AFTER THE MYCENAEAN COLLAPSE AND THE DARK AGE, ART AND ARCHITECTURE DEVELOPED CONTINUOUSLY; AND ALTHOUGH THEY ARE DIVIDED FOR CONVENIENCE INTO PERIODS IT SHOULD BE REMEMBERED THAT THESE ARE USEFUL WAYS OF ORGANIZING THE SUBJECT, NOT HARD-AND-FAST DIVISIONS. FROM THE GEOMETRIC TO THE HELLENISTIC, OVER ALMOST A THOUSAND YEARS, THE GREEKS WERE RESPONSIBLE FOR AN UNSURPASSED OUTPOURING OF VISUAL AND TACTILE CREATIVITY.

The Vaphio Cup, one of two Mycenaean gold goblets from c.1500 BC, named after the site in the Peloponnese where they were found. The repoussé (hammered relief) design on this one shows men capturing bulls in a net.

MYCENAEAN ART

When the Greeks appeared in the Aegean around 2000 BC, the area had already produced some notable art and architecture. The Cycladic islanders had traded their pottery up and down the Mediterranean, and had mined their native marble to fashion smooth, beautifully balanced little figures. And, on a larger scale, the Minoans of Crete were engaged in creating an opulent palace culture with colourful decorative styles and a range of skilled craftwork. The impact of Cretan styles and skills on the Mycenaeans is evident from the 16th-century treasures recovered from the shaft graves at Mycenae itself. Many of these were items that rarely survive the centuries, since they are usually melted down or destroyed: the gold masks used to cover the faces of the dead; gold ornaments – hammered, granulated, engraved and drawn into wire patterns; engraved and inlaid bronze swords and daggers; and vessels of carved rock crystal. The ornamental subjects are different in spirit from the festive scenes of Cretan art, for the Mycenaeans delighted in hunting and warfare, decorating their metalwork and pottery with sieges and sea battles, and carving war chariots on their stone grave-markers, which are consequently the earliest Greek relief sculptures.

A few later finds, such as the Vaphio cups from a tomb near Sparta, suggest that Mycenaean art was developing a virile individual style; and examples of weapons, armour, ivory and jewellery have come to light. But from later centuries only pottery, as usual, survives in any quantity, thanks to its peculiar combination of qualities – it is cheap and easily broken, but almost impossible to destroy completely. Greek vessels, with stylized or pictorial decorations, have been found in many places between Italy and Syria, bearing witness to the scope of Mycenaean trade at its height. Equally, the feebler decorative treatment of later times is a symptom of the decline of Mycenaean Greece and the closing-in of the Dark Age.

Fragments of wall paintings from Pylos and elsewhere suggest that Greek work in this art was also derived from the Minoans. But the layout and construction of Mycenaean buildings are related to a different tradition. The great citadels of Mycenae and Tiryns consist of huge irregular stones, closely fitted together so that they hold in place (and could hold off attackers) without cement; later Greeks, understandably awe-struck by the gloomy grandeur of these sites, believed that they were the work of the Cyclops, one-eyed giants of myth; and this type of masonry is still called 'cyclopean'. Around a gateway the stones were more carefully dressed into rectangles, no doubt to make the structure look more impressive. The most famous example is the Lion Gate at Mycenae, which has the earliest known Greek monumental carving, relief sculpture (lionesses on either side of a pillar) inset above the gateway. The triangular slab carrying the relief also had a functional role; only 70cm (27½in) thick, it conceals what would otherwise be a void (technically known as a relieving triangle) left to reduce the weight of the masonry pressing on the lintel.

The 'beehive' or *tholos* tombs of the Mycenaeans, which were more common and somewhat later in date than the shaft graves, were also cyclopean constructions. The roofs were not made on the arch or lintel principle, but by overlapping stones inwards from the sides until they met; this procedure (known as corbelling) is crude, but lends itself to ruggedly impressive effects, as in the famous tomb at Mycenae miscalled 'the Treasury of Atreus'. Inside the citadel lay the palace, made of a timber framework filled in with rubble and plastered over. At its heart was a large rectangular chamber which must have been where the king sat in state; his throne was on one side of the room, which had a hearth in the centre surrounded by four columns. Here, perhaps, kings and heroes feasted, Homeric-style, seated at long tables; but this is only speculation. The palaces survive as archaeological sites, not as buildings; they – and, presumably, most Mycenaean art – were destroyed in the general collapse that ushered in the Dark Age.

The beautifully fitted roof of this 'beehive' tomb bears witness to the building skills of the Mycenaeans; it has been variously miscalled 'the Treasury of Atreus' and 'the Tomb of Agamemnon'; c.1250 BC.

EASTERN INFLUENCES

Archaeological finds at Lefkandi, on the island of Euboea, suggest that the Dark Age had its brighter spots: this Mycenaean city seems to have survived, and to have flourished as a trading centre, right down to the 9th century BC. However, the general picture of impoverishment and illiteracy during the period 1100–750 BC still appears to be correct, and is necessary to account for the fact that Mycenaean achievements had very little influence on the later development of Greek art.

Even during the Dark Age there were new forces at work. From about 1050 Athenian potters and painters started producing wares decorated with bold concentric circles, semicircles and other abstract patterns, precisely applied with compass and rule or multiple brushes. The style spread to other Greek centres, although their wares never equalled the quality of Athenian potting and painting; the leading role played by Athens during this period lends credence to the Athenian tradition that Attica escaped the worst during the Mycenaean collapse and served during the Dark Age as a haven for refugees from other areas. By about 900 BC this impressively simple

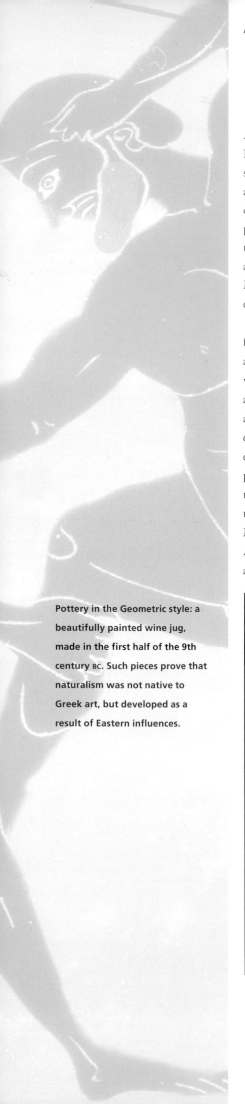

Pottery in the Geometric style: a beautifully painted wine jug, made in the first half of the 9th century BC. Such pieces prove that naturalism was not native to Greek art, but developed as a result of Eastern influences.

'Protogeometric' was developing into a full-blown 'Geometric' style in which the vase was covered with dense ornament in horizontal bands. Painters elaborated a range of new motifs – zigzags, swastikas, meanders squared off into key patterns – and crammed them on to every inch of the surface, even filling the interiors of the patterns with hatchings to minimize the empty spaces. The first sign of a break with geometric abstraction came in the 8th century, when little human and animal figures began to appear in some of the bands, although they were represented schematically and as silhouettes, often repeated with the regularity of paper cut-outs. Later still, huge vases used as memorials in Athens' cemetery carried action scenes such as funeral processions, scenes of warfare and parading chariots; it is possible that some of these were intended to represent episodes from Greek myth.

A surprising feature of these indigenous Greek wares is the extent to which the decoration takes the form of pattern-making rather than the naturalism for which Greek art has since become famous. The first significant impulse in a new direction in fact came from outside, in the form of images and techniques from the Near East. This 'Orientalizing' phase reflects the renewal of trading and other contacts with the outside world, probably begun by Greek merchants at Al Mina by 800 BC and quickened by their appropriation of the Phoenician alphabet at this or some nearby settlement. The results were again most apparent in pottery decoration, this time from about 700 BC. Griffins, sphinxes and other imaginary beasts appeared along with lions, deer, goats, birds and plants, gradually growing larger and occupying more and more of the available space. Experiments were also made with outline drawings of the human figure, executed with greater freedom and realism. Athenian potters worked in their 'Protoattic' version of the new style, continuing to produce many large vessels; but the leading place was taken by Corinth, which was at the height of its commercial

The 'Orientalizing' style. Though horizontally banded like the wine jug on the opposite page, this vessel of the same type has new animal motifs learned from the East: it comes from Rhodes and was made in the 7th century BC.

prosperity in the 7th century. Protocorinthian and (from about 625 BC) Corinthian vase painting was notably precise and delicate, featuring black silhouettes that were animated by incising the internal details — that is, scratching through the black so that the natural colour of the vessel showed through as drawn lines. In this way the Corinthians anticipated the black-figure painting style that the Athenians would later use to even greater effect.

Eastern influence also seems to have been responsible for the revival and elaboration of metal working techniques and miniature craft work such as ivory carving. Numbers of bronze and terracotta statuettes have been found, mainly in graveyards or as votive offerings in sanctuaries of the gods. And before the 7th century was over, developments in architecture and large-scale sculpture heralded a new phase of artistic achievement.

THE ARCHAIC ACHIEVEMENT

Noble remains: the temple of Apollo at Corinth, built in the Doric style late in the 6th century BC. These are all that is left of the city of Corinth, destroyed by the Romans in 146 BC.

In art and architecture the years between about 600 and 480 BC are conventionally known as the Archaic period. The term sounds faintly derogatory, as though Archaic art was no more than a primitive phase, superseded by the Classical art that followed in the 5th century; but such an attitude is now itself obsolete, and the beauty and vitality of Archaic sculpture and vase painting are universally acknowledged.

Archaic buildings were at least as important in the history of Greek architecture, although painfully little survives above ground level from this period. Now and later, what can be seen are communal rather than familial or individual structures. Most Greek houses were relatively humble places throughout the Archaic and Classical periods; time, money and skill were lavished on public buildings, and above all on the temples that embodied the religious and the civic spirit of the *polis*. In a sense, architecture was the queen of the arts, to whom the others paid tribute. Most sculpture was for or associated with a temple in the form of votive statuary, relief carvings on the friezes at roof level, and free-standing figures made to be set into the pediments (triangular gables) at each end of the building. The important commissions of the great 5th- and 4th-century painters were panel and wall paintings for temples – famous in their own time and for centuries afterwards, carefully described by Roman connoisseurs such as Pliny, but long since vanished. Even pottery was widely used for dedications to the gods and for burial with the dead, though, of course, it had equally important secular functions in the kitchen, on the table and (in the case of the finer pieces) at drinking parties and similar occasions for display.

This public art would have been much more colourful than we can easily imagine: the buildings and statues that survive represent Greek art after the paint has worn away and the accessories have been destroyed or looted. Apart from mural decorations, many of the mouldings and other architectural details of buildings were brightly painted; statues had coloured clothes, hair, eyes and lips; polished bronzes with inlaid eyes, lips and nails flashed with yellow brilliance in the sunlight; and the three-dimensionality of reliefs was emphasized by the now-vanished earrings the figures wore, the spears they carried, the bridles attached to their horses. The Acropolis of Athens and the sacred cities of Delphi and Olympia must have been strikingly colourful patches on the Greek landscape, evoking feelings of awe in pilgrims and visitors.

The Greek temple was not a place of worship in which believers expected to gather and hold services: it was a house for the god or goddess, presided over by a cult figure of the deity and looked after by his or her priests; public ceremonies took place outside, at an altar in front of the building. But although the splendour of the temple was naturally felt to reflect the splendour of the god, the Greeks built in wood and mud brick until the 7th century, when a slow transi-

tion began to building in stone; the initial impulse probably came from the sight of Egyptian temples, with which Greek merchants must have become familiar during this period. As late as 590 BC some of the upper parts of the temple of Hera at Olympia are believed to have been made of wood; so were the surrounding columns, but these were gradually replaced by stone, and their remains are now virtually all that is visible on the site above ground level.

Like the Egyptians, the Greeks built in a simple lintel-and-pillar style, derived from wooden buildings in which vertical posts held up a roof of horizontal beams. They made no use of such devices as arches and vaults; and indeed their engineering feats went little further than widening the distance between the internal columns needed to support a large building. The subtle beauty of the Greek temple was created from

The orders of architecture. The decorative styles developed by the Greeks influenced architecture for two and a half millennia. This 17th-century illustration shows Doric, Ionian and Corinthian.

The *kouros* Dionysermos, a statuette of c.600 BC. In mainland Greece standing figures of young men (*kouroi*) were always naked, unlike this and other examples from Asia Minor. But its face wears the characteristic 'Archaic smile' and it is stiffly upright.

even triple colonnade). The upper structure, known as the entablature, was divided into horizontal registers including a frieze, and culminated in a cornice. The gables at the front and back of the temple took the form of an imposing triangular frame, the pediment, which was filled with sculptures.

The improvements made in temple-building were aesthetic rather than constructional: the use of *entasis*, a slight swelling in the body of a column that prevented it from appearing to shrink in the middle; the slight inward inclination of the colonnade, also for optical reasons; and other subtle adjustments. One great advantage of the relative simplicity of building techniques was that public works could be sub-contracted without difficulty, involving large numbers of independent craftsmen in each project. This way of doing things was characteristically Greek (as opposed to employing a large, permanent, drilled and disciplined workforce), and invites speculation concerning the subterranean relationship between the general outlook of a culture and the techniques and methods of organization developed by its members.

By the beginning of the Archaic period, two main decorative styles, or orders, had developed in temple building: Doric and Ionic. Doric, which predominated on the mainland and in Greater Greece, was massy, powerful and relatively simple. The columns were thick and fluted (with vertical grooves); they had no bases, and each culminated in a large, cushion-shaped capital (the 'head' of the column, immediately below the entablature). Another very distinctive feature was the frieze, which consisted of alternating panels: metopes, sometimes painted or carved in relief, and triglyphs, decorated with three vertical bars. (The bars, like certain other details, are believed to be translations into stone of once-functional features of construction in wood.)

The Ionic order developed somewhat later, in Asiatic Greece and the nearby islands. It seems to have been based on decorative motifs of the Near East, particularly the distinctive Ionic capital, which swells out into two large scroll-like features known as volutes. The order is generally lighter but more ornate than Doric, with slender

very simple elements: a rectangular walled structure with a pitched roof, surrounded by a colonnade. The rectangular structure, the *naos* or *cella*, was the heart of the temple, holding the cult statue of the god or goddess. The upper structure and roof extended beyond the *cella* block and were supported by the columns of the colonnade (or, in grander buildings, a double or

columns standing on bases. Instead of being divided into metopes and triglyphs, the frieze was unbroken, lending itself to continuous carving all the way round. During the 6th century three famous Ionic temples were built, two of them on the island of Samos and one at Ephesus – the colossal Temple of Artemis, which ranked as one of the Seven Wonders of the Ancient World. All three have perished, as have most Doric buildings of the Archaic period, including splendid temples and other public buildings known to have been erected in Athens under the Pisistratid tyranny and, in a competitive spirit, under the democratic regime that replaced it. The best remaining example of Archaic architecture in Greece itself is the temple of Apollo at Corinth, built around 560; but this is in truth a romantic ruin rather than a temple. Outside Greece there are the temples of Hera (c. 550) and Athena (c. 500) at Posidonia (Paestum) in southern Italy, which at least preserve a skeletal colonnaded grandeur.

Monumental sculpture, like large-scale architecture, began to be created during the Archaic period and seems to have been directly inspired by Egyptian models. During the 7th century small bronze and terracotta figures had been made, and so had statuettes carved from soft limestone; the best-known example, the 65-cm (25½-in)-high Lady of Auxerre (c. 640 BC), illustrates the 'Daedalic' style, with a flat, triangular face, wig-like hair, and other generally stylized and simplified features. In the later 7th century life-size and over-life-size figures appeared, cut from marble quarried at Naxos, Paros, Samos and other Greek islands. The earliest life-size sculpture, the Nicandre statue from Delos, is a female figure that is still (as far as it is possible to tell from its worn condition) in the Daedalic style. But in the 6th century the most characteristic life-size statues were standing figures of young men and women, put up as dedications in temples or monuments on graves; whatever the purpose served, each wore the distinctive 'Archaic smile', faint and – to modern eyes – rather ambiguous. They were made all over the Greek Aegean area, but as so often Athens provides the best evidence – in this instance

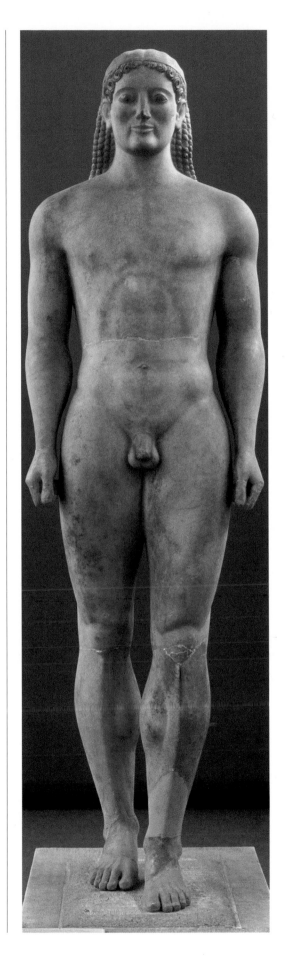

Kouros from Anavissos in Attica; marble, c.530 BC. Like many *kouroi*, this one was put up to mark the site of a tomb. By contrast with the older figure opposite, he is stepping out, his arms are cut away from his body, and the musculature is indicated.

through sheer chance: when the Persians sacked Athens in 480 they destroyed the buildings on the Acropolis and threw down the votive statues on the site; the Athenians reverently buried the remains, and consequently these were preserved for posterity without being further damaged or re-used.

Egypt may have supplied the original models, but Greek monumental sculpture was never purely imitative. In direct contrast to Egyptian conventions, the standing figures of young men were always shown naked; and even the earliest of them were rather more human and less intim-

The *kore*, or standing figure of a maiden. This example, rigid and highly stylized, dates from about 575 BC and is the earliest known from Attica. In its right hand the figure holds a pomegranate, symbol of eternal life.

idating than their Egyptian prototypes. But the emphasis on symmetry and frontality was very marked, as if the figure had barely been released from the block of marble and did not yet dare to stretch out his arms. This remained broadly true throughout the Archaic period, but during its course sculpture did in other ways become less hieratic and more human and natural. Gradually the young man, or *kouros*, stepped forward with a new suppleness; his musculature, originally indicated by schematic surface patterning, was articulated with increasing detail and accuracy; and finally he ceased to look rigidly upright, as if stood against a wall, and was given a natural, relaxed stance with his weight on one foot. His female equivalent, the *kore*, followed a different line of development: she was always shown clothed, so in her case the sculptor made his chief innovations in the treatment of her head and the detailing of her tunic, at first scoring a pattern on the smooth surface to indicate drapery and later carving folds that were progressively more emphatic and natural-looking.

A few other statues in the round are known from the mid-6th century, notably the Moschophorus, or Calfbearer, a votive figure from the Acropolis at Athens. Some pediment sculpture has also survived, culminating in a number of pieces from the very end of the period (*c.* 500–480) which stood in the temple of Aphaia on the island of Aegina; the near-complete group from the west pediment, with the goddess Athena in the centre, illustrates the range of dynamic poses that sculptors had mastered and the skill with which they could fit figures into the awkward triangular frame. Life-size figures were also made in bronze but, as in other periods, the ease with which the metal could be melted down and re-used means that very little has survived (smaller pieces fared a good deal better). However, excavators have unearthed one *kouros* from about 520, with outstretched arms (one of them originally holding a bow), that shows a considerable advance in naturalness on its marble counterparts.

Relief sculpture, unhampered by problems arising from the need for three-dimensional treatment, advanced towards naturalism even more quickly. Reliefs were carved on temple friezes, on the plinths of statues, and on stele (upright slabs that served as tombstones), where they usually pictured a young athlete or warrior. By the early Classical period even a colonial town in Greater Greece could afford and appreciate a masterpiece such as the Ludovisi Throne, with its subtle and moving carvings of the birth of Aphrodite and other female figures.

Meanwhile, the 'minor' arts were helping to create the wealth that would finance the great building and sculptural projects of the 5th century. With the new refinement of gold and metalworking techniques, Greek craftsmen produced statuettes, decorated armour and jewellery for export as well as home consumption. A large bronze wine-making bowl was discovered in a Celtic royal tomb at Vix in eastern France, and Scythian gold objects in the native 'animal style', found in the Crimea, are often the work of Greek craftsmen.

At Athens, where olive oil and wine exports were so important to the economy, there was a concomitant need for containers; so potters were assured of a steady demand for utilitarian wares between commissions that called for more sophisticated potting and painting skills. Few workshops can have been highly specialized; even many individual painters seem to have worked as potters too, perhaps specializing later in life as their talent became apparent and opportunity offered. It is doubtful whether they expected or received any recognition as artists, although they might be known and respected as citizen-craftsmen who had made a success in life; but their own opinion is clear from the fact that they often signed their best pieces as potter and/or painter.

By about 600 the Athenians had mastered the new black-figure style of painting. This was pioneered by Athens' commercial rival, Corinth, but its very popularity encouraged the Corinthian potters to over-produce and lower standards; the Athenians took it up and by the mid-6th century were dominating the export market. By contrast with the Corinthian taste for animal subjects, Athenian painters displayed a preference for narrative that carried

over into the black-figure period. The new style still involved using silhouettes, but now the figures were larger, fuller and more realistic, painted in black against the unpainted reddish-buff background of the fired clay. Drapery, musculature and other internal details of figures and objects were drawn in by

Kore carved in about 520 BC; the difference in freedom and naturalism between this and the older figure on the opposite page is patent. Like her male counterpart, the *kore* served as a votive offering or tomb monument.

Vase painting in the black-figure style: the painting was done in black on the reddish pottery ground, which was left uncoloured; internal details were incised so that they showed through in the ground colour. This is a Dionysian scene, c.560-530 BC.

scratching through the paint to the clay; other details were sometimes touched in with red and white paint. With their high Attic glazes, black-figure vases are superbly distinctive works of art; scenes of war and death on them have a sinister intensity (partly, no doubt, through colour association), but the range of subjects is already very wide, from myth to bibulous merrymaking. In the hands of the greatest black-figure painter, Exekias, the style was capable of achieving an emotional intensity appropriate to the more tragic mythical episodes such as the slaying of the Amazon queen Penthesilea by Achilles, and Ajax's preparations for his suicide.

Around 530 BC a new technique was introduced at Athens and quickly superseded the black-figure everywhere; for well over a century or more, Athens' supremacy as a producer of fine pottery remained unchallenged. The red-figure technique was the reverse of the black-figure: the painter filled the areas around his figures with black, leaving the figures themselves in unpainted reddish-buff. Internal details could now be painted in, with an immediately notice-able gain in freedom of drawing; the main disadvantage was the starker overall effect created by red-on-black. Greater freedom encouraged greater realism: three-quarter views, eyes shown in profile instead of frontally (Egyptian-style), and a variety of movements and gestures were mastered over the following decades, culminating in the works of such masters as the Cleophrades Painter, the Berlin Painter and the Brygos Painter; and apart from its own merits, Athenian pottery is the main visual source for information about the development Greek painting, which, at least in terms of drawing techniques, is known to have been meeting and overcoming the same problems.

The Moschophorus, or Calfbearer, was discovered on the Acropolis at Athens, where it had been buried after the 5th-century Persian onslaught. Despite the complexity of the pose, it dates from the mid-6th century and the man's face wears the 'Archaic smile'.

THE CLASSICAL AGE

The Classical age is usually defined as the years between 480 and 323 BC; that is, between the victory over the Persians at Salamis, which effectively ensured Greek independence, and the death of Alexander the Great, when the Greek world expanded to take in the eastern Mediterranean and western Asia. In art and architecture, the period witnessed the sculptor's

The Discus Thrower (Discobolus), one of the most renowned works of Classical Greek sculpture – despite the fact that it is known only in marble Roman copies; the mid-5th-century original, by Myron of Eleutherae, was a bronze, and as such would certainly have been more finely articulated.

achievement of full mastery over his material and the collaboration of builders, sculptors and painters on the Parthenon and other great Athenian works – pre-eminent in their own generation, but now unnaturally isolated in their grandeur because most of their rivals, such as the Temple of Zeus at Olympia, have disappeared.

Early Classical sculpture – before *c.* 450 – is often described as Transitional, or as belonging to the Severe Style because of a certain austerity of expression and treatment. It completed the transformation of the Archaic *kouros* and *kore* into naturally posed figures that could be viewed from any angle. Instead of standing foursquare, with only one foot advanced to suggest movement, the *kouros* began to raise his arms, turn his head and shift his weight. The female figure was still treated with greater reserve, but a new awareness of the female body is shown by the substitution of the linen *chiton*, following the contours of the body more closely, for the *peplos*. Such developments must have made this a time of intense excitement for sculptors, who revelled in their freedom to create never-before-seen stances and gestures in marble and bronze. The most famous, in his own day and since, was Myron of Eleutherae, who fashioned the bronze Discus Thrower (Discobolus), a superb work even in the marble Roman copies by which it is known. The difficult posture and accurately rendered musculature seem a world away from the older standing figures, and do in fact represent something new: the fully active human figure, as convincing in its parts as in the whole. Among the other outstanding figures that survive are a number from the pediments of the Temple of Zeus at Olympia, notably the Apollo placed in the centre of the west pediment; a more sober figure than the Discus Thrower, he stands with arm outstretched, decreeing victory for the lapiths in their struggle against the centaurs.

The copy of the Discus Thrower and the damaged Apollo exemplify the survival situation as far as Classical and much later Greek art are concerned: most of the great individual works are known only by repute, in Roman copies (not always of a high standard and substituting marble for the original bronze), or

A mighty deity – but no one is certain whether he is Zeus, king of the gods, about to fling a thunderbolt, or the sea god Poseidon brandishing his trident. Over life size, this magnificent bronze, dating from c.460 BC, was found in the sea off Artemisium.

from coins or engravings on jewels. The other remains are purely architectural and more or less fragmentary: reliefs or free-standing statuary for pediments, both intended to be admired not just for themselves but for the skill with which they were fitted into awkward shapes and integrated into the architectural whole. It says a good deal for the Greek achievement that even its broken and incomplete history has been taken as the 'Classical' norm by so many people.

Like the Discus Thrower, The Tyrannicides by Critios and Nesiotes was a bronze, now known only in a Roman marble copy. It shows two figures, Harmodius and Aristogeiton,

brandishing the weapons with which they struck down the Athenian joint-tyrant Hipparchus in 514. The group was set up in the *agora* at Athens in 477, replacing earlier figures of the heroes that had been carried off by the Persians. It is a remarkably early representation of figures in the round engaged in violent action and, although not in any sense a double portrait, unusual in commemorating a historical event; it is, in effect, political propaganda celebrating a deed that led on to the establishment of Athens' democratic system.

Thanks to some happy accidents, four important bronzes are known from the early Classical period. The earliest, the Charioteer of Delphi, was made to celebrate the victory of the Sicilian tyrant Polyzalus at the Pythian Games of 478 or 474; it owes its survival to an earthquake that buried it for centuries. Rather more stiff and impersonal than most figures of this date, the figure is deeply impressive – perhaps more so than if it stood in its original setting, a chariot drawn by four horses. By contrast, a majestic bronze figure of Zeus or Poseidon is more obviously poised for action, legs braced and arms outstretched as he prepares to fling a thunderbolt or trident. (The absence of the thunderbolt/trident is the reason why the identity of the figure remains in doubt.) Zeus escaped being melted down because he was lost at sea off Euboea and raised from the depths only in the 1920s. A similar rescue was effected as recently as 1972, when two slightly over-life-size bronzes of warriors were recovered from the sea off Riace in Southern Italy. By contrast with the shaven faces and boyishness of so many male figures from this period, the intensely charged physical presence of these bearded, confidently muscular beings in the prime of life is disconcerting – all the more so because there is no evidence that they were regarded as of any great note in antiquity; the fairly extensive ancient literary record provides no scholarly niche into which they can be fitted. The discovery of such important yet unrecorded figures brings home just how much there must be about the ancient Greeks that we do not know and are not even aware of not knowing. Though similar enough to suggest that they belong together, the figures are not identical and may not even be the work of the same artist. Each was evidently equipped with the spear and round shield of the hoplite, which suggests that they belonged to a larger group; their combination of relaxation and alertness is perhaps that of men on guard duty. The location where they were found makes it likely that they were cultural loot, on their way to Rome when the vessel they were in was wrecked.

The Persians' destruction of the buildings and statuary on the Athenian acropolis was a disaster, even for such a commercially prosperous city as Athens. Apart from rebuilding the fortification wall of the citadel, the Athenians did relatively little to make good the damage for the space of a generation. They may also have been restrained by an oath taken by the city-states just before the battle of Plataea in 479, pledging themselves not to rebuild the shrines that had been destroyed by the Persians; the ruins were to remain a permanent and visible testimony to Persian barbarism. But in 454 the funds of the Delian League were transferred to an increasingly dominant, imperial Athens, and Pericles announced that a percentage of the annual contributions would be dedicated to the goddess Athena – which turned out to mean the city of which the goddess was patron. The oath of Plataea forgotten, ambitious plans were made soon after 450 BC for a group of splendid marble buildings that would celebrate Athens' imperial greatness and astonish Hellas. There is no doubt that Pericles masterminded the project, though it was of course approved by the Assembly and financed by the state – insofar as the expenses were not paid for by Athens' allies. The project was carried out over the next 50 years (with some economies) in spite of Pericles' death and in the teeth of an exhausting war and ultimate defeat.

The results are still visible above the modern city in the ruined glory of the Parthenon, the Propylaea, the Temple of Athena Nike and the Erechtheum. In order to visualize the full splendour of the Acropolis in (say) 400 BC we should also have to conjure up a host of smaller shrines and votive statuary, with a processional throng winding uphill from the city during the great festivals. On the highest point stood the Parthenon, dedicated to Athena Parthenos (Athena the Virgin), the largest Doric temple built on mainland Greece. Though less isolated, and therefore less dominant, than it now appears, the Parthenon provided a visual climax to the colourful, crowded mass of buildings and even rose clear above them when viewed (as the architects must have intended) from the north-west; and every optical refinement known to the Greeks was employed to enhance its beauty. The colonnade consisted of eight columns at the front and back (six was more usual) and 17 down each side. The *cella* was divided into two chambers, each with a separate entrance behind a six-columned porch; one chamber held the temple treasury, the other the cult statue of the goddess, a colossal figure by the great sculptor Phidias, its wooden core covered with gold and ivory (a combination described as chryselephantine).

Not much is known about the architects of the Parthenon, Ictinus and Callicrates. Ictinus also designed the Temple of Apollo at Bassae in Arcadia, of which a notable feature was the appearance of a new order. This was Corinthian, a variant of Ionic in which the volute capital on top of the column was replaced by a mass of acanthus leaves; it was used only occasionally by the Greeks, but its showy character made it a favourite with the Romans. Overall supervision of the Parthenon project seems to have been entrusted to the native Athenian sculptor Phidias, the universal genius of his time. However, the architects' contribution cannot have been negligible, since Ictinus is known to have written a book about his work on the Parthenon. The building was carried out with incredible speed, taking only nine years (447–438 BC); both the temple and its 12-m (39½-ft)-high statue were ready for consecration at the Panathenaea of July 438. The pediment sculptures took another six years to finish, probably from designs by Phidias. Inevitably, the cult figure of Athena Parthenos has not survived; nor has Phidias' colossal gold and ivory Zeus for the temple of the god at Olympia, which ancient commentators considered his masterpiece (it was one of the Seven Wonders of the World).

Opposite: bronze figure of a warrior, c.450 BC. It is one of two over-life-size bronzes, recovered as recently as 1972 from the sea off Riace in Southern Italy. It no longer carries a spear and round shield, but its face still has its original copper lips and silver teeth.

The Parthenon – the temple of Athena Parthenos (the Virgin) – is a masterpiece of architectural beauty. It stands on the Acropolis, or citadel, of Athens, alongside other late 5th-century buildings erected to replace those destroyed by the Persians and proclaim the greatness of Athens.

The sculptures integrated into the Parthenon itself were exceptionally lavish in number and treatment. The metopes all round the building – 92 of them – included some carved in such high relief that they are almost free-standing. They portray mythical conflicts that the Greeks interpreted as victories for civilization over barbarism: between the lapiths and the drunken centaurs who had tried to carry off the lapiths' women; between Greeks and Amazons; and between gods and giants. They are in effect coded references to the Greek triumph over the Persians, and reflect the conviction, reinforced by the wars, that barbarians (slaves of an autocrat, like the Persians) could never be a match

for civilized, free men (that is, Greeks). The two pediments were filled with free-standing sculptures honouring Athena: the east pediment celebrated her birth from the head of the supreme deity, Zeus, liberated with a blow of the axe wielded by the blacksmith god Hephaestus; while the west pediment showed her victorious struggle against the sea-god Poseidon for domination over Attica. The other major sculpture was a 160-m (525-ft) frieze in low relief that ran all the way round the outside of the *cella*: an unorthodox Ionic touch on this greatest of all Doric masterpieces. Appropriately – from every point of view – the subject of the frieze was the procession at the four-year Great Panathenaea, filled with young men on horseback, charioteers driving their vehicles, officials, musicians and other celebrants bearing animals to the sacrifice and the new robe that was woven for the goddess and presented to her every four years.

Like other temples, the Parthenon suffered over the centuries from religious fanaticism, war and vandalism; the worst damage was inflicted by an explosion in 1687, when a Venetian fleet besieged Turkish-occupied Athens and one of their shells ignited gunpowder stored in the temple. In 1812 the majority of the surviving sculptures were taken down and shipped to Britain by Lord Elgin, whose otherwise dubious actions may well have saved them from further damage, not least from industrial pollution. Purchased by the British government, the 'Elgin Marbles' became part of the British Museum collection in London; in recent years there has been much controversy over the Greek government's demands, so far rejected, that the sculptures should be returned to their country of origin.

The surviving reliefs and sculptures from the Parthenon have always been regarded as the climax of Classical art – men, gods and beasts superbly natural, noble and balanced, individually and as groups. But they represent something of a deviation from the realistic tendency of the earlier period, perhaps because the elevated subject matter encouraged a more poised, hieratic rendering even of battle scenes: the men and women of the Parthenon sculptures, whatever actions they are engaged in, have the unmoved serenity of the gods they are glorifying. It is possible, too, that this treatment

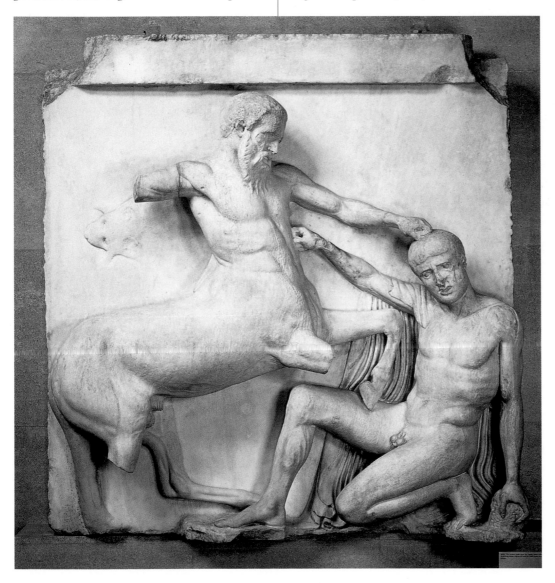

Lapith versus centaur: a scene from one of the metopes (panels) on the Parthenon. The figures are relief carvings, but the relief is so high that they are almost free-standing. The battle between the lapiths and the centaurs was interpreted as one between civilization and barbarism.

reflects something in the mood of the late 5th century; for Phidias' most famous contemporary, Polyclitus of Argos, is said to have treated *kouros*-like subjects in a very restrained style, and on the evidence of his Spear Carrier (Doryphorus, known from marble Roman copies of the original bronze) this appears to have been the case. Polyclitus actually defeated Phidias in the only recorded competition between the two for a commission. He was possibly the more influential, writing a book, *The Canon*, in which he laid down ideal proportions; these, exemplified by the Doryphorus, are believed to have been followed by many later sculptors.

Of the other Classical buildings on the Acropolis, the small Ionic Temple of Athena Nike (Athena Bringer-of-Victory) was designed by Callicrates at about the time the Parthenon was begun. But its construction was deferred until the 420s, by which time the design had to be modified to accommodate the Propylaea, the

grand marble gateway to the Acropolis, designed by Mnesicles and built from 437. A balustrade was added to the temple of Athena Nike from *c.* 410 which marks a stage in the treatment of the female body. In a well-known group of three goddesses from the east pediment of the Parthenon, the draperies have become moulded to the bodies, suggesting the forms beneath; the balustrade reliefs go further, carrying lighter, more 'transparent' fabrics with an unmistakable erotic appeal and foreshadowing the appearance of the female nude in Greek sculpture.

The last of the great Classical buildings on the Acropolis was the Erechtheum, not finished until 406. Though small, it is one of the great masterpieces of Ionic. It housed the joint cults of Athena and Poseidon, as well as that of Erechtheus, a legendary king of Athens said to have been reared by Athena herself. (This joint household was doubtless specially arranged to mollify Poseidon, who had been defeated in his

Youths about to mount and join the Panathenaic procession. The scene was part of the 160-metre frieze that ran round the building behind the colonnade of the Parthenon; its masterly low relief contrasts strikingly with the more or less free-standing figures elsewhere on the temple.

attempt to become the city's patron, while ensuring that the victorious Athena was not offended by honours paid to her rival.) A curious feature of the Erechtheum is the use of female figures as columns, their heads supporting the 'maidens' porch' on the south side of the building. The Romans occasionally copied the idea of using such figures, which are called caryatids; a British architect, more literal, applied a copy of the maidens' porch to St Pancras' Church in London, where a line of load-bearing Greek girls still confronts the Euston Road.

Of the many building projects carried out in Athens during the Classical age, only one other survives in any substantial form. Below the Acropolis, on a hill in the city itself where it looks down on the *agora*, stands the Temple of Hephaestus, an unassuming Doric building

begun in 449; its dedication to the blacksmith god was appropriate and intentional, since the temple itself was near the potters' and metal-workers' quarters. Time has been less kind to the civic architecture that also flourished at Athens and elsewhere, in the form of assembly and music rooms, theatres and *stoas* (shops and offices with covered colonnades).

During the Classical period Athenian red-figure pottery continued to dominate the market, maintaining a high standard all through the 5th century and into the 4th, when a decline began to set in; it may represent a response to changing public taste, since after *c*. 400 the vase-painting tradition came to a surprisingly rapid end. Quantities of red-figure ware survive, but a different style of painting developed in the mid-5th century of which there are all too few

Attendant goddesses, Demeter, Kore and possibly Artemis; they were originally shown on the east pediment of the Parthenon as part of a group of divinities present at the birth of Athena. Despite the missing heads, the sloped grouping (to fit them into the pediment triangle) is apparent.

The Erechtheum, a small temple on the Athenian Acropolis, built about thirty years after the Parthenon; it was finished in 406 BC. Whereas the Parthenon is Doric in style, the Erechtheum is Ionic, characterized by (among other things) the volutes, or scrolls, at the top of its columns.

Opposite: the caryatids on the south porch of the Erechtheum, facing the Parthenon. These supporting pillars in female form were a novelty from the East when they were installed; later they were copied by the Romans and by classically inclined Europeans.

examples. The tall cylindrical oil jar (*lekythos*) was covered with a white ground on which artists such as the Achilles Painter drew in outline, broadly colouring the drapery and other details in a much more 'painterly' manner than was possible with the black-figure or red-figure techniques; lekythoi were used almost exclusively for funereal and religious purposes because of the fragility of the white ground, which made it unsuitable for frequent handling.

The often exquisite charm of the painted figures on *lekythoi* suggests more vividly than anything else what treasures have been lost through the disappearance of wall and panel paintings; often quite full descriptions have survived of the painting techniques of the great Classical artists from Polygnotus to Zeuxis, Parrhasius and Apelles, but they are no substitute for the works themselves. However, in recent years

excavations of royal Macedonian tombs at Vergina have uncovered some wall-paintings from about 340 that were probably executed by imported Greek artists. The one in best condition shows Hades carrying off Persephone in his chariot; despite its curiously sketchy style it is technically accomplished, and the violent anguish of Persephone looks forward to the emotional expressiveness of Hellenistic art.

Much 4th-century art has also been lost, making it hard to trace the development of Classical sculpture away from the Parthenon style, which has so often been taken as the Classical norm. Sculptors now began to explore new subjects and to use a more expressive and dramatic style in representing emotions, gestures and movements: the development is so pronounced that it must have been warmly approved, if not directly stimulated, by patrons,

civic and private. The most immediately obvious change was in the female form, already provokingly semi-visible in the balustrade reliefs on the late 5th-century temple of Athena Nike. By the 360s the leading sculptor of the day, Praxiteles, was confidently carving a divine Aphrodite in the nude; this figure, the Aphrodite of Cnidus, is known only through what seem to be quite poor Roman copies, but it was regarded by the ancients as definitely inviting. Unlike most of the Greek sculptors known by name, Praxiteles preferred to work in marble rather than bronze, achieving soft, smooth effects that are visible on the surviving group of Hermes with the infant Dionysus, which is though it may not be the original; its almost lazy sensuality may well have characterized the Aphrodite of Cnidus as carved by Praxiteles himself. The other great 4th-century masters were Scopas, credited with introducing violently emotional facial expressions, and Lysippus, master of large-scale compositions involving dramatic movements and swirling draperies.

Lysippus' skill was such that Alexander the Great is said to have allowed no other sculptor to portray him. Alexander's evident wish for a true (if possibly flattering) likeness marks the coming-of-age of portraiture, which had earlier been infrequent, idealized and often even posthumously executed, although some earlier images – of Themistocles and Pericles, for example – do carry a certain conviction. As early as the mid-4th century, individual self-assertion was combined with a new taste – for the colossal – when the Hellenizing governor of a Persian province was provided with a gigantic marble tomb filled with large friezes and hundreds of statues. The governor was Mausolus of Caria, in the southwest of Asia Minor, and his tomb was the Mausoleum, another of the Seven Wonders, which has given its name to all structures of this type; it appears to have been a temple-like building crowned with a huge pyramid. A new sense of personal uniqueness and a taste for the colossal, along with personal emotion, violence, realism and much else, became components of the new age that was ushered in by the career of Alexander the Great.

Lekythos decorated with the figure of a robed woman; 5th century BC. The *lekythos* was a type of funerary oil jar; along with some cups used in religious ceremonies, it was painted freely in more than one colour and on a white ground, with results that were often enchanting.

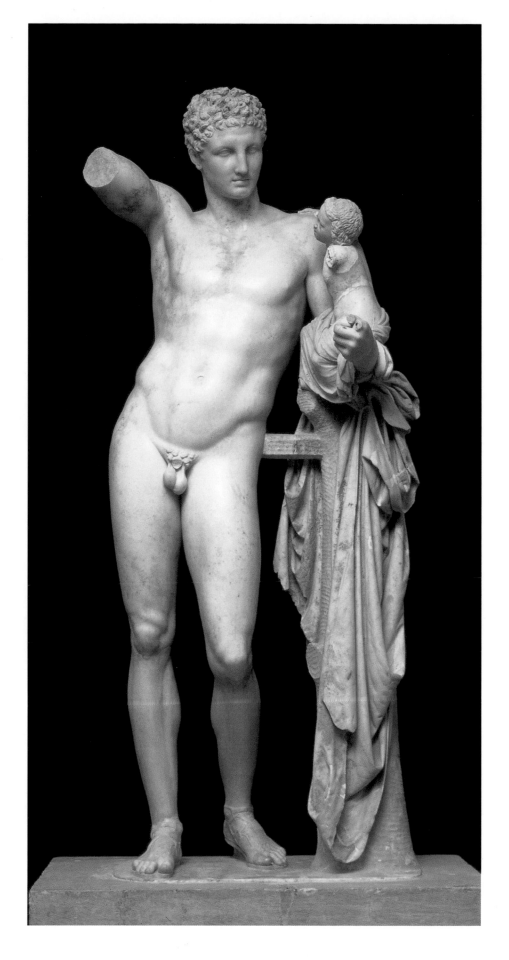

Hermes with the infant Dionysus. This marble group is by the 4th-century Athenian sculptor Praxiteles. Its style is notably softer, more sensual, more lively and more frivolous than the Classical sculpture of the 5th century BC.

CRAFT AND ART

The ancient Greeks had no word for art and, except perhaps in the late Hellenistic period, no concept of it as an aesthetic fact or activity that could be separated from other aspects of life and contemplated for its own sake. Significantly, there were muses of tragedy and history, but there was no muse of painting or sculpture. What we regard as works of art were objects made to be used, whether as votive offerings to gods or heroes, grave goods, or, in the cases of jewellery and painted pottery, means of personal adornment or conveniences for everyday living. Of course this does not mean that the Greeks could not appreciate beautiful and well-made things. There was no art, but there was *techne*, craft, and skilled workmanship was certainly admired, although without any presumption that it would confer immortality on the craftsman.

However, as time went on some architects, sculptors and painters did become famous, and notice was taken of their innovations, especially when these were associated with major public and religious projects. By contrast, the names of vase

Early Greek craftsmanship: a 7th-century plaque, picked out in filigree and granulation, showing the winged Near Eastern goddess Astarte. Found in a cemetery on the island of Rhodes, it is one of a set of seven plaques that were designed to be strung together and worn on the chest.

painters were never recorded except by a few individuals who signed their works. So the long-lived distinction between fine (or major) arts and the applied (or minor) arts implicitly existed in ancient Greece even though all its arts were in some sense applied. Modern opinion tends to dismiss the distinction as unhelpful or even untenable, and as a result there has been a markedly increased appreciation of 'minor' arts, albeit often, if old items are in question, as 'antiques'.

A wealth of examples survive from ancient Greece, although vast quantities of works in materials such as textiles and wood have perished. Objects made of gold and silver are rare for a different reason (their intrinsic value made it tempting to melt them down for re-use or as currency), but excavation of Mycenaean sites has uncovered hammered (*repoussé*) gold masks and relief-decorated cups from early in the known history of the Greeks. Any loss of skills during the ensuing Dark Age must have been made good surprisingly quickly, for goldwork from the Geometric period – mainly small objects of adornment such as rings and brooches – is executed with great delicacy and in extraordinary detail, displaying a mastery of techniques such as granulation (soldering grains of gold on to the surface to create bead patterns) and filigree (openwork decoration using threads and little balls of gold or silver). Later gold work includes superb export items found in South Russian tombs and lavishly wrought objects made for the luxury-loving Hellenistic courts.

Bronzes have a more continuous history, since many small items escaped the fate of most of the large figures. Figurines were made as independent works, but were also often designed as handles (for example, of mirrors, which were themselves made of polished metal) or attached to cauldrons or cups. Early examples were solid cast (that is, bronze all the way through), and this remained the norm for statuettes; but by the 6th century the Greeks had mastered the hollow-casting technique which made it possible to create large bronze figures. In the most advanced method, known as *cire perdue* (lost wax), a clay core was covered with a thin skin of wax on which the modelling of the figure was done. The figure was placed in a mould, which was heated so that the wax drained away; then the molten bronze was poured into the mould, replacing the wax skin.

When the mould and core were removed, the hollow figure was assembled and finished off.

Figures in terracotta (baked clay) served as cheap, mould-mass-produced substitutes for bronze offerings. However, in some periods they had distinctive features (for example, the curious 6th-century paint-striped figures made in Boeotia), and in Hellenistic times the use of several moulds to produce single figures made possible the creation of refined objects such as 'Tanagra' statuettes.

Marble was by no means the only medium in which carving was done. During the 7th century ivory was used for figures and for intaglio designs on seals; the intaglio (cut down into the surface) produced a relief design when the seal was pressed on to clay or some similarly receptive material. Later, chalcedony and other semi-precious stones replaced ivory. Similar skill in intaglio was developed by the craftsmen who carved the die-stamps from which coins were struck, and it is possible that seals and die-stamps were made by the same individuals. Carving of gemstones for rings and other forms of personal jewellery reached a high standard in the Classical period, but Hellenistic workmanship in engraving, inlaying, cameo-carving and other techniques was, as in most other respects, climactic in its virtuosity.

Later Greek craftsmanship: an intricate example of Hellenistic gold work, possibly made in Ptolemaic Egypt. It takes the form of a stalk of wheat which is divided into three stems with ears; the image was probably associated with the cult of the grain goddess Demeter.

HELLENISTIC ART

The Hellenistic age is conventionally dated from the death of Alexander the Great in 323 BC to 30 BC, when Egypt, the last of the great Greek-ruled kingdoms, was absorbed into the Roman Empire. Although artistic developments can rarely be fitted into precise dates, the career of Alexander can reasonably be taken as a watershed, separating the age of the small-scale republican societies in Greece from the era in which Greek monarchies dominated the post-Alexandrian East. During this last period, new centres of Greek culture grew up, and their rulers displayed large ambitions, cultural as well as political, as a result of the wealth their kingdoms commanded and their rivalry with their fellow-monarchs.

The Apollo Belvedere; the archer god originally held a bow in his left hand. Once regarded as the apogee of ancient Greek art, the Apollo Belvedere is now seen as exemplifying one of the new directions taken by Hellenistic art; Roman marble copy of a 4th-century BC bronze.

There were important consequences for artists and architects. The old pieties were observed, but working for kings and wealthy private individuals meant that palaces became as important as temples, and that sculpture was much concerned with glorifying individuals and commemorated their famous victories with un-Classical ostentation. Eastern autocrats with almost unlimited resources were able to promote a cult of the colossal, so that their monuments dwarfed those of the Classical age. At the same time a new interest in the idiosyncrasies of individual appearance became apparent; though no doubt owing most to the self-regard of Alexander and his successors, it probably also represented a response by artists to their liberation from Classical priorities, which favoured the making of more generalized images of gods and heroes.

Hellenistic art varied greatly in mood and form, taking in (among other things) the colossal, emotional, dramatic, realistic, grotesque and sentimental. The common denominator was the virtuosity to which these genres gave free rein. Often dismissed in the past as showy and vulgar, Hellenistic works are now appreciated for their astonishing technical accomplishment, and for the range of emotions and subjects they introduced; without these to widen the scope of Greek art, the narrow limits of classicism might seem a good deal less admirable.

The grid-planned cities of the Hellenistic age, with their palaces, temples, libraries, baths, theatres and monuments, have already been described; some notion of their grandeur can be obtained by seeing the still-extensive ruins of Ionian cities such as Pergamum and Didyma. Here, and at other Hellenistic centres, the more ornate Ionic order was favoured and a decorative treatment of theatres and other civic buildings became common. Although no longer politically powerful, Athens benefited from its past prestige, which persuaded Hellenistic rulers to demonstrate their cultural credentials by lavishing gifts on the city. The best extant example of a Hellenistic shopping mall is the reconstructed

The Stoa of Attalus, Athens; reconstruction of the 2nd-century BC original. During the Classical period marble was reserved for solemn structures such as temples; grand civic building for secular purposes (here a shopping mall) was a distinctive new feature of the Hellenistic period.

Stoa of Attalus, presented to Athens by the ruler of Pergamum in about 150 BC. It stood on the east side of the Athenian *agora* and consisted of two storeys of shops (21 on each floor) behind a very spacious double colonnade; the columns on the ground floor were Doric, those of the upper floor Ionic and Pergamene (a new type with a capital of stylized palms). The colonnades of this and other stoas served as covered meeting places for large numbers of people; one group of philosophers who took advantage of this facility were named after such buildings – the Stoics. Attalus may have been competing with the Seleucid king Antiochus IV, who at about the same time took up and financed work on a far-from-complete 6th-century Athenian project on the other (eastern) side of the Acropolis. Begun under the Pisistratid tyrants, the temple of Olympian Zeus had been neglected since their fall. Antiochus employed a Roman architect to go on with it, for the first time using the Corinthian order throughout – appropriately, since the temple was of un-Classical height and vastness, with 124 columns almost 17m (56ft) high; it was finally completed under the Roman emperor Hadrian in

AD 132. Only 15 columns are still standing, but they are a spectacular sight.

The drama and emotionalism of Hellenistic sculpture are particularly marked in surviving works from Pergamum. The kingdom had successfully repelled invading tribes of Gauls, and the fact was celebrated on a scale clearly intended to evoke comparisons with Greek victories in the Persian wars and the works in which these were represented as civilization triumphing over barbarism. But the Pergamene sculptors introduced a new note of pathos in picturing the defeated tribesmen, and displayed an interest in the appearance and behaviour of a non-Greek people that was also new. The Dying Gaul is a closely observed study of a Celtic warrior, moustached and wearing a torque round his neck. Preoccupied with his own fate, he is not recumbent but can just manage to support himself; and his pose sharpens the viewer's sense that death is about to overtake him. Another sculpture, possibly belonging to the same group as The Dying Gaul, shows a Gaulish warrior about to kill himself rather than face capture and slavery; with one hand he still half-supports his wife, whom he has

The Dying Gaul; Roman copy of a bronze Pergamene original of the late 3rd century BC. The figure was probably part of a large monument celebrating Pergamum's victory over its Gaulish invaders. However, there is a palpable sense of sympathy for the dying man.

Opposite: the Great Altar at Pergamum was constructed early in the 2nd century BC to celebrate military victories. Its most striking feature is the battle between gods and giants, fought out round the outer walls and up the sides of the steps to the altar.

already slain for the same reason. Both of these sculptures survive only in Roman copies, but the original Altar of Zeus, constructed some 40 years later (c. 180 BC) still stands, albeit in the Berlin museum entirely dedicated to it. This huge edifice consists of a monumental staircase, flanked by projecting wings, that leads to a platform on which stood the altar itself; the platform and wings are colonnaded. The most celebrated feature of the altar is a frieze, once 110-m (361-ft) long, that stretched round the outer walls and up the sides of the staircase. It follows Classical precedent in showing the Pergamene victory over the Gauls obliquely, through the battle between the gods and the giants; but in scale, style and mood it represents a climax of the grandiose, theatrical and dynamic trends in Hellenistic art, which have often been labelled 'baroque' because of their resemblance to similar aspects of the later (17th-century) European movement of that name. Expressing extremes of terror and pain, the

frenzied figures are carved in a very high relief that minimizes their dependence on the wall behind, and the illusion that their struggling, writhing forms are real is intensified by the way in which those closest to the altar steps crawl out on to them; such illusionism, blurring the boundaries between art and reality, is a characteristic of baroque styles. The interior of the altar held another frieze in a quieter mood, narrating the life of Telephos, a legendary ancestor of the Pergamene kings; it is notable for creating a sense of depth by placing figures in a group above one another (instead of showing them all standing on a base line), introducing to relief sculpture a technique said to have been long-established in Greek painting.

Conveying movement by twisting poses and swirling drapery was a favourite Hellenistic device. One of its most spectacular manifestations is on the famous Winged Victory of Samothrace, a now-headless, almost 3-m (10-ft) -high, figure alighting on the prow of a ship and so guaranteeing its success in battle; it was probably set up near the sanctuary of Samothrace, along with the vanished marble ship, to commemorate a naval victory by one of the Hellenistic powers.

A suggested attribution of the Winged Victory is to Pythocratus of Rhodes, whose native state may well have been the unidentified victor. If this is correct, the island had a particularly distinguished sculptural tradition, since Rhodians are linked with not only the fabled Colossus but also the Laocoön group, celebrated in antiquity and influential (on Michelangelo among others) 17 centuries later when it was dug up on the Esquiline Hill in Rome. Laocoön was a Trojan priest who tried to warn King Priam of the danger represented by the wooden horse that the Greeks had left behind; he was silenced by two sea serpents despatched by Apollo, which killed him and his young sons. The sculptural group shows the three caught in the coils and struggling in vain to free themselves; those who saw it in antiquity would have known the story and would have realized that while it showed the fate of Laocoön it also implied the doom of Troy. The subject lent itself to virtuoso display, and the artists concerned created an appropriately complex composition,

The Winged Victory of Samothrace; Hellenistic,
3rd or early 2nd century BC. The colossal figure
of the goddess Victory was originally shown
alighting on the marble prow of a ship.

agonized expressions and a variety of twisting and turning poses featuring a plenitude of tensed muscles. According to the later Roman writer-administrator Pliny the Younger, the Laocoön was the work of three Rhodians, Hagesandrus, Athenodorus and Polydorus; however, much controversy surrounds the group, which many scholars believe to be a copy or adaptation of a 2nd-century BC original, with the Rhodians serving their Roman masters as copyists and probably working in or just after the 1st century BC.

Single nude figures of gods and heroes continued to be made, but now constituted only one genre among many. They were often shown in novel poses or with an erotic or jokey frisson. Aphrodite, goddess of love, remained a popular subject, although, because many Greek works became known throught Roman sources, she is often miscalled by the Roman version of her name, Venus. The Crouching Venus shows Aphrodite at her ablutions, not only crouching but with the distinctive Hellenistic body-twist; the Capitoline Venus represents her as making an unconvincing attempt to conceal her nakedness with her hands. A third Roman copy, featuring Eros (Roman Cupid) kissing his lover Psyche, is unabashedly sentimental, while sex is treated in the most light-hearted way in an idiosyncratic group with a smiling nude Aphrodite making a mock-threatening gesture with the slipper she holds in her hand, while an amused winged Eros pushes an urgent Pan away from her. Two sculptures with hermaphrodites also provide evidence of art as mildly erotic amusement: both a Sleeping Hermaphrodite and a group in which a hermaphrodite fends off an amorous satyr are arranged so that the unusually endowed figure is seen from behind and looks like a beautiful woman; when the viewer moves round to the other side, some unexpected sexual apparatus is revealed, evidently with the intention of amusing and titillating.

Deservedly or otherwise, the Venus de Milo (properly Aphrodite of Melos) is certainly the most famous statue in the world, having made an indelible impression on the public imagination after its discovery on the island of Melos in 1820; much of its reputation derived from its mistaken identification as a work of the Classical period. Dating from

the later 2nd century BC, it was probably influenced by the Classical revival that occurred in late Hellenistic times, but despite its sobriety it is very much of its period in its turning pose and the use of insecure-looking drapery at hip level.

Although the Classical cult of ideal beauty continued to be influential, the Hellenistic sculptor was also able to create a wider range of types. He recorded the ugly and the unusual with unsparing realism, alongside other subjects that had been neglected: childhood and emaciated old age, dwarf, boy jockey and boxer, and

Sleeping Hermaphrodite; copy of a 2nd-century BC original. This smoothly sensual, unusually endowed figure shows an impish side of Hellenistic sculpture.

also sympathetically presented non-Greek individuals such as Gauls and Africans. Perhaps the most strikingly anti-Classical of these is a well-known bronze of a seated boxer, with visibly battered and swollen features and fresh cuts in his face indicated by strips of inlaid copper.

A keen interest in the specific and idiosyncratic helped to make individual portraiture a major Hellenistic art. It had a special appeal for autocrats who were vain enough to want to perpetuate their own images and wealthy enough to patronize artists with the requisite skills. In earlier times there seems to have been a feeling that a portrait was a form of *hubris*, displaying a dangerous ambition and perhaps offensive to the gods. However, some portraits – notably heads of Themistocles and Pericles – have survived and have an individuality that suggests they may be likenesses; still, it is impossible to be quite certain that they are not idealized posthumous images. This is to some extent true of representations of Alexander the Great in statuary and on coins; although consistent in their rendering of the king's youthful features, upward gaze and cascading leonine hair, they are known to represent an officially approved Alexander, his public image defined by his chosen portraitist, the sculptor Lysippus. The image may be a truthful one, but its evident propagandist intention leaves the matter in some doubt: if the pictured Alexander looked less handsomely god-like, less the heroic world-conqueror, it would be easier to believe that it corresponded to the reality.

From this point of view many Hellenistic portraits do convince by their warts-and-all character, although the fact that every ruler is shown as possessing a superabundant head of hair is suspicious, suggesting that Alexander's celebrated mane had made this feature indispensable to the Hellenistic conception of royalty. Still, Ptolemy I of Egypt appears on his coins with a large and powerful hooked nose, unmistakably an individual personality. So is the over-life-size bronze from about 150 BC of an unidentified ruler, standing in heavy muscular nakedness and holding a long staff; his face and attitude convey a palpable, unappealing arrogance, and it is hard to imagine who was intended to see and be impressed by it.

There are also excellent, sharply individuated portraits of philosophers and writers; some, such as a much-copied, long-headed bust of Epicurus, are probably likenesses, but others seem to have been influenced by the wish to make larger statements, for example contrasting the keen mind and ageing body of the philosopher.

The spread of a more affluent lifestyle during the Hellenistic age is reflected in the number of small craft works that have survived, representing household ornaments or tomb offerings. Among them are small bronze and terracotta figures of considerable artistic quality. Especially popular and accessible, then as now, were terracotta figures of slender young women in neatly draped everyday costumes. These, along with similar images of children, young men, Eros and Aphrodite, are known as 'Tanagra' figures, after the cemetery in Boeotia where large numbers were found; but they were in fact made all over the Greek world, evidently satisfying a demand for offerings that would bring sweetness and light into the tomb.

From the end of the 4th century most pottery was Megarian ware, made in moulds and carrying relief decoration. The disappearance of scenes painted on vases means that this important evidence about the techniques used by painters on a larger scale is absent for the Hellenistic period. Its place is supplied to some extent by another art form, the mosaic, in which differently coloured pieces of stone or glass are assembled to create a picture. The earliest known examples are 4th-century pebble mosaics from northern Greece and Macedon. By about 300 BC vigorous, action-packed hunting scenes were being created at Pella, the capital of Hellenistic Macedon; thanks to the Macedonian kings' conscious promotion of their court as a centre of Hellenistic culture, famous artists such as Apelles are known to have worked in the north, and the mosaics are believed to be copies of contemporary paintings. Roman imports and copies of Greek art certainly extended to paintings, and a good many of the murals excavated from the volcano-smothered city of Pompeii are probably copies of Greek originals. Some give great prominence to landscape features, a devel-

opment known to have originated in Hellenistic times. However, the most nearly certain derivation is that of the Alexander Mosaic, a tremendous set-piece representing a critical moment in the battle of Issus at which Alexander and Darius confront each other; this Pompeian floor mosaic (not a pebble mosaic but executed in the more advanced technique, with tiny cubes of coloured stone) is held to be a copy of a late-4th-century painting by Philoxenus of Eretria, described by Pliny the Younger. The thrilling quality of the copy makes the loss of the original seem an even more poignant matter for regret.

Opposite: the Venus de Milo is a Hellenistic work, from the 2nd century BC. Stylistically it is a revival of Classicism - although like most revivals it remains imbued with the spirit of its own age.

The Rape of Europa. Terracotta statuettes were popular votive offerings. Like this one, the best-known figures came from Tanagra. The subject here makes a change from the more common sweet, modestly draped figures.

7 WORDS AND IDEAS

IF THE GREEKS ARE THE FIRST PEOPLE IN HISTORY WHO SEEM TO SPEAK TO US FULLY AND FREELY, PART OF THE REASON LIES IN THE NEW TOOL THEY ACQUIRED FROM THE PHOENICIANS IN THE 8TH CENTURY BC: THE ALPHABET. THE OLDER FORMS OF WRITING INVOLVED USING HUNDREDS OF PICTURES OR SIGNS TO STAND FOR OBJECTS OR SYLLABLES; KNOWLEDGE OF THEM MUST HAVE BEEN THE MONOPOLY OF A NARROW CASTE OF PROFESSIONAL SCRIBES WHOSE TIME AND ENERGY WAS DEVOTED TO COMPILING CIVIL SERVICE RECORDS RATHER THAN COMPOSING WORKS OF LITERATURE. BUT THE ALPHABET, WITH ONLY TWENTY-ODD LETTERS THAT COULD BE PERMUTATED TO CONVEY EVERY KNOWN WORD, WAS EASY TO LEARN AS WELL AS QUICKER AND MORE CONVENIENT TO USE. WRITING BECAME RELATIVELY WIDELY PRACTISED AND UNDERSTOOD, AND SERVED AS A MEDIUM FOR RECORDING AND GIVING ARTISTIC FORM TO ALL KINDS OF FACTS, EXPERIENCES, THOUGHTS AND FEELINGS. CONFRONTED WITH WONDERFUL OPPORTUNITIES, THE GREEKS PIONEERED MOST OF THE MAIN BRANCHES OF LITERATURE AND CREATED WORKS THAT HAVE PERHAPS BEEN EQUALLED BUT HAVE NEVER BEEN SURPASSED.

SPOKEN AND WRITTEN WORDS

The earliest tangible result of adopting the alphabet was the writing down of the *Iliad* and the *Odyssey*. Scholars have debated endlessly about the identity of the author and the subject-matter of the poems. Did Homer write one, both, or neither of them? Was he, as tradition insisted, a blind bard from one of the Ionian cities? Or is 'Homer' just a tag for the collective efforts of many generations? The 19th-century English writer Samuel Butler asserted that Homer was a woman; Lawrence of Arabia, who translated the *Odyssey*, regarded the author as a landlubber, ignorant of the seafaring that he (or she) described. Modern scholars are quite certain that the epics are products of a long oral tradition; Homer, if he existed, was perhaps an Ionian genius who linked, shaped and polished a mass of traditional material at the time when it was being written down. Oral transmission of the poems over the centuries accounts for many of their most puzzling features including their historical inconsistencies. Clearly, the Homeric and Mycenaean worlds are in many respects similar, for example in the forms of the names mentioned and the places listed; and, as we have seen, Schliemann was able to discover the site of Troy through his belief in the documentary value of the *Iliad*. Equally clearly, the bards of the Dark Age adapted traditional matter so that it squared with the world they knew: the supposedly Bronze Age heroes are familiar with iron; they cremate their dead instead of burying them as the Mycenaeans did; and their kings are simple war-leaders, not the bureaucrats we glimpse in the Linear B tablets. Among the distinctive features of the epics are the use of fixed epithets – the sea is always 'the wine-dark sea' – and some even longer formulas, which may have originated as aids to improvisation. Although our knowledge of other Greek epics is fragmentary, it is clear that the *Iliad* was exceptionally long. Even so, it does not narrate the entire story of the Trojan War but dwells on a single

episode in which Agamemnon and Achilles quarrel; Achilles withdraws from the fighting and the Greeks get the worst of things; the death in battle of Achilles' friend Patroclus brings the hero back into the field; and there he slays the Trojan champion Hector. Achilles' own death and the ultimate destruction of Troy are only hinted at.

Once written down, the Homeric poems were fixed, so that they seemed to later Greeks to represent an increasingly remote past; their all-pervading influence has already been indicated. Although the withering of the oral tradition has often been regretted, the literature that replaced it was of unexampled variety and expressiveness. Language and literature, together with religion and ritual, became significant unifying elements among a widely scattered and politically divided people.

However, the use of writing did not immediately bring with it the reading of literature as a private activity. Down to the 4th century Greek poetry was a largely public art, primarily intended to be recited or sung to an audience, large or small. The introduction of writing made literary composition easier, and provided

An idealized portrait bust of the epic poet Homer; 2nd century BC. Even in antiquity Homer was a shadowy figure; modern scholars doubt whether the *Iliad* and the *Odyssey* had a single author.

Apollo and the Muses. Apollo was the god of poetry and music and the leader of the Muses, the goddesses who inspired the nine creative arts. Here he plays on his lyre while the Muses dance. Attic black-figure *lekythos*.

a permanent record of it; it also ended the cumulative composition and adaptation by bards that characterized the oral tradition and produced the Homeric epic. But solitary reading of books was rare, although there are occasional references to book collectors, and the dramatist Euripides is supposed to have lived in a book-lined cave by the sea-shore. Until the Hellenistic era the book (a roll of papyrus) was a 'script' rather than an object of private study. This applies even to the wealth of poetry produced between Homer and his near-contemporary Hesiod and the 5th-century Athenian drama. Alcman wrote lovely choruses for Spartan girls to perform; Sappho of Lesbos and other poets of direct, personal emotion composed their verses as lyrics, to be accompanied by a lyre or flute; the epitaphs of Simonides are public memorials (famously of the dead at Thermopylae: 'Tell the Spartans when you see them, passer-by,/At their command, obedient, here we lie.'); and the odes of Pindar are works of public celebration, commissioned and paid for as such. This wealth of poetry, falling between the impersonalities of Homer and the drama, constitutes the first great outburst of directly stated emotion and opinion in literature; but (in a fashion typical of the Greeks) it is very much emotion on display, whether recorded and shaped for a small circle of friends or designed for the world at large.

Prose developed later than poetry, becoming the medium of a reasoned search for the truth in history, natural science and philosophy, and still later the medium of imaginative expression. The first of the great Greek prose writers whose work survives is the historian Herodotus, though he must have had predecessors whose efforts have been lost, since part of his declared purpose was to correct them. He was born at Halicarnassus (modern Bodrum, Turkey), travelled in Egypt and other lands, spent some time in Periclean Athens, and by about 440 had settled at Thurii, an Athenian foundation in Greater Greece. His *History* is no mere compilation: the material, for all its diffuseness, is skilfully related to the grand theme of the Greco-Persian wars and the triumph of Athens

'The Father of History', Herodotus; fragment of a statue from Ptolemaic Egypt. He was the first writer to travel in order to research the past, and the first to write a historical narrative rather than a chronicle of events.

in particular. However, although Herodotus is not entirely uncritical, he is above all a collector and teller of wonderful stories with human interest rather than analysis as his chief concern.

Within less than a generation an Athenian, Thucydides, had brought the writing of history to a level of accuracy and impartiality never again equalled in antiquity. Thucydides served as a general in the Peloponnesian War until 424, when he failed to save the city of Amphipolis from the great Spartan general Brasidas; as a result he was sent into exile and only returned to Athens 20 years later, dying soon afterwards. His history of the war is therefore contemporary history, but written from the sidelines and with an earnest attempt at fairness despite his passionate attachment to his native city. It is also the first piece of sustained historical research, based on documents and eye-witness accounts that have been carefully examined and compared with one another. With its tense, compressed style and narrative excitement,

Thucydides' history ranks as a masterpiece of both literature and history. At his death he had brought his account down to 411 BC. It was continued and completed by Xenophon, an Athenian aristocrat disillusioned by post-war Athens who spent part of his later life as a pensioner of Sparta. Xenophon had little of Thucydides' historical rigour, but his many works do include a masterpiece: the *Anabasis*, a splendid eye-witness narrative of war and adventure, about the fighting retreat from Babylon to the Black Sea undertaken by 10,000 Greek mercenaries, with Xenophon himself as one of the leaders, in order to escape from Persia, where they had ended up on the losing side in a civil war.

Scholarship flourished during the Hellenistic period, and the great library at Alexandria was a treasure-house of original manuscripts, copies and critical commentaries. In the early 4th century three important poets, Callimachus, Apollonius of Rhodes and Theocritus, were associated with the city. Apollonius wrote an epic *Voyage of the Argo* that is the only full surviving account of the adventures of Jason and the

Argonauts; though replete with echoes of Homer, it reflects the spirit of a new age in its psychological tensions and characterizations of Jason and Medea. From the point of view of posterity the outstanding poet was Theocritus, who introduced one of the most enduring of literary conventions, the pastoral. This celebrates the simple lives and loves of shepherds and their sweethearts – the kind of quasi-nostalgic subject that makes its appeal to city-dwellers in every age who feel their existence has become artificial and over-refined.

After this brief Alexandrian renaissance, Greek poetry never again reached the heights, although much accomplished verse continued to be written. When the Romans became masters of the eastern Mediterranean, Greek culture became part of the equipment of educated people throughout the empire; and if no great Greek poetry was written, important advances were made in several prose forms. It was a Greek historian, Polybius, who made the first sustained attempt to chronicle the rise of Rome and analyse the reasons for its success. The Jewish historian Josephus wrote in Greek when he com-

A girl reading a scroll; it would have been made of papyrus imported from Egypt. Parchment, introduced later, led to the codex or book with leaves. Athenian red-figure vase painting, 5th–4th century BC.

posed his *Jewish War*, describing the events culminating in the destruction of the Temple (AD 70). Plutarch (*c.* AD 40–120) produced parallel biographies of the most eminent Greeks and Romans in a narrative style so attractive that they influenced writers down the ages including Montaigne and Shakespeare; his essays, too, though less widely known, are exceptional in their charm and wisdom. A number of other historians of the 1st and 2nd centuries AD, notably Arrian, Appian and Cassius Dio, also wrote in Greek; they were not great writers, but their works contain a good deal of information no longer to be found in any other sources.

Tourism and antiquarian interest in the Greek past elicited another pioneering effort, Pausanius' site-by-site *Guide to Greece* (*c.* AD 180). More imaginative prose was written in the 140s by Lucian of Samosata, author of satirical essays and dialogues and fantastic stories, some of which have been described as early science fiction. An even more intriguing development was the appearance, possibly as early as the 1st century BC, of longer prose fictions that are increasingly being recognized as early novels, although some authorities still prefer the dismissive term 'romances'. The plots of the handful of more or less complete novels that survive are certainly escapist, falling into one general pattern: true lovers are parted by misfortune, undergo various trials and, chastity intact against all the odds, are finally reunited. The emphasis on chastity, male as well as female, is a little surprising and suggests that novel-readers mainly came from a respectable urban middle class that may not have been so very different from the British readership of 'classic' novels during the 18th and 19th centuries; however, this impression may be false, since some novel fragments have come to light that seem to be less high-minded. The best of the Greek novels is *Daphnis and Chloe* by Longus, which is more pastoral in setting and tone than other examples of the genre. Daphnis and Chloe are both foundlings, discovered and adopted by, respectively, a goatherd and a shepherd on the island of Lesbos. The story describes their discovery of their mutual love and the barriers to their happiness; inevitably, both turn out to be well-born and all ends satisfactorily; but within the superficially conventional plot are surprisingly sophisticated reflections on feeling and convention, innocence and experience, and the city and the country.

The rise of Christianity did not put an end to Greek literature. But it did radically change its content and purpose, taking it into a new world that is beyond the scope of this book.

Genius of biography. Written under the Roman Empire, Plutarch's parallel lives of great Greeks and Romans had an immense influence on later literature; title page of an English edition of 1656.

THE BIRTH OF THE DRAMA

Perhaps the most remarkable thing that Greek religion brought into the world was an entirely new art form: the drama. Shakespeare, Molière, Schiller, Eugene O'Neill and Bernard Shaw owed the medium of which they were masters to the city of Athens; and more specifically they owed it to the god Dionysus.

Dionysus had had to force his way into the company of the Olympians. His worship involved darker, more dangerously ambivalent emotions than theirs, and in historical times there were still vivid folk-memories of his female followers, or maenads, tearing to pieces animals and even human beings. In time Dionysus settled down in the Greek pantheon as a more or less respectable fertility god; but in late 6th-century Athens his cult could still occasion a vigorous mixture of obscene play and poignant emotion; and this was the starting-point of the world's drama.

The 6th-century tyrant Pisistratus founded the greatest Athenian festival dedicated to the god, the City Dionysia; and it may have been the newness of the festival that made another innovation possible. This was the addition of a speaking actor to the ritual singing and dancing performed by the Dionysian chorus; when the actor became involved in verbal exchanges with the leader of the chorus, the drama was born. This innovation is attributed to one Thespis, who had established it firmly enough to be awarded a prize for his work in about 534 BC; none of it survives, and Thespis is otherwise remembered only as the first 'thespian'.

A second actor was introduced by the tragedian Aeschylus, the first dramatist whose works have survived – those that were performed in his last years, from 472 BC. In less than 20 years a third actor was added, and that was the limit: if there were more parts than three, one or more of the

Theatre of Dionysus, Athens. This was the first true theatre, built on the slopes of the Acropolis in the early 5th century BC; all the surviving Greek tragedies and comedies were performed here. The present theatre dates from the 4th century BC.

actors had to double up, a feat made easier by the fact that all the participants wore masks. Obviously, no scenes could be written in which more than three speakers were on stage at the same time. The chorus continued to play an important part. In tragedy they commented on the action in the guise of courtiers, citizens or other groups, expressing the conventional man's moral values and common-sense spirit of compromise in the face of the main characters' heroic principles or obsessions. In comedy their role may well have been closer to the Dionysian original, involving rollicking fantastic impersonations of frogs, birds or wasps.

The first true theatre was built in the open air on the southern slopes of the Acropolis, next to the temple of Dionysus – presumably because the new form of entertainment was so popular that special arrangements had to be made to allow everybody to see it. 'Entertainment' is not really the right word for a spectacle that remained so closely associated with Dionysus and the city: after a day of sacrifices and processions the young men brought the cult-figure of the god into the theatre so that he could see the performance; and before it began there were solemn civic ceremonies. The theatre of Dionysus was originally built of wood, so a description of some parts of its layout can only be a matter of educated guesswork. The audience sat on benches arranged in a semi-circle on the slopes; below, the chorus chanted, sang and danced in a circle (the orchestra), while the actors performed behind it on a low platform, with some kind of raised structure (the *skene*) representing a palace or other setting. Later, wood was replaced by stone; the orchestra contracted to a semi-circle, neatly dovetailing with both stage and seating; and painted scenery was introduced. The best-preserved of ancient Greek theatres is not the theatre of Dionysus at Athens, but one at Epidaurus, restored in recent times, used for present-day performances of Greek classics, and celebrated for its perfect acoustics.

By modern standards performances were tests of an audience's powers of endurance. Except in wartime, when the programme was curtailed, there were five days of solid dramatic fare. On each of the first three days, three tragedies and a satyr play (a kind of parody), all by a single dramatist, were presented. On the fourth day no less than five comedies were put on. It is hard to believe that spectators who sat through the entire festival can have avoided emotional exhaustion, especially since some of the greatest figures in world literature were writing for them, often in direct competition with one another. Aeschylus (525–456) had all his surviving plays staged in the lifetime of his younger contemporary Sophocles (c. 496–406); and the third of the great tragedians, Euripides (484–406), also began his career before Aeschylus' death.

Aeschylus' plays have a magnificent set-piece quality – more oratorio than opera, so to speak, though to contemporaries their introduction of a second (and later a third) actor would have made them seem intensely dramatic by comparison with anything they had seen before. Sophocles was the master-craftsman of Greek drama, creating believable characters and situations, and developing them to inevitable, harrowing climaxes. He also gave expression to moral conflicts of permanent importance; *Antigone*, for example, concerns the conflict between religious piety (or conscience) and duty to

Sophocles, probably the Greek dramatist who speaks most directly to modern audiences in tragedies such as *Oedipus the King* and *Antigone*. He lived to a great age, and this 3rd-century bronze, idiosyncratic and expressive, may be a true likeness.

Scene from a boisterous comedy; here, in contrast to the high seriousness of tragedy, the accent is obviously on the farcical and grotesque. Apulian red-figure bell crater; by the Dijon Painter.

performance, the Athenians were intending to finance the construction of a new fleet.

These four writers are the only ones whose plays survive from the great age of Athens. Some of their plays: only 43 out of the several hundred they are known to have written. After Euripides, tragedy seems virtually to have disappeared. But comedy continued to flourish, although the absence of anything but fragments makes it impossible to trace how it evolved from the Old Comedy of Aristophanes to the New Comedy of Menander (c342–c.293) some 70 years later; even Menander's work is known only thanks to relatively recent papyrus finds in the Egyptian desert. His plays are recognizably the ancestors of the Western comedic tradition. The chorus now takes no part in the main action, merely appearing between acts. The dialogue is less inventive but more natural than Aristophanes'. The plots are full of love crises caused by unsympathetic parents or differences in the lovers' social status, along with foundlings who prove to be kidnapped sons or daughters of respectable parents, and elaborate confidence tricks pulled off by crafty slaves; the ending is always a happy one. The characters are mainly types: misers, garrulous cooks, soldiers who are cowardly braggarts, scoundrely servants. These durable elements reappear in early Greek novels, Roman comedy, the improvised Italian *commedia dell'arte*, Shakespeare, Molière and many later, if generally less distinguished, productions.

The organization of the drama, and of the Dionysia as a whole, was entrusted to one of the *archons*, who acted on behalf of the state. He chose which playwrights should be represented, but the cost of the performance was borne by a wealthy producer, the *choregus*; the job was usually taken by people with political ambitions who hoped to win popularity by putting on a good show, although it was possible to appoint a reluctant rich man who was felt to be lax in making contributions to the general welfare.

Many conventions of the Greek theatre must have derived from its sheer size and open-air setting. Performers had to be seen and identified at distances of almost 100m (300ft) and from many different angles; and so masks, strongly patterned and brightly coloured costumes, large formalized

the state. In Euripides' tragedies the atmosphere is less nobly remote: there is more realism, more ordinary human passion and weakness, and also more melodrama. Euripides remodelled and implicitly criticized the myths, yet this no-nonsense playwright had a distinct taste for ending his tragedies with a *deus ex machina* – the 'god out of a machine' (literally a machine: the god was lowered by a theatre crane) who resolved the conflicts of the plot and foretold the future. Though contemporaries such as Aristophanes considered Euripides a cynic and misogynist, his works seem to be a curious, rather enigmatic mixture of myth, 'modern' realism and personal religious feeling.

The great comic writer Aristophanes (c. 448–c. 380) was a younger contemporary of Sophocles and Euripides, living to see the defeat of Athens in the Peloponnesian War and the city's partial recovery. His plays were a mixture of knockabout farce and wild poetic fantasy, combined with political satire that was bang up to date: in *Lysistrata*, for example, the women seized the Acropolis and secured the very emergency fund with which, at the time of the

gestures and intelligently pointed dialogue were necessary; at a later date tragic actors started to wear thick-soled buskins to make them taller, and these eventually became platform boots 20cm (8in) high. Such conventions determined the limits of the drama; they ensured that violent action would take place offstage, and they made intimate effects impossible even if the writers and spectators had wanted them.

Actors and chorus were all men, and one of the functions of a mask was to conceal the sex of performers who took female roles. Costumes were adapted to the same purpose: in the theatre, unlike everyday life, they were long-sleeved and ankle-

length. The actor's chief instrument must have been his voice, and presumably the finest performers could project their words to the farthest edge of the auditorium while convincingly imitating the emotions and tones of both sexes. In the earliest plays the author himself is said to have taken the main part, but the special skills of the actor were recognized by 449 BC at the latest, when prizes began to be awarded for the best performances.

At Athens the price of admission to the theatre for the day was two obols, most of a poor man's day's wages; but from the time of Pericles the state paid it for them. The Theatre of Dionysus must have seated at least 15,000 people (Plato says 30,000), and

Epidaurus in southern Greece. The best-preserved of ancient theatres, Epidaurus is celebrated for its acoustics: words whispered by the actors can be heard in the highest tier of seats.

evidence of various enlargements suggests that it was often packed to capacity. As its fame spread, not only citizens and *metics* but also foreign visitors flocked to the Dionysia; women, children and slaves may have been admitted in some circumstances, though perhaps only in the company of influential or privileged men. These included priests, officials and ambassadors, all of whom had stone seats (not mere benches) at the front of the auditorium. Not much is known about the behaviour and responses of audiences at tragic performances: it is perfectly possible that they appreciated nice points of verse technique and dramatic irony; but it is equally possible that most of them responded on a simpler level to awe-inspiring enactments of legends that were common property. Some tragedies did deal with contemporary events, though only one has survived: Aeschylus' *The Persians*, set at the Persian court as it awaits the news from Salamis. However,

Aristophanes' comedies are full of broad, impudent contemporary references which presuppose a politically aware and appreciative audience as well as an extraordinary licence granted to the author, who is forever poking fun at the sexual aberrations and political intrigues of prominent writers and politicians. Again, audiences may have enjoyed the knockabout fun rather than the lyrical beauty of Aristophanes' choruses, but there is no record of their objecting to them, although we know that when they disliked a comedy they showed it by taking out their packed lunches and eating them noisily, presumably crunching down as hard as they could on their onions. There were evidently connoisseurs too, or at least fans: not content with a single performance of each new play, they followed the 'company' as it toured the rural Dionysia celebrated by the parishes of Attica in December. These, incidentally, were the only repeat performances given of

Ceramic theatre mask, 5th century BC. This must have been a souvenir or decoration, since real actors' masks were lighter objects, made of cork or stiffened fabric. Tall masks dignified tragic actors; a grotesque mask, combined with padded clothes, created the appropriate comic mood.

Masked actor-musicians performing in a comedy. Discovered in the buried Roman city of Pompeii, this mosaic scene is signed by a Greek craftsman, Dioscurides of Samos. He made it in about 100 BC as a copy of an earlier Hellenistic painting.

the 5th-century masterpieces in the lifetimes of their authors. So great was the prestige of Aeschylus that revivals of his tragedies began shortly after his death; but the works of Sophocles and Euripides were not seen again until the 4th century.

Like so many public events in Greek life, the dramatic festival was a competition, with prizes for the best tragedy and comedy as well as the best actor. Careful precautions were taken to prevent corrupt verdicts, a clear enough indication that, if the opportunity offered, the will to win was likely to overcome the scruples of any writer or actor.

The Hellenistic theatre appears to have been popular but uncreative. The age was one in which reverence for the past was combined with a taste for virtuoso display in the present. The works of the great tragedians began to be regularly revived, and in 330 BC authorized texts were established (although a century later the Athenians had to pawn them to the culture-hungry Alexandrians when they needed cash to buy off the Macedonian garrison). Papyrus finds show that these 'classics' were widely read and performed. At about the same time theatres were spreading all over the Greek world and soon

became a required amenity for any city that cared about its reputation; performances were given not only at Dionysia but during any other festivals and celebrations for which the financial backing was available. But if the theatre flourished, the drama went into a decline: thousands of plays must have been written, but they have vanished – and not entirely by accident, it seems, since contemporaries never considered them remotely comparable with 5th-century works, and quoted them far less often in their writings. It has been plausibly suggested that Hellenistic drama consisted of imitations of 'Classical' drama for highbrows, and otherwise of overblown set-piece 'scripts' which served as vehicles for the virtuosos of the theatre: the actors. Hellenistic theatrical conventions encouraged 'performances' rather than serious drama: actors became grotesque giants, wearing padded costumes, built-up shoes and masks conveying wildly exaggerated emotions, looming above the orchestra on a 3- or 4m (10- or 13-ft)-high stage. The 'star system' was in full swing by the 4th century and famous actors could command fortunes for a few performances; but there is now no way of recreating their virtuosity.

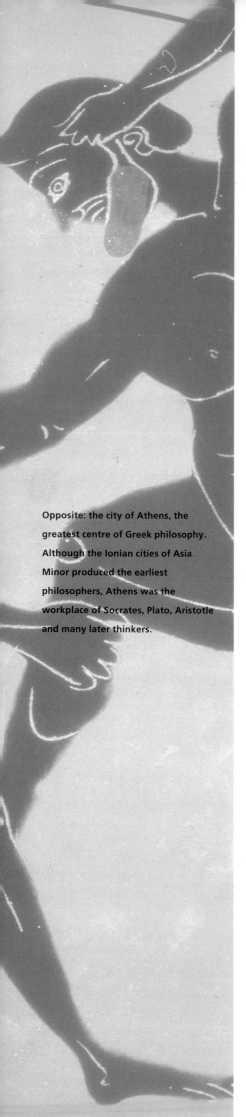

THE FIRST PHILOSOPHERS

For most purposes philosophy may be defined as a quest for truth, undertaken by means of thought, without relying on religious or other dogmas. It poses questions that, at the time when the philosophizing is being done, cannot be answered by conducting scientific investigations or by collecting facts. The first philosophers in human history appeared in early 6th-century Ionia, their works surviving in often enigmatic fragments. They asked such questions as: What is the primal stuff from which the universe is made? By what process did this change and diversify into the world as we know it? Or are change and diversity mere illusions? Thales of Miletus held that water was the primal substance, whereas his fellow-citizen Anaximines believed it was air. Heraclitus of Ephesus asserted that 'all is in flux'; the Southern Italian philosopher Parmenides of Elea argued that since the One can never become the Many, real change is impossible; and Empedocles the Sicilian attempted to reconcile their conflicting views by positing a universe made of Earth, Air, Fire and Water, set in motion by the operation of two forces he called Love and Discord.

The extraordinary thing about these speculations is that they made no concessions to the cosmological myths and supernatural agencies that pervaded Greek life. There is no entirely convincing explanation for this development, although part of it may lie in the commercial prosperity which brought the Ionian cities into extended contact with Egypt and Western Asia. Apart from acquiring mathematical and astronomical skills from abroad, the Ionians may have developed a certain scepticism through realizing the infinite variety of gods worshipped in their world. Certainly the earliest Greek philosopher, Thales, and two of his successors, Anaximander and Anaximines, were citizens of Miletus, a notably prosperous and powerful city until its destruction by the Persians in 494.

Little is known of the lives or teaching methods of these early philosopher-scientists. We have a fuller picture of Pythagoras, the supposed discoverer of the famous theorem, although the evidence is largely based on tradition and legend. He was born on the island of Samos, off the Ionian coast, but about 531 settled at Croton in Southern Italy. There he founded a school, or rather something approaching a religious order, following an austere rule of life, which is said to have governed Croton for some time with great success. So Pythagoras appears to have introduced two elements into philosophy that were very influential on later Greeks: the idea of philosophy as a way of life, and the idea of philosophers as proper persons to rule a state. He is also credited with a belief in the transmigration of souls (reincarnation) and with the discovery that musical intervals could be expressed as mathematical proportions. Mathematics remained an important element in Pythagorean beliefs, which long survived the master's death; numbers were valued for their mysterious properties and relationships, which seemed to reflect some absolute, unchanging order of things.

At Athens the scientific-cum-philosophical outlook seems to have been introduced by another Ionian, Anaxagoras, who became a friend of Pericles. His true successors, however, were not Athenians but Leucippus and Democritus, who put forward an atomic theory of matter more than 2,300 years before its correctness was demonstrated. At Athens, philosophy was dominated by ethical and political concerns in the teaching of Socrates (469–399) and Plato (c. 427–348), no doubt reflecting the intense character of Athenian public life. Socrates' importance in the history of philosophy is such that his predecessors are often referred to as 'pre-Socratics'. He seems to have been interested in natural science as a young man, but most of his career was devoted to ethical problems. The oracle at Delphi is said to have told one of his friends that Socrates was the wisest man in Greece – and Socrates, all too conscious of his ignorance, concluded that his wisdom lay in the fact that he knew that he knew nothing. He therefore adopted his celebrated habit of cross-examining everybody he met, exposing the flaws in their thinking and the unjustified assumptions

Opposite: the city of Athens, the greatest centre of Greek philosophy. Although the Ionian cities of Asia Minor produced the earliest philosophers, Athens was the workplace of Socrates, Plato, Aristotle and many later thinkers.

on which it rested. Although he had done the state good service, fighting bravely as a hoplite in several battles of the Peloponnesian War, in 399 Socrates was accused of impiety and corrupting Athenian youth, sentenced to death, and, following Athenian custom, given the poison hemlock to drink. Although his questioning of accepted beliefs may have irritated some people (he called himself the city's gadfly), he was probably condemned on political grounds, as one who had associated with many members of the recently defeated oligarchic party.

Socrates' great contribution to philosophy lay in subjecting the whole field of human conduct to the test of reason. More than that it is

difficult to say, since he appears to have written nothing. If he had any positive doctrines, they cannot now be distinguished from those of his disciple, Plato, who makes Socrates the hero of many of his writings, and often no doubt attributes his own views to the older man. In return (so to speak), Plato made Socrates immortal; for Plato was a great literary master and one of the most influential philosophers in history. He invented his own literary form, the dialogue, which was admirably suited to portray philosophical conversation and Socrates' long chains of critical reasoning. As a thinker he initiated one of the main philosophical traditions, based on the conviction that every object, thought or

Far left: Socrates, whose questioning of accepted ideas finally led him to be condemned to death by the Athenians; marble copy of a Greek original of the early 4th century BC.

Second from left: Plato, the disciple of Socrates. A major philosopher in his own right, he founded the long-lived Idealist tradition in philosophy. Marble Roman head, 1st century AD.

Left: Aristotle, a native of Stagira, settled in Athens as Plato's disciple and became a philosopher of encyclopaedic range. His writings dominated medieval European thought.

concept in the universe is the imperfect shadow of pure, unchanging Forms which are the true reality, knowable through reason and contemplation. The Forms are also known as Ideas, and this type of philosophy is called Idealism (rather confusingly in view of the modern everyday meaning of the word).

Plato's dialogues show Socrates debating and teaching in quite ordinary social circumstances; the *Symposium*, for example, with its famous disquisition on the nature of love, is set at a drinking party whose members include the rising young politician Alcibiades and the comic dramatist Aristophanes. But Aristophanes, in his *Clouds*, presents Socrates as running a school in his own

house, with pupils boarding there; and Plato, as we have seen, set up his Academy as a permanent institution (in one form or another it survived for nine hundred years). Both men evidently intended to exercise influence, on the leaders if not the citizen body, and both had students who became men of power; Alcibiades attached himself to Socrates, and Lycurgus and Phocion, the chief figures in the struggle to maintain Athenian independence against Macedon, both studied at the Academy. To what extent they regarded such studies as more than a course in persuasion and analysis, useful to their careers, is another matter. And since Plato lived in an age when the city-state was dying as an independent institution, neither he nor his pupils achieved more than temporary practical success. Paradoxically, these Greeks – characteristically obsessed with public and contemporary effectiveness – exercised their deepest influence posthumously.

During the Hellenistic age Athens remained the philosophers' capital; although none of the major figures were born in the city, all of them gravitated to it, evidently preferring freedom and congenial company to the fleshpots of Alexandria and Pergamum. The greatest of them, Aristotle, was not fully a man of the new age, since his life (384–322) bridged the Classical and Hellenistic periods. Born at Stagira in the Chalcidice peninsula of Thrace, he came to Athens to study under Plato at the Academy; his early interest lay in zoology, and he left the Academy after Plato's death, when the philosophizing became too unfactual for his taste. Later he became Alexander the Great's tutor, though whether Alexander's career owed much to his philosophy is doubtful. Returning to Athens in 335, Aristotle set up a school in a grove sacred to Apollo Lyceius (whence Lyceum); however, his taste for discussion in the open air, while walking up and down with his pupils, caused the philosopher and his followers to be nicknamed 'the Peripatetic school'. He was one of the most fact-minded of the ancients, strikingly unlike his master Plato in preferring to discover and analyse realities rather than reason about perfect entities and how things ought to be. Though by no means always correct in his information and inferences, Aristotle possessed a brilliant and all-inclusive intellect, ranging over every subject of study from logic to natural history, from metaphysics to rhetoric. Aristotle's encyclopaedic learning made him the major non-religious authority of the European Middle Ages: he, Socrates and Plato are the greatest philosophical thinkers of ancient Greece.

But some of Aristotle's contemporaries and successors had a far more direct influence on the way men behaved in the centuries immediately ahead. Mentally, Aristotle lived in the age of the *polis*; his *Politics* described and compared the constitutions of Greek states at the very time when their independence and importance were being demolished by his pupil Alexander. Diogenes, Epicurus and Zeno the Stoic spoke to men who needed a new kind of philosophy, suited to an age when the ordinary citizen could no longer control events, was conscious of himself as an individual rather than as a member of a community, and consequently sought for individual or universal – not community – values. Some truth-seekers turned from the Olympian gods (who in their local aspects were identified with the city-state community) and embraced mystery religions or oriental cults such as Egyptian Serapis and Isis; others found the answers they sought in the ideas of the new philosophers.

The most radical of these was Aristotle's contemporary Diogenes, the best-known of the Cynics. The Cynics were not the disillusioned scoffers of modern usage, but 'drop-outs' who believed in reducing their needs to a minimum, living according to nature, and detaching themselves from the world and its vanities. Diogenes' Cynicism is said to have included such eccentricities as living in a tub and rebuffing Alexander the Great; nevertheless his philosophy was a serious one and intermittently found followers in the Greco-Roman world.

The Epicurean and Stoic philosophies had even greater influence, since they were more compatible with living an ordinary life in the world. Epicurus, though born on Samos, was the son of an Athenian and eventually set up his school in the city; he taught in the garden of his house, and thanks to misunderstandings of his philosophy 'the garden of Epicurus' had become a by-word for private self-indulgence even in antiquity. For Epicurus taught that pleasure was the only object of existence; however, he added that desire only bred greater desire, so that happiness could not be achieved by the pursuit of pleasure in the ordinary sense. Instead, Epicurus recommended temperance, the enjoyment of friendship, and the cultivation of contentment. Above all, the wise man should have no fear of the gods: the universe was material, a collection of atoms as Democritus held, and if the gods did exist they did not concern themselves with human affairs.

Epicureanism became the philosophy of men able to retire from the world in modest comfort; Stoicism appealed to those who were compelled by circumstances or temperament to act or endure. Its founder, Zeno, was a Cypriot who taught in the shelter of an Athenian *stoa*, which gave the name to his philosophy. Stoicism held that the soul of man was a spark from the cosmic fire, to which it would eventually return if it was faithfully tended. This meant that a man must live according to nature and reason, which in practice involved virtuous, 'stoical' acceptance of fate and diligent performance of the duties appropriate to it; while acting as he should, the stoic remained self-sufficient, cultivating a happiness that was independent of his circumstances. Stoicism was to have a long history as the philosophy most congenial to the future masters of the Hellenistic world, the Romans.

Philosophers disputing in a rural setting; they may represent the Academy of Plato in session. The mosaic dates from the 1st century AD and comes from a site close to the Roman city of Pompeii.

SCIENCE AND TECHNOLOGY

The Greeks may be said to have invented scientific speculation when the 6th-century pre-Socratic philosophers of Ionia put forward a variety of theories about the primal substance of the universe. But during the great age of the city-state, actual science made little progress except in a few subjects – mathematics, astronomy, medicine – where some impetus had been given by the older civilizations of the Near East.

Evidently the ethos of the city-state was inimical to the painstaking life-style of the scientist, although the work of Aristotle in classifying fields of study was of enduring importance. But in general more impressive results were achieved after 300 BC in the cities of the Hellenistic world, and especially in Alexandria. At around that time Euclid was teaching in the city; his *Elements* summarized and systematized all that the ancients had learned about geometry, and for over two thousand years Euclid and geometry were virtually synonymous. Astronomy was studied from very early times because of its importance in regulating the calendar. Most astronomers believed that the earth was a fixed point around which the sun, planets and stars moved, but Aristarchus of Samos seems to have been a lone voice in asserting (*c.* 275 BC) that the earth went round the sun. Though he happened to be correct, in antiquity the geocentric school had the better of the argument, especially as refined by a brilliant mathematician and astronomer, Apollonius of Perge, who worked in Alexandria early in the 2nd century BC. Apollonius' explanation of celestial movement in terms of eccentric and epicyclical orbits was enshrined in the *Almagest* of the 2nd-century AD astronomer Ptolemy, which was transmitted to the medieval West via Islam and, through no fault of Ptolemy's, acquired an authority that was to hinder further progress. Ptolemy's work contained much that was of value, including the observations of Hipparchus of Nicaea, who was antiquity's most successful practical astronomer. Active around 135 BC in another of the great Hellenistic centres, Rhodes, Hipparchus improved the instruments used by astronomers, observed the precession of the equinox, and produced an improved star map.

Technological change was also very slow. Various explanations have been put forward to account for this, including the effects of cheap – slave – labour in removing any pressing motive for improvement. However, it is hardly necessary to look for explanations, since technological conservatism has been the rule in most cultures. (The 'problem' can be more usefully reversed: why was the West, unlike other cultures, so innovative – and so receptive of innovations – from the 18th century onwards?)

The Tower of the Winds at Athens. The roof of this unusual octagonal building supported a weather vane; the relief at the top of each side represents the appropriate wind. The interior was a weather clock.

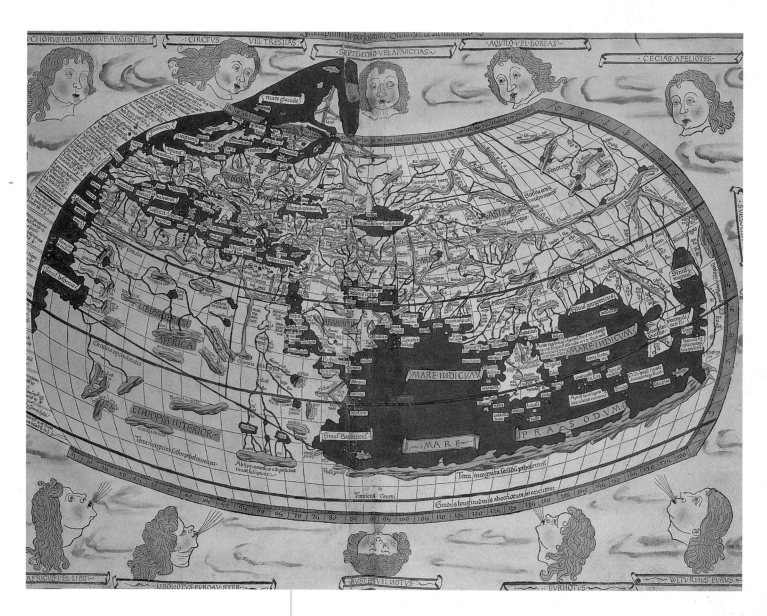

Again it was the Hellenistic age, and Alexandria in particular, that proved most creative. However, the most celebrated of Greek engineers, Archimedes, was a native of Syracuse in Sicily and, although he may have studied at Alexandria, spent most of his life in his native city working for its ruler, Hiero II. Archimedes was an outstanding mathematician, invented the science of hydrostatics, and formulated the law of leverage; one of his most famous remarks was 'Give me a place to stand and I can move the world.' Even more celebrated is his 'Eureka!', said to have been uttered on emerging from the bath and running jubilantly (and naked) through the streets after grasping the relationship between his immersed body and the amount of water displaced by it. Archimedes also did good service to the state when the Romans besieged Syracuse: he is credited with having designed a giant lens that could focus the sun's rays on an enemy ship and set it on fire. But the city fell despite his efforts; and Archimedes is said to have been slain by a Roman soldier.

Hellenistic rulers were eager to exploit new military technology, but other inventions aroused little interest. Around 270 BC an Alexandrian engineer named Ctesibius devised an accurate water clock and a fire pump; but when, around AD 60, Hero of Alexandria harnessed steam power, its application was confined to automata and other small gadgets of no practical significance. This confirms that even when Greek society produced individuals who conceived new technological means, it lacked the attitudes and institutions required to make use of them.

Influential for 1300 years: this map of the world, published in 1486 at Ulm in Germany, was based on the descriptions and co-ordinates given by Ptolemy of Alexandria in the 2nd century BC.

8 THE LEGACY OF ANCIENT GREECE

DURING THE 2ND CENTURY BC THE ROMANS BECAME MASTERS OF THE LANDS AROUND THE MEDITERRANEAN, INCLUDING THE GREEK CITY-STATES, MACEDON AND THE GREEK NEAR EAST. BUT CULTURALLY THE TIDE OF CONQUEST FLOWED IN THE OPPOSITE DIRECTION, AS THE ROMAN RULING CLASS SUCCUMBED TO GREEK ARTS AND IDEAS. LATER ON, A NEW RELIGION, CHRISTIANITY, CAME OUT OF THE GREEK EAST AND ULTIMATELY TRIUMPHED THROUGHOUT THE EMPIRE. BY THIS TIME ROME'S WESTERN PROVINCES WERE COMING UNDER INCREASING PRESSURE FROM BARBARIAN TRIBES AND WERE BEGINNING TO DECLINE AND LOSE COHESION. BY CONTRAST, THE URBAN GREEK WAY OF LIFE IN THE EAST REMAINED RELATIVELY PROSPER-OUS, AND THE CHANGE IN THE BALANCE OF POWER BETWEEN THE TWO HALVES OF THE EMPIRE WAS SIGNALLED IN AD 330 BY THE FOUNDATION OF A NEW IMPERIAL CAPITAL, CON-STANTINOPLE, WHICH GRADUALLY WAXED AS ROME AND THE WEST WANED. AFTER THE FINAL COLLAPSE OF THE WEST, THE ROMAN EMPIRE WAS CONFINED TO THE EASTERN MEDITERRANEAN; AND ALTHOUGH MANY OF THE OLD NAMES AND FORMS WERE RETAINED, THIS 'EAST ROMAN' EMPIRE DEVELOPED INTO AN AUTOCRATIC, CHRISTIAN, GREEK-SPEAKING SOCIETY WHICH HISTORIANS CALL THE BYZANTINE EMPIRE. IN THIS FORM GRECO-ROMAN SOCIETY SURVIVED UNTIL THE FALL OF CONSTANTINOPLE TO THE TURKS IN 1453. MEANWHILE THE DEVELOPMENT OF WESTERN EUROPEAN CIVILIZATION WAS INFLUENCED BY THE EXAMPLE OF ANCIENT GREECE, MOST OBVIOUSLY DURING THE RENAISSANCE AND SUBSEQUENT 'CLASSI-CAL' REVIVALS; AND ITS ENDURING LEGACY IS STILL TO BE SEEN ALL AROUND US.

GRECO-ROMAN CIVILIZATION

In the 2nd century BC the Hellenistic monarchies began to fall before the rising power of Rome. The Romans were initially drawn into the affairs of Greece by a wish to prevent other powers from dominating the area, and were therefore able to present themselves to the Greeks as liberators. In 196 BC, having defeated Philip V of Macedon, the Roman general Flaminius proclaimed 'the freedom of the Greeks'; and in 191–190 the Romans inflicted a humiliating rebuff to Seleucid invaders. But the protectors soon turned into masters. After the Roman victory at Pydna (167), Macedon was dismantled; and when the Macedonians attempted to stage a revival and the Greek cities of the Achaean League tried to arrest their decline, they were crushed: Corinth was razed to the ground and Macedon and Greece became a Roman province (146). The same fate overtook Pergamum (133), the Western Asian dominions of the Seleucids (64) and Egypt (30).

Over the next few centuries Greece had much to endure. When Mithridates of Pontus (on the shores of the Black Sea) challenged Rome, some Greek cities supported him and were punished for it; in 80 BC Athens itself was sacked by the future Roman dictator Sulla. Greece also suffered during the Roman civil wars, when the climactic battles of Pharsalus (48) and Philippi (42) were fought on its soil.

Nevertheless the Greeks became thoroughly integrated into the Roman Empire and played a very considerable part in it. The Greek character of the eastern Mediterranean and the Near East was hardly affected by Roman rule, whereas the Roman conquerors were profoundly influenced by Greek culture. The Romans had come into direct contact with the Greeks in Southern Italy, especially after they captured the great Sicilian city of Syracuse (211 BC). After this campaign, and the 2nd-century victories won by the Roman army in Greece itself, quantities of booty poured into Rome, delighting the recipients with their beauty and craftsmanship. Roman conservatives fought a rearguard action against the vogue for what they saw as Greek-inspired decadence, but in vain. Educated Romans began to employ Greek tutors and came to pride themselves on their ability to speak and write the language. The gods of Rome, though not Greek in origin, were identified with those of Hellas – Jupiter with Zeus, Mars with Ares, Venus with Aphrodite, and so on. Greek myths became part of the Romans' inheritance, linked with their own origins through Aeneas, their supposed Trojan ancestor. Greek epics and dramas provided models for Roman writers. Athletic competitions in the Greek style were introduced. The naturalism of Greek art was copied, and the

Perseus freeing Andromeda: a 1st century AD painting, found at the Roman city of Pompeii in Southern Italy. Such copies of Greek originals exemplify the way Greek art and myths permeated the Roman (and later the European) mind.

Justinian and his entourage;
mosaic in the Church of San Vitale,
Ravenna, 6th century AD. Residing
in Constantinople, the former
Greek city of Byzantium, Justinian
ruled a 'Roman' Empire that was to
become increasingly Greek in
character.

Romans employed the Greek orders and decorations on their temples. They also visited Greece as tourists with Pausanius' book as their guide, and those with intellectual ambitions studied philosophy at Athens. The emperors Nero and Hadrian were passionate philhellenes, while Marcus Aurelius became the most famous exponent of Greek Stoic philosophy. Of course the Romans made their own substantial contributions in engineering, law, literature and other fields, and it was as part of a composite Greco-Roman culture that the Greeks' achievements would eventually be transmitted to the European societies that developed after the fall of Rome.

In the centuries that followed the conquest of Greece, Rome made the transition from republic to empire, and periods of stability alternated with upheavals caused by the rivalries of would-be emperors and barbarian attacks on the frontiers. In the 4th century Christianity became the state religion under the Emperor Constantine and his successors; although it originated in the Jewish provinces of the empire, its sacred book (the New Testament) was written in Greek, and Greek thought certainly influenced the way in which the new doctrines were elaborated and put into practice.

By this time there was an increasing tendency for the western and eastern halves of the empire to be ruled separately, with the Greek East controlled from Constantinople (modern Istanbul), the city founded by Constantine in AD 330. Greece and the rest of the Nest East suffered from the depredations of Visigoths and other Germanic tribes that crossed into the empire from the late 4th century, but in the event it was the West that collapsed; the last emperor was deposed in 476 and the Roman dominions were replaced by Germanic kingdoms.

The East survived, and with it great Greek cities such as Constantinople, Antioch and

Alexandria. Early in the 6th century the Emperor Justinian regained control of Italy and most of the Mediterranean coastline, but after his time the empire was confined to the East and, outside the court, the law and the army, it was essentially Greek in character. It was also changing in many ways; most of the changes were too gradual to be dated to a single year, but two events may perhaps be taken as marking the end of antiquity: Theodosius' laws forbidding pagan worship and establishing Christianity as the sole religion of the empire (392) and Justinian's decree (529) closing the Academy at Athens founded by Plato and effectively outlawing the kind of unfettered thought pioneered by the Greek philosophers. Theodosius' abolition of the Olympic Games (393) also signalled the passing of the older customs and values.

The dominions of Justinian and his successors are generally described as the East Roman Empire. At some indeterminate date after this, historians use a new label, the Byzantine Empire. (Byzantium was a Greek city on the site later occupied by Constantinople.) The renaming acknowledges the evolution of the empire into a different kind of society that was essentially Greek, although the Byzantines continued to describe themselves as Romans.

Byzantine history is beyond the scope of this book, and only a few crucial events can be described here. In the 7th century the Byzantines lost their Levantine and Egyptian territories to warriors who surged up from the Arabian peninsula, fired by the new religion of Islam, and carried everything before them. Byzantium remained a great power, based on Anatolia (Asia Minor) and the Balkans, while its cultural influence had a decisive impact on Eastern Europe; the Bulgars, Russians and other Slav peoples were converted to Christianity by Byzantine missionaries, and the Greek Orthodox Church took shape as an institution effectively separate from the Roman Catholic Church in the West. In 1071 the Byzantine army was crushed by the Muslim Seljuk Turks at Manzikert, a terrible blow that cost the empire its Anatolian territories. In the West, the First Crusade of 1094 was launched partly at least to relieve the pressure on the Byzantines. But there was soon little love lost between the Crusaders – known as Latins or Franks – and the 'Greeks' they had come to help. Constantinople, still by far the greatest city in Christendom, aroused the greed of the Franks, and their visions of rich plunder were realized during the Fourth Crusade of 1204, in which the city was sacked and the Byzantine Empire divided between the Crusader leaders. This 'Latin Empire' was relatively short-lived, but Byzantium, though reconstituted, never really recovered. Miraculously, Constantinople itself held out against the Ottoman Turks until 1453, when the city was stormed and the last emperor, Constantine XI, died fighting.

Byzantine art. This mosaic shows the 10th-century-AD Emperor Constantine IX Monomachus and his empress Zoe, on either side of the enthroned Christ; the jewel-like colours and remote, hieratic atmosphere have left the classical world far behind.

LASTING INFLUENCES

During the centuries when Greek Byzantium was civilized and powerful, western Europe slowly emerged from tribal chaos and developed into a new kind of society. Feudal states in the West had only intermittent contacts with distant Byzantium before the Crusades, and their known and admired models were more often Roman. But since Rome had absorbed so much from ancient Greece, elements such as the architectural orders passed in modified form to the medieval West, where they became part of a 'classical' tradition that stretched from 10th-century Romanesque through the Renaissance, Baroque and Neo-classical styles and on into the early 20th century.

The Middle Ages were most keenly aware of Greek history in the person of Alexander the Great, whose exploits inspired often wildly inaccurate romances and epics both in the West and in the East (where he became 'Iskander'). Greek was hardly studied in Europe, but much Islamic learning was based on Greek scholarship, and some knowledge of Greek authors reached the West via Muslim Spain; in particular, Aristotle's encyclopaedic learning and speculations became available in the 1150s and caused a virtual revolution in medieval thinking.

From the 14th century, beginning in Italy, there was a great revival of Greek and Roman studies which formed the core of the Renaissance. Great advances were made in knowledge of ancient Greek mythology, philosophy, history and literature, especially after the fall of Constantinople in 1453 caused many Greek scholars to flee to the West. Plato's writings pervaded Renaissance thinking, and the Idealist tradition derived from Plato became one of the principal schools of European philosophy. Study of the New Testament in the original Greek brought fresh insights and sparked controversies which helped to launch the Protestant Reformation that split western Christendom in the 16th century. Directly, or indirectly through Roman poets such as Ovid, Greek mythology became a prime subject for

artists like Titian, and also inspired literature: Chaucer and Shakespeare wrote of the Trojan War, dramatists composed tragedies, and poets sang in Theocritan vein of shepherds and their loves. Greek tragedy – misunderstood – also served as the model for early operas.

Such was the immense prestige of Classical Antiquity that, as late as the 17th century, there were Ancients-and-Moderns controversies in England and France in which one side held that no modern works had equalled, let alone surpassed, the masterpieces of antiquity. In England the dispute generated more heat than light, and Jonathan Swift, author of *Gulliver's Travels*, satirized the proceedings in *The Battle of the Books* but nevertheless came down on the side of the ancients.

This sense of cultural inferiority passed, but nevertheless the dominant movement in 18th-century architecture, painting and sculpture was Neo-classicism. As Greece became more accessible (though still ruled by the Ottoman Turks) architects studied her monuments at first hand and a purist Greek Revival movement began which produced, among other buildings, the British Museum in London. The British diplomatist Lord Elgin removed many sculptures from the Parthenon and brought them to Britain; two hundred years later, controversy continues to rage over the propriety of their 'rescue', the quality of the British Museum's stewardship, and whether the 'Elgin Marbles' should remain in Britain or be returned to Greece. So steeped in the classics were Europe's educated classes that the Greek revolt against Turkish rule was greeted with a wave of sympathy, and volunteers went out to fight for them, including the English Romantic poet Lord Byron.

During the 19th century England developed a system of public schools (actually private schools for the education of the upper class) in which study revolved around Greek and Latin, while the sports regime can fairly be described as a Spartan training in hardness that was modified by promotion of the team spirit. However, the most consciously Greek-inspired innovation of the 19th century was the revival in 1896 of the Olympic Games, organized as an international rather than a Panhellenic event.

Even in the 20th century, when past conventions were so often rejected in the name of modernism, homage was paid to ancient Greece in many ways, from Freud's Oedipus complex and the 'Grecian' dancing of Isadora Duncan to the pseudo-classicism of Nazi art. Writers – especially French dramatists from Giraudoux to Sartre – reworked Greek myths to cast light on the dilemmas of their own age. Modernist architecture abolished ornament, including Greek ornament; but then Post-modernism reinstated it, making eclectic use of key patterns, the orders and other features. Film-makers more frequently ventured on to classic ground, creating art movies such as Cocteau's *Orpheus* as well as 'sword and sandal' blockbusters like *The Three Hundred Spartans* and *Jason and the Argonauts*. Coming down to the present day, although Greek and Latin may not be widely studied, translations of Homer sell in surprisingly large numbers and Classical Civilization courses have proved popular in schools and colleges. Absorbed into the western bloodstream, the Greek legacy is still hard at work.

Below: Classicism, 18th-century British style; bacchanalian scene designed by the sculptor John Flaxman for Josiah Wedgwood's crisp Neo-Classical pottery, which became world famous.

Above: into the 20th century. This classically inspired semicircular arcade stands in the Plaza de Espana at Seville, Spain. It was built between 1914 and 1928 to the designs of Alvarez Osorio.

INDEX

Page numbers in *italics* refer to illustrations.

PHOTOGRAPHIC
ACKNOWLEDGEMENTS

In source order

AKG, London 5 bottom right, 15, 18, 21, 27 top, 29, 57, 142 main picture, 147, 155, 182, /John Hios 13 right, 23, /Erich Lessing front cover, back cover background, back cover centre, front flap, 2, 4, 5 top centre, 5 centre left, 5 bottom centre, 8-9 background, 10 left background, 11, 14 main picture, 14 left background, 16, 17 right background, 18 left background, 20 left background, 22-23 background, 24 left background, 26 left background, 27 right background, 30 left background, 31 top right, 31 bottom, 32 left background, 33 centre, 33 bottom, 34 left background, 35 top, 35 right background, 36 main picture, 36 left background, 37 bottom, 38-39 background, 40 left background, 43, 46 main picture, 46 left background, 47 right background, 48, 49 bottom, 49 right background, 50-51 background, 51 right background, 52 main picture, 54 left background, 55 right background, 58, 59 right background, 60 left background, 61, 62 left background, 63 main picture, 63 right background, 64, 65 main picture, 65 right background, 66 main picture, 66 left background, 68 main picture, 69 top, 69 bottom, 70 centre, 70 left background, 72, 73 bottom, 74 main picture, 74 left background, 75, 76 left background, 78 main picture, 78 left background, 84, 86 left background, 88 main picture, 88 left background, 92 left background, 93 bottom, 94 main picture, 94 left background, 96 left background, 98 left background, 102 main picture, 102 left background, 106 main picture, 106 left background, 107, 110, 111 top, 111 bottom left, 112 top, 112 bottom, 113, 114 left background, 115, 116 bottom, 118, 119, 120, 121, 122, 122 left background, 123 right background, 124 left background, 125, 126 bottom, 126-127 background, 127 right background, 128 bottom, 128 left background, 130 main picture, 130 left background, 136 left background, 138 left background, 150 left background, 151 right background, 152 left background, 160-161 background, 161 centre, 161 right background, 166 left background, 172 left background, 178 left background, 180-181 background, 183, 184 left background, /Schutze/ Rodemann 169

Ancient Art and Architecture Collection 39 bottom, 51 centre right, 54 main picture, 86 bottom centre/G.T. Harvey 59 main picture, /Michelle Jones 90, /R. Sheridan 60 Bottom Centre, 96 main picture, 105 bottom, 129, 153, 164, 167

Bridgeman Art Library, London/New York/Acropolis, Athens, Greece 166 main picture, /Acropolis, Athens, Greece/ Bildarchiv Steffens 5 centre right, 173, /Antiquarium, Locri, Calabria, Itlay 92 main picture/Archaelogical Museum, Olympia, Archaia, Greece 149, /Archaeological Museum, Delphi, Greece 28/Archaeological Museum, Thessaloniki, Macedonion, Greece 39 top, /Architectural Museum, Istanbul, Turkey 40 main picture, /Ashmolean Museum, Oxford, UK 79, 80, 81, 82, 83, 93 centre, 104, 109 right/British Museum, UK 3 right background, 19, 20 main picture, 25 right background, 32 main picture, 34 main picture, 37 right background, 45 right background, 52 left background, 68 left background, 76 centre, 77, 85, 101 right background, 108, 116 left background, 117, 134 left background, 139 right background, 142 left background, 143, 145, 150 main picture, /Bury Art Gallery and Museum, Lancashire, UK 185 bottom/Fitzwilliam Museum, University of Cambridge, UK 22 main picture, 47 main picture, 174 right/Freud Museum, London, UK 97, /Galleria e Museo Estense, Modena, Italy 109 left, /Hermitage, St Petersburg, Russia 1, 24 main picture, /Kunsthistorisches Museum, Vienna, Austria 175, /Louvre, Paris, France 132, 156, 157, 162, /Musee Conde, Chantilly, France/ Giraudon 159, /Museo Archeologico Nazionale, Naples, Italy 99, 171, 174 left, 177, 181, /Museo Archeologico, Bari, Italy 168, /Museo e Gallerie Nazionali di Capodimonte, Naples, Italy 42, /Museo Nazionale, Reggio Calabria, Italy 140, /National Archaeological Museum, Athens, Greece 5 top left, 9, 17 main picture, 67, 89, /Pergamon Museum, Berlin, Germany 134 centre, /Persepolis, Iran 5 bottom left, 44, /Plaza de Espana, Seville, Spain 185 top/Private Collection 38 Bottom, 131, 165, /Private Collection/ Index 45, /Royal Geographical Society, London, UK 179, /Vatican Museums and Galleries, Vatican City, Italy 91, 114 main picture, 152 main picture /Vatican Museums and Galleries, Vatican City, Italy/ Index 5 top right.

Corbis UK Ltd 103, 154, /Yann Arthus-Ber 100, /Bettmann 158, /Burstein Collection 8 Centre, 148, /Kevin Fleming 105 top, /Chris Hellier 178 main picture, /Mimmo Jodice 170, /Wolfgang Kaehler 133, /Gail Money 10 main picture, /Gianni Dagli Orti 3 Centre, 71, 138 main picture, /Third Eye Images 12, /Vanni Archives 139 main picture, /K.M. Westermann 124 main picture, /Roger Wood 13 left

E.T. Archive/British Museum, London, UK 98 bottom centre

Octopus Publishing Group Ltd. 127 right

Hirmer Verlag 87

Ny Carlsberg Glyptotek/Jo Selsing 56

Tony Stone Images/George Grigoriou 6-7, 53

Werner Forman Archive 95, 136 main picture, 146, /Acropolis Museum, Athens 135, 137, /British Museum, London, UK 50 centre, 73 top, 144, /Museo Ostia, Italy 30 main picture, /Private Collection, New York 163/Sotheby's New York 151 Bottom Centre